The
Bad-Ass Librarians
of Timbuktu

AND THEIR RACE TO SAVE THE WORLD'S MOST
PRECIOUS MANUSCRIPTS

Joshua Hammer

Simon & Schuster

NEW YORK   LONDON   TORONTO   SYDNEY   NEW DELHI

Simon & Schuster
1230 Avenue of the Americas
New York, NY 10020

Copyright © 2016 by Joshua Hammer

First Simon & Schuster hardcover edition April 2016

SIMON & SCHUSTER and colophon are registered trademarks
of Simon & Schuster, Inc.

For information about special discounts for bulk purchases,
please contact Simon & Schuster Special Sales at 1-866-506-1949 or
business@simonandschuster.com.

The Simon & Schuster Speakers Bureau can bring authors to your
live event. For more information or to book an event contact the
Simon & Schuster Speakers Bureau at 1-866-248-3049
or visit our website at www.simonspeakers.com.

Interior design by Ruth Lee-Mui
Front endpaper: Map of Timbuktu. Copyright bogdanserban/iStock via Getty Images.
Back endpaper: Manuscript page. Photo by Xavier Rossi/Gamma-Rapho via
Getty Images.

Manufactured in the United States of America

10   9   8   7   6   5   4   3   2

Library of Congress Cataloging-in-Publication Data is available.

ISBN 978-1-4767-7740-5
ISBN 978-1-4767-7743-6 (ebook)

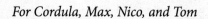

For Cordula, Max, Nico, and Tom

The Bad-Ass Librarians
of Timbuktu

Prologue

He shifted nervously in the front passenger seat of the four-wheel-drive vehicle as it approached the southern exit of the city. Down the tarmac road, in the pink light of the desert morning, two gunmen stood beside a checkpoint made from a rope strung across a pair of oil barrels. They were lean men with beards and turbans, Kalashnikov semiautomatic rifles slung over their shoulders. Take a deep breath, he told himself. Smile. Be respectful. He had already been arrested once by the Islamic Police, hauled before a makeshift tribunal, interrogated, and threatened with Shariah punishment. That time he had managed—just barely—to persuade them to set him free. He couldn't count on being lucky a second time.

He cast a glance at the rear compartment. There, covered with blankets, lay five padlocked steamer trunks, each one filled with treasure: hundreds of illuminated manuscripts, including some from the fifteenth and sixteenth centuries, the Golden Age of Timbuktu.

Encased in goatskin covers with inlaid semiprecious stones, they were gorgeous works composed by the most skillful scribes of the era, fragile pages covered with dense calligraphy and complex geometrical designs in a multitude of colors. Al Qaeda in the Islamic Maghreb, the terrorist group that had seized the north of the country four months earlier, had several times vowed on television and radio to respect them, but few in the city believed their promises. The extremists had declared jihad against anyone and anything that challenged their vision of a pure Islamic society, and these artifacts—treatises about logic, astrology, and medicine, paeans to music, poems idealizing romantic love—represented five hundred years of human joy. They celebrated the sensual and the secular, and they bore the explicit message that humanity, as well as God, was capable of creating beauty. They were monumentally subversive. And there were thousands of manuscripts just like these hidden in safe houses in Timbuktu. Now he and a small team had set out to save them.

The driver stopped at the roadblock. The two Al Qaeda gunmen peered into the car.

"Salaam Aleikum," he said, with all the equanimity he could muster. Peace be upon you. They were young men, barely out of their teens, but they had dead eyes and the hard, fanatical look of true believers.

"Where are you going?"

"Bamako," he said, the capital in the south.

The men circled the car, and peered into the back.

Wordlessly they waved him onward.

He exhaled. But they still had another six hundred miles to go.

1

Abdel Kader Haidara was a small boy when he first learned about the hidden treasures of Timbuktu. In the Haidaras' large house in Sankoré, the city's oldest neighborhood, he often heard his father mention them under his breath, as if reluctantly revealing a family secret. Dozens of young boarders from across the Sahel region of Africa, the vast, arid belt that extends from the Atlantic Ocean to the Red Sea, came to study mathematics, science, astrology, jurisprudence, Arabic, and the Koran at the traditional school that his father ran in the vestibule of their home. Consisting of three three-hour sessions beginning before dawn and continuing, at intervals, until the early hours of the evening, the Haidara School was a throwback to the informal universities that had flourished in Timbuktu during its heyday as a center of learning in the sixteenth century. There were thousands of manuscripts at the house in Timbuktu, locked away in tin chests in a storage room behind a heavy oak door. Haidara had a sense of their importance, but he knew very little about them.

Sometimes his father would rummage through the storage room and emerge with a volume from his family's collection—a treatise about Islamic jurisprudence from the early twelfth century; a thirteenth-century Koran written on vellum made from the hide of an antelope; another holy book from the twelfth century, no larger than the palm of a hand, inscribed on fish skin, its intricate Maghrebi script illuminated with droplets of gold leaf. One of his father's most prized works was the original travel diary of Major Alexander Gordon Laing, a Scotsman who had been the first European explorer to reach Timbuktu via Tripoli and the Sahara, and who was betrayed, robbed, and murdered by his Arab nomadic escorts shortly after departing from the city in 1826. A few years after Laing's murder, a scribe had written a primer of Arabic grammar over the explorer's papers—an early example of recycling. Haidara would peer over his father's shoulder as he gathered students around him, regarding the crumbling works with curiosity. Over time he learned about the manuscripts' history, and how to protect them. Haidara spoke Songhoy, the language of Mali's Sorhai tribe, the dominant sedentary ethnic group along the northern bend of the Niger River, and in school he studied French, the language of Mali's former colonial masters. But he also taught himself to read Arabic fluently as a boy, and his interest in the manuscripts grew.

In those days—the late 1960s and early 1970s—Timbuktu was linked to the outside world only by riverboats that plied the Niger River when the water level was high enough, and once weekly flights on the state-owned airline to Bamako, the capital of Mali, 440 air miles away. Haidara, the sixth child among twelve brothers and sisters, had little awareness of his town's isolation. He, his siblings, and their friends fished and swam in a five-mile-long canal that led from the western edge of Timbuktu to the Niger. The third

longest river in Africa, it is a boomerang-shaped stream that origi-
nates in the highlands of Guinea and meanders for one thousand
miles through Mali, forming lakes and floodplains, before curving
east just below Timbuktu, then flowing through Niger and Nigeria
and spilling into the Gulf of Guinea. The canal was the most vibrant
corner of the city, a gathering point for children, market women,
and traders in dugout canoes, or pirogues, piled high with fruits
and vegetables from the irrigated farms that flourished beside the
Niger. It was also a place redolent with bloody history: Tuareg warriors hiding on the reed-covered bank on Christmas Day 1893 had
ambushed and massacred two French military officers and eighteen
African sailors as they paddled a canoe up from the Niger.

Haidara and his friends explored every corner of the Sankoré
neighborhood, a labyrinth of sandy alleys lined with the shrines of
Sufi saints, and the fourteenth-century Sankoré Mosque—a lopsided mud pyramid with permanent scaffolding made from bundles
of palm sticks embedded in the clay. They played soccer in the sandy
field in front of the mosque and climbed the lush mango trees that
proliferated in Timbuktu in those days, before the southward advance of desertification caused many of them to wither and die, and
the canal to dry out and fill with sand. There were few cars, no tourists, no disturbances from the outside world; it was, Haidara would
recall decades later, a largely carefree and contented existence.

Abdel Kader's father, Mohammed "Mamma" Haidara, was a
pious, learned, and adventurous man who deeply influenced his
son. Born in the late 1890s in Bamba, a village hugging the left bank
of the Niger River, 115 miles east of Timbuktu, Mamma Haidara had
come of age when Mali, then known as French West Sudan—a mé-
lange of ethnic groups stretching from the forests and savannah of
the far south, near Guinea and Senegal, to the arid wastes of the far
north, toward the Algerian border—had still not fallen under total
French control. Fiercely independent Tuareg nomads in the Sahara

were carrying on armed resistance, galloping on camels out of the dunes, ambushing the colonial army with spears and swords. It was not until 1916 that they would be completely subdued. After learning to read and write in French colonial schools, Mamma Haidara had commenced a life of travel and study. He had little money, but he was able to hitch rides on camel caravans, and, because he was literate, he could support himself along the way holding informal classes in the Koran and other subjects.

At seventeen he journeyed to the ancient imperial capital of Gao, two hundred miles along the river east of Timbuktu, and to the desert oasis of Araouan, a walled town famed for its scholars and a stop on the ancient salt caravan route through the Sahara. Driven by a thirst for knowledge and for an understanding of the world, he traveled to Sokoto, the seat of a powerful nineteenth-century Islamic kingdom in what is now Nigeria; to Alexandria and Cairo; and to Khartoum, the Sudanese capital situated at the confluence of the White and Blue Niles, and its twin city, Omdurman, across the river, where the army of Major General Horatio Herbert Kitchener defeated a force led by an Islamic revivalist and anticolonialist called the Mahdi in 1895 and established British rule over Sudan.

After a decade of wandering Mamma Haidara returned an educated man, and was named by the scholars of Bamba the town's *qadi*, the Islamic judicial authority responsible for mediating property disputes and presiding over marriages and divorces. He brought back illuminated Korans and other manuscripts from Sudan, Egypt, Nigeria, and Chad, adding to a family library in Bamba that his ancestors had begun amassing in the sixteenth century. Eventually Mamma Haidara settled in Timbuktu, opened a school, made money trading grain and livestock, purchased land, and wrote his own manuscripts about reading the stars, and the genealogy of the clans of the city. Scholars from across the region often stayed with the family, and local people visited to receive from the Islamic savant a fatwa—a ruling on a point of Islamic law.

In 1964, four years after Mali won its independence from France, a delegation from the United Nations Educational, Scientific and Cultural Organization in Paris convened in Timbuktu. UNESCO historians had read books written by Ibn Batuta, perhaps the greatest traveler of the medieval world, who visited the land that is now Mali in the first half of the fourteenth century; and Hassan Mohammed Al Wazzan Al Zayati, who wrote under the pen name Leo Africanus while held under house arrest by the pope in Rome during the sixteenth century. The travelers described a vibrant culture of manuscript writing and book collecting centered in Timbuktu. European historians and philosophers had contended that black Africans were illiterates with no history, but Timbuktu's manuscripts proved the opposite—that a sophisticated, freethinking society had thrived south of the Sahara at a time when much of Europe was still mired in the Middle Ages. That culture had been driven underground during the Moroccan conquest of Timbuktu in 1591, then had flourished in the eighteenth century, only to vanish again during seventy years of French colonization. Owners had hidden manuscripts in holes in the ground, in secret closets, and in storage rooms. UNESCO experts resolved to create a center to recover the region's lost heritage, restore to Timbuktu a semblance of its former glory, and prove to the world that Sub-Saharan Africa had once produced works of genius. UNESCO gathered notables to encourage collectors to bring the manuscripts out from their hiding places.

Nine years later, Mamma Haidara, then in his seventies, started working for the Ahmed Baba Institute of Higher Learning and Islamic Research, created by UNESCO in Timbuktu and funded by the ruling families of Kuwait and Saudi Arabia. Mamma Haidara lent fifteen volumes to the Ahmed Baba Institute's first public exhibition, then traveled house to house in Timbuktu, knocking on doors, trying to persuade other collectors to donate their hidden manuscripts. He was part of a great campaign of education, Abdel Kader Haidara recalled, that was greeted, for the most part, with suspicion and incomprehension. The work intrigued Abdel Kader, but he couldn't imagine following in his father's footsteps. There didn't seem to be much of a future in it.

Mamma Haidara died after a long illness in 1981 in his mid-eighties, when Abdel Kader was seventeen. The notables of the town, along with officials responsible for distributing inheritances, called a meeting of the Haidara family. Abdel Kader, his mother, many of his siblings, and representatives of several brothers and sisters who couldn't attend jammed the vestibule of the family house in Timbuktu's Sankoré neighborhood to listen to a reading of the will. The elder Haidara had left behind land in Bamba, much livestock, a sizable fortune from a grain-trading business, as well as his vast manuscript collection—five thousand works in Timbuktu and perhaps eight times that number in the ancestral home in Bamba. The estate executor divided up the patriarch's businesses, animals, property, and money among the siblings. Then, following a long-standing tradition within the Sorhai tribe, he announced that Mamma Haidara had designated a single heir as the custodian of the family's library. The executor looked around the room. The siblings leaned forward.

"Abdel Kader," the executor announced, "you are the one."

Haidara received the news in astonished silence. Although he was the most studious of the twelve siblings, read and wrote Arabic fluently, and had long shown a fascination for the manuscripts, he could not have imagined that his father would entrust their care to somebody so young. The executor enumerated his responsibilities. "You have no right to give the manuscripts away, and no right to sell them," he said. "You have the duty to preserve and protect them." Haidara was unsure what his new role would portend, and was concerned whether he was up to the job. He knew only that the burden was great.

In 1984, Haidara's mother died after a five-month illness, a loss that deeply affected him. She had been a warm, loving counterpart to Mamma Haidara, who could be a stern disciplinarian. At six years old, Abdel Kader had earned a reputation for fighting with other neighborhood boys, and his father, to rein him in, had dispatched him to study at a Koranic school deep in the Sahara, an austere encampment 150 miles north of Timbuktu. Haidara would describe with affection years later how his mother had labored over the cooking fire in the family courtyard, preparing perfumed rice, couscous, and other treats, then had packed the food into a basket to help ease the journey and provide sustenance throughout the month-long Koranic course. When his mother's food had run out, young Haidara had stopped eating, and the sheikh in charge had shipped him back in exasperation to his parents in Timbuktu.

Immediately after the funeral of Haidara's mother, the director of the Ahmed Baba Institute came to the Haidara home to pay his respects. "I need you to come and see me," he told Haidara, cryptically. A month later Haidara hadn't shown up. Still coping with his grief, he had totally forgotten about the request. The director dispatched his driver to Haidara's home. "Please come with me," the driver said.

The director, Mahmoud Zouber, greeted Haidara at the Ahmed Baba Institute, a quadrangle of limestone buildings with Moorish archways enclosing a sand courtyard planted with date palms and desert acacias. Then in his thirties, Zouber was already regarded as one of the most accomplished scholars in northern Africa. He had started his career as a teacher at a French-Arabic high school in Timbuktu, studied on a Malian government fellowship at Al Azhar University in Cairo, the world's most prestigious center of Islamic scholarship, and earned his PhD in West African history at the Sorbonne in Paris. Zouber had written his doctoral thesis on the life of Ahmed Baba, a famous intellectual of Timbuktu's Golden Age, who had been captured by the Moroccan invaders in 1591 and taken as a slave to Marrakesh. Chosen director of the Ahmed Baba Institute in 1973, while still in his twenties, Zouber had raised hundreds of thousands of dollars from Kuwait and Iraq to construct the institute's headquarters. Then he had built up the archive from nothing—starting with the fifteen manuscripts borrowed from Mamma Haidara's collection.

A small, courtly man from Mali's Peul tribe, traditionally farmers and herders who lived along the bend in the Niger River between Timbuktu and Gao, he took Haidara gently by the arm and escorted him through the courtyard and into his office. "Look," said Zouber. "We worked a lot with your father. He did a great job collecting and educating the population about the manuscripts. And I hope that you will come to work with us as well."

"Thanks, but I really don't want to," Haidara replied. He was contemplating a career in business, perhaps following his father into livestock and grain trading. He wanted to make money, he would explain years later. What he did not want to do, he was quite sure, was spend his days toiling in or for a library.

The director chased Haidara down a second time a few months later. Again he dispatched his driver to Haidara's home, and summoned him back to the institute. "You have to come," he said. "I'm going to train you to do this. You've got a great responsibility."

Haidara again mumbled his gratitude for the offer, but politely declined.

"You are the custodian of a great intellectual tradition," Zouber persisted.

The institute was facing difficulties, the director confided. For the past ten years, a team of eight prospectors had embarked on one hundred separate missions in search of manuscripts. In a decade of driving through the bush in a convoy of four-wheel-drive vehicles, they had accumulated just 2,500 works—an average of less than one a day. After decades of thievery by the French colonial army, the owners had become fiercely protective of their manuscripts and deeply distrustful of government institutions. The appearance of Ahmed Baba prospectors raised alarms that they had come to steal their precious family heirlooms. "Every time they drive into the villages, people are terrified. They hide everything," Zouber told Haidara, looking him in the eye. "I think that if you come and work for us you're going to help us bring out the manuscripts. It's going to be a challenge, but you can do it."

In 1509 Hassan Mohammed Al Wazzan Al Zayati, a sixteen-year-old student from an aristocratic Muslim family of Granada, which had settled in Fez after the expulsion of the Moors from Spain, arrived in Timbuktu with his uncle, a Moroccan diplomat, and found a vibrant commercial and cultural crossroads. In a classic travel book that he published under the pen name Leo Africanus in 1526, *The History and Description of Africa and of the Notable Things Therein Contained*, he described markets overflowing with goods from across the world, weaver's shops filled with textiles from Europe, and a large limestone palace inhabited by "the rich king of Tombuto [who] hath many plates and scepters of gold, some whereof weigh 1,300 pounds."

Al Zayati was astonished by the scholarship that he encountered in Timbuktu. About one quarter of the city's population of 100,000 were students who came from as far away as the Arabian

Peninsula to learn at the feet of the Songhai Empire's masters of law, literature, and science. The king, Al Hajj Askia Mohammed Touré, gave lands and financial support to scholars and invited architects to Timbuktu to build mosques and palaces. The University of Sankoré, a loose affiliation of mosques and private homes, developed into the most prestigious of 180 scholastic institutions in the city. A Sudanese proverb from the time declared that "Salt comes from the north, gold from the south, and silver from the country of the white men, but the word of God and the treasures of wisdom are only to be found in Timbuctoo." According to the *Tariq al Fattash*, a history of Timbuktu written in the seventeenth century, the city's reputation for scholarship was so great that, when a famed Tunisian professor arrived in town to become a lecturer at the University of Sankoré, he quickly realized he didn't qualify, and retreated to Fez to bone up for fourteen years.

Al Zayati was most impressed by the flourishing trade in manuscripts that he observed in Timbuktu's markets. The books were made of rag-based paper sold by traders who crossed the desert from Morocco, Tunisia, Libya, and Algeria, where the process had taken root after making its way from China and Central Asia. By the end of the twelfth century, the city of Fez had 472 paper mills and was exporting south to the Sahel and north as well to Majorca and Andalusia. Superior Italian paper soon penetrated the Maghreb, the region of northern Africa that lies west of Egypt, derived from the Arabic word for "sunset," transshipped via Mediterranean ports such as Cairo and Tripoli. (Some Italian brands bore Christian cross watermarks, making them a difficult sell in Islamic markets.) By the time that Al Zayati arrived in Timbuktu, most paper was being imported from Venice—typically watermarked with the *tre lune* or three crescents—via the land that is now Libya. Craftsmen extracted ink and dyes from desert plants and minerals, and made covers from the skins of goats and sheep. Binding, however, was

unknown in northern Africa at that time; loose, unnumbered folios were enclosed inside leather binders, tied shut with ribbons or
strings. Al Zayati noted that the sale of manuscripts was far more
profitable than that of other goods.

Four hundred years before Al Zayati's visit, a clan from the Tuareg
tribe, the veiled, free-ranging pastoralists of the Sahara, made its
annual summer migration from a bleak region of salt mines and
dunes to a grassy plain beside the Niger River, 150 miles to the
south. A plague of mosquitoes and sand flies, an infestation of toads,
and the stench of decaying marsh grass made their usual encampment intolerable, so they picked up stakes and moved with their
camels, cattle, and goats to a more congenial spot they discovered,
a few miles north, on a tributary of the Niger formed by seasonal
flooding. A shallow well provided clean, sweet water. When they
migrated north in September, they left their heavy baggage in the
care of a local Tuareg woman they called Bouctou—"the one with
the big belly button." Word spread about this hospitable meeting
place of camel and canoe. The next year, other nomads asked them
where they were heading. "We are going to Tin-bouctou," they replied, the well of Bouctou.

During the next hundred years Timbuktu grew from a collection of tents and mud-and-wattle houses along the riverbank into
a crossroads of the world and a collision point of two cultures—
bringing together desert and river traffic in continuous and mutu-
ally enriching exchanges. Farmers, fishermen, black Tuareg slaves
known as *bellas*, their aristocratic Tuareg masters, and Arab and
Berber traders fleeing an animist despot of the then declining Ghanaian Empire—located in what is today southern Mauritania and
western Mali—settled in the town. Camel caravans laden with salt,
dates, jewelry, Maghrebi spices, incense, European fabrics, and

other goods from as far away as England arrived in Timbuktu after weeks crossing the Sahara. Boats sailed north on the Niger, bringing to Timbuktu, at the river's highest bend, the products of jungle and savannah—slaves, gold, ivory, cotton, cola nuts, baobab flour, honey, Guinean spices, cotton, and shea butter, an ivory-colored fat extracted from the nut of the African shea tree. Traders, middlemen, and monarchs made fortunes in the main currency—gold. When Mansa Musa, otherwise known as Musa I, the ruler of the Malian Empire—a vast territory that subsumed parts of the collapsed Ghanaian Empire and also comprised modern-day Guinea and northern Mali—traveled in 1324 on the hajj to Mecca from Timbuktu, he brought several thousand silk-clad slaves and eighty camels carrying three hundred pounds of gold dust each. "The emperor flooded Cairo with his benefactions," wrote an Arab historian of the time. "He left no court emir nor holder of a royal office without the gift of a load of gold." The emperor dispensed so much gold during his stopover in Cairo, wrote the historian, that he suppressed its value in the city's markets for a dozen years.

In the late fourteenth century, Timbuktu began to emerge as a regional center of scholasticism and culture. Mansa Musa brought back from the hajj a famed poet from the Andalusia region of Spain, and invited one of Cairo's preeminent architects to design Timbuktu's most imposing mosque, Djingareyber. In 1375, the city appeared on a European map drawn by the Jewish cartographer of Majorca, Abraham Cresques, in an atlas made for Charles V of France, a sign of Timbuktu's prominence. But this age of intellectual ferment was not to last. In 1468, the warlord Sunni Ali and his army marched and rode toward Timbuktu. Born in Gao, a Niger River port two hundred miles to the east, Sunni Ali came from a line of local chieftains who had controlled the Gao region since the 1330s, but he had his eyes on a bigger prize. Islamic chronicles portray him as a brilliant military tactician; a skillful horseman who led his own cavalry into battle; a practitioner of an animist faith who opposed Islam and partook in the casting of spells and the use of talismans and animal parts for good luck and fortune-telling; an avid slaver; and an insecure ruler who, after capturing the city, initially welcomed the savants to Timbuktu, then turned against them, convinced they were plotting his overthrow. "The great oppressor and evildoer Sunni Ali . . . killed so many human beings that only God most high could count them," one Timbuktu historian declared. "He tyrannized scholars and holy men, killing them, insulting them, and humiliating them. He perpetrated terrible wickedness in the city, putting it to flame, sacking and killing large numbers of people." Eventually he built up a kingdom—the Songhai Empire—that stretched for two thousand miles along the Niger River.

Sunni Ali reigned without serious rivals, but a bloody succession battle followed his death in 1492. A forty-nine-year-old general and devout Muslim—and a nephew of Sunni Ali, according to some historical texts—named Mohammed Touré put together an army and defeated the forces of Sunni Ali's son near Gao in April 1493. As would happen often in Timbuktu's history, the nightmare of violent repression would give way to a golden age of openness and tolerance. Declaring himself the new ruler of the Songhai Empire, and renaming himself after his pilgrimage to Mecca for the hajj, King Al Hajj Askia Mohammed Touré ushered in an era of peace and prosperity that would endure for one hundred years.

By the time that Askia Mohammed consolidated his power over Timbuktu, the literary tradition was well entrenched in the city, despite Sunni Ali's antischolastic purges. Visiting academics had brought from Cairo, Córdoba, and beyond the classic tools of Islamic scholarship: Korans, the Hadith (the pronouncements of the Prophet Mohammed as compiled by his companions); inquiries into Sufism, the moderate and mystical form of Islam that had spread from Morocco across most of North Africa; and works of the Maliki school of jurisprudence, the dominant legal system in the Sahel, centered at the Great Mosque of Kairouan in Tunisia. The thirst for such works had inspired a thriving cottage industry. Scribes made elaborate facsimiles of the imported volumes for the libraries of professors and wealthy patrons. Working side by side in ateliers in the alleys of Timbuktu, the most prolific copied works at the rate of one every two months—writing an average of 150 lines of calligraphy per day—receiving their compensation in gold nuggets or gold dust. These scribes employed proofreaders who pored over every Arabic character, receiving a percentage of the payment. A *colophon*—Greek for "finishing touch"—at the end of each work recorded the manuscript's start and completion date, the place where the manuscript was written, and the names of the scribe, proofreader, and vocalizer, a third craftsman who inked the "short vowel" sounds that are not usually represented in Arabic script. The patron who commissioned the work frequently received a mention as well. The scribes also produced so-called *ajami* manuscripts, transliterating into classical Arabic script a multitude of local languages—Tamasheq, the language of the Tuaregs; Fulani; Hausa; Bambara; and Soninké.

Despite the dedication to religious scholarship, the Islam that took root in Timbuktu was never very strict. Leo Africanus (Al Zayati) wrote that many residents "spend a great part of the night singing and dancing through all the streets of the city." Most of Timbuktu's residents, one traveler noted, didn't observe the Ramadan fast, consumed alcohol, and restricted their observance of Islam to the practice of circumcision and going to mosque for Friday prayers. The imams of Timbuktu and the general population were receptive to secular ideas, many of which had been exported to the Saharan entrepôt by moderate scholars of Cairo, a more cosmopolitan city. Over time, the scribes widened their scope. They copied surveys of algebra, trigonometry, physics, chemistry, and astronomy. They

translated into Arabic the works of the greatest Greek philosophers, Ptolemy, Aristotle, and Plato; the "father of medicine," Hippocrates; and the eleventh-century Persian philosopher and scholar
Avicenna, who wrote dozens of manuscripts about ethics, logic,
medicine, and pharmacology. Scribes reproduced a twenty-eight-
volume Arabic language dictionary called *The Mukham,* written by
an Andalusian scholar in the mid-eleventh century. An analysis of
poetry by Al Khalil Ibn Ahmad, a ninth-century linguist and literary historian from Iraq, used complex circular diagrams to depict
the metric patterns of Arabic verse.

Great original books as well came out of Timbuktu, by a swelling
number of local scientists, historians, philosophers, and versemak-
ers. Anthologies of poems celebrated everything from the Prophet
to romantic love to more mundane subjects such as green tea. The
Tariq Al Sudan presented, in thirty-eight chapters, an unparalleled
history of life on the Middle Niger under the Songhai emperors,
describing in great detail trade routes, battles, invasions, and daily
life in cities such as Djenné, famed for its thirteenth-century Great
Mud Mosque. "The land of Djenné is prosperous and densely inhabited, with major markets every day of the week. It is said there
are 7,077 villages in that land, all close to one another," the author
observed. "If the sultan wants to summon to Djenné someone living near Lake Debo [a seasonal lake north of Djenné, formed by the
flooding of the Niger River basin], his messenger goes to a gate in
the wall and calls the name of the person in question. People pass
on the message from village to village, and it reaches the person immediately, and he comes and presents himself."

The city's legal experts compiled vast scholarship about Islamic
jurisprudence, or *fikh,* some of which provided insights into the
progressive nature of Timbuktu's society. "I have read your question and carefully considered it," many of these volumes begin, before the author provides a fatwa, or Islamic legal ruling, on issues

ranging from the distribution of inheritances to the withdrawal of sexual privilege from the marital bed. One fatwa supported a woman's decision not to sleep with her husband by arguing that men had often exercised the same right. Another consists of a lengthy disquisition on obligatory alms, or *zakat*, declaring that acceptance of charity from thieves and oppressors is the equivalent of abetting their crimes, and that the duty of alms giving belongs to everyone who possesses a minimum degree of wealth, not just aristocrats.

Timbuktu's astronomers studied the movement of the stars and their relationship to the seasons, accompanying their writings with elaborate charts of the heavens. Manuscripts contained precise diagrams of the orbits of the planets, based on complex mathematical calculations. The astronomers instructed readers on the use of a gnomon, or the shadow-casting edge of a sundial, to time the five daily Islamic prayers; used spherical trigonometry to calculate the exact direction of the *Qibla*, the direction to be faced during prayer; advanced arguments for the adoption of the earth-centered model of the solar system; tested a formula to calculate leap years; and diagrammed the "mansions," or stations of the moon in its orbit around the earth, a means of tracking the time at night, the lunar calendar, and the passage of the seasons. They documented a range of celestial phenomena, including a 1593 meteor shower: "In the year 991 in God's month of Rajab the Godly, after half the night had passed stars flew around as if fire had been kindled in the whole sky—east, west, north and south," wrote one astronomical observer. "It became a nightly flame lighting up the earth, and people were extremely disturbed. It continued until after dawn."

Physicians issued instructions on nutrition and described the therapeutic properties of desert plants. They prescribed herbal remedies to help ease women through labor, toad meat to treat snakebites, and droppings from panthers mixed with butter to ease the pain of boils. Ethicists debated such issues as polygamy,

moneylending, and slavery. There were catalogues of spells and in-
cantations; astrology; fortune-telling; black magic; necromancy, or
communication with the dead by summoning their spirits to discover hidden knowledge; geomancy, or divining markings on the
ground made from tossed rocks, dirt, or sand; hydromancy, reading
the future from the ripples made from a stone cast into a pool of
water; and other occult subjects that would prove to be especially
odious to Timbuktu's future jihadi occupiers.

One of the most eye-opening volumes, *Advising Men on Sexual
Engagement with Their Women*, served as a guide to aphrodisiacs
and infertility remedies and provided counsel on winning back
wives who had strayed from the marital bed. At a time when wom-
en's sexuality was barely acknowledged in the West, the manuscript,
a kind of Baedeker to orgasm, offered tips for maximizing sexual
pleasure on both sides. "Drinking cow-milk and mixing the powder from a burned cow horn with food or drink increases sexual
potency," the manuscript advises. "For abundant sexual activity and
sexual climax a man must drink the dried, pulverised testicles of
a bull. If a man suffers from impotence he must take the nail of a
cock's right leg, burn it and fumigate himself with the smoke and he
will be cured." The manuscript continued with an ever more exotic
list of potions and remedies, some based on animist practices that
had existed in the region for millennia. "The dried, pulverised penis
of a lizard placed tenderly into honey then licked will let a man
experience full sexual desire and satisfaction and will increase his
sperm count," it declared. The manuscript asserted that sexual pleasure was sanctioned by Islam, and even recommended prayer as a
means of prolonging erections and intensifying orgasms. "In order
to strengthen his penis and enjoy sexual intercourse," it declares,
"the husband must recite the following Qur'anic verses: 'Allah is the
One Who created you from [your state of] weakness and made out
of the weakness strength'; Say '[O Muhammed] O you disbelievers';

and 'Li Ila fi Quraysh' until its end." The author recommended reciting these verses three times a day for a week while standing over seven water-soaked leaves from an acacia tree, then drinking the water before sex. The application of Koranic verses as sexual stimulants suggested both the deep-rootedness of religion in Timbuktu's quotidian life, and the daring nature of the Islam that was practiced here. The zealots who would occupy Timbuktu repeatedly over the centuries would regard such use of the Koran as disrespectful, even blasphemous.

Timbuktu's manuscripts were as prized for their aesthetic splendor as for their subject matter. The city's scribes drew upon a variety of complex calligraphic styles: the western African tradition known as Hausa, marked by thick brush strokes; the Kufic form from Persia, with exaggerated horizontals and sharply angled letters that leaned and bent as if prostrating before God; and the most popular style, Maghrebi, characterized by rounded, bowl-shaped letters and sweeping curves and loops. Unlike Middle Eastern calligraphers, who traditionally used pens sharply cut from the full circumference of a reed, giving their letters a hard edge, Maghrebi scribes sliced the reed into flat slats with blunt, rounded ends, resulting in a distinctly softer and to many eyes a more pleasing outline. Calligraphers also wrote with a pen fashioned from the branch of a local shrub or a bird quill.

They alternated standard black ink made from charcoal or gum arabic, with a variety of earth colors—yellows derived from an arsenic sulfide known as orpiment, found in hydrothermal veins, fumaroles, and hot springs, and once used in the Roman Empire and ancient China as an arrow-tip poison; crimsons extracted from the powdered mineral cinnabar or, alternatively, from the cochineal, a scale insect that produces carminic acid as a deterrent to predators, which was then mixed with aluminum or calcium salts. The illustrators filtered in other ingredients, such as gelatine, to make the letters glow more brightly, or iron rust, to ensure their indelibility. The finest works contained page after page illuminated by gold leaf, typically twenty-two-karat gold hammered into thin sheets and carefully layered over the paper.

Discouraged by the Koran from representations of the human form, the manuscript artists filled margins and broke up text blocks with geometric designs in the same earth tones as the calligraphy. Sinuously intertwined and endless repeating arabesques—leaves, vines, palmettes, and flowers—strikingly reminiscent of the mosaics at the Great Mosque of Damascus and the Alhambra Palace in Granada, conveyed the bounty and infiniteness of God's universe. Kaleidoscopic latticeworks of diamonds, octagons, stars, and other geometric forms communicated balance and symmetry. Some illustrations replicated the patterns of Middle Eastern or Berber carpets—rectangular fields filled with concentric circles of cream, red and green, each aswirl with petals, loops, and abstract calligraphy. The four sides represented the basic elements of existence—fire, water, earth, and air—while the circles were meant to symbolize the physical world. One page from a Koranic manuscript is an exact replica of a Zemmoura flat weave from Morocco's Middle Atlas Mountains. Patterns of diagonals and zigzags arranged in rectangular panels resembled the bogolanfini—dyed mud cloths found throughout Mali, typically done by sewing together narrow strips of cotton. Occasionally scribes enlivened their texts with realistic images: delicate pen-and-ink renderings of mosques, medieval stringed instruments, mountain ranges, Saharan oases with shimmering pools and date palm trees. Amber-, turquoise-, and silver-inlaid tooled leather covers were made from the skins of goats, sheep, or camels.

The city was filled with notable savants, but one figure stood far above the rest: Ahmed Baba Al Massufi Al Timbukti, an eccentric black polymath, born in the salt-mining oasis of Araouan in the deep Sahara in 1556, known for his brilliant mind and his lugubrious appearance. Ahmed Baba wore black eye shadow and dressed entirely in black. Nicknamed "As Sudani," or "The Black One," and often referred to by his admiring colleagues as "The Unique Pearl of His Time," he composed sixty books for the University of Sankoré's library—an unparalleled outpouring of astronomical treatises (one written entirely in verse), commentaries on the Koran and the Hadith, and a vast biographical dictionary of Islamic savants belonging to North Africa's Maliki Sufi sect.

In one work, *On the Lawfulness of Tobacco Usage*, he pondered the ethics of smoking, writing in response to a religious movement in Timbuktu that favored banning the habit. Ahmed Baba determined, perhaps influenced by commercial considerations, that tobacco was neither stimulating nor addictive, and therefore acceptable in the realm. In another, he proposed methods of conflict resolution, arguing for dialogue, forgiveness, and tolerance. His most famous manuscript, *Ahmed Baba Answers a Moroccan's Questions About Slavery*, otherwise known as *The Ladders of Ascent*, argued that freedom is a fundamental right of human beings, except under rare conditions governed by Islamic law. In such cases, the scholar urged compassion and empathy: "God orders that slaves must be treated with humanity, whether they are black or not," he wrote. "One must pity their sad luck, and spare them bad treatment, since just the fact of becoming an owner of another person bruises the heart, because servitude is inseparable from the idea of violence and domination, especially when it relates to a slave taken far away from his country."

In only one respect was the Golden Age of Timbuktu blighted by regressive thinking: the prevailing attitude toward the Jews.

Thousands of them had settled in the Maghreb after their expulsion from Palestine by the Romans in the first century CE. By the fifteenth century, despite the entrenchment of Islam throughout the region, the Jews had gained a share of the salt trade, earned the privileged designation *Tujjar Al Sultan*, or the Sultan's Merchants, by the rulers of Morocco, and even produced some of the region's most splendid manuscripts, written in Hebrew. But the fragility of their status was made terribly clear in 1495. That year, a Maghrebi fundamentalist scholar, cleric, and vicious anti-Semite named Muhammed Al Maghili, incensed by their prominent economic role, organized the destruction of a synagogue in the oasis of Touat on the Saharan salt route, in what is now Algeria, and expelled the Jews from the town. "Rise up and kill the Jews," Al Maghili wrote after the attack, just as King Askia Mohammed was consolidating power. "They are indeed the bitterest of enemies who reject Mohammed." Askia Mohammed had been influenced early in his reign by a moderate Egyptian scholar he had met during a stopover in Cairo on the way to the hajj in Mecca, and who had urged the emperor to tolerate non-Muslims in his realm. But the king reversed course following his encounters with the fiery Al Maghili. Heeding Al Maghili's counsel, Askia Mohammed imprisoned the Jews of Gao, the administrative seat of the Songhai Empire, and banned them from the rest of his domain. He backed down only when a delegation of *qadis* from Timbuktu visited him in his palace in Gao—a sprawling, palisade-enclosed complex where visitors were obliged to pour dust on their heads before meeting the king—and pleaded with him to exercise compassion.

The confrontation between these two Islamic ideologies—one open and tolerant, the other inflexible and violent—would bedevil

Timbuktu over the following five centuries. In the case of King Askia Mohammed, a complex figure who encouraged a balance between secular and Islamic values, while expressing his intolerance toward non-Muslim peoples, both strains seemed embodied in a single personality. "The King is an inveterate enemy of the Jews," observed Leo Africanus. "He does not wish any to live in his town. If he hears it said that a Barbary merchant . . . does business with them, he confiscates his goods."

Eighty-two years after Leo Africanus documented Timbuktu's intellectual ferment, in 1591, the golden era abruptly ended. The Moroccan sultan demanded that the last independent king of the Songhai Empire, Askia Ishak II, surrender control to Morocco of the great Saharan salt mines of Taghaza. When the king refused, 42,000 Moroccan soldiers and 10,000 horses and camels crossed 1,700 miles of desert and laid siege to Timbuktu. Armed with cannons and harquebuses, a powerful matchlock gun invented in the fifteenth century that was fired from a support, the invaders faced a force that knew nothing about mechanized warfare: 10,000 Songhai infantrymen fighting with only bows and arrows and 18,000 spear-carrying cavalrymen. King Askia Ishak II was killed while fleeing. His brother succeeded him and pledged his fealty to the Moroccan sultan.

Ahmed Baba and other scholars urged the population to resist the occupiers. In retaliation, Moroccan troops stormed the Sankoré Mosque, looted Ahmed Baba's library, and dragged him in chains into captivity. "Why did you conquer Timbuktu?" he demanded as they led him and dozens of other Timbuktu scholars on the arduous journey across the desert, during which his chains became entangled and he broke his leg in a fall from a camel. "We are Muslims like you, and we should be brothers." Ushered into a meeting with the Moroccan sultan, he bitterly complained about the loss of his precious manuscripts. "I had the smallest library of many of my friends," he said, refusing to make declarations of obeisance or otherwise show humility before the king, "and your soldiers took from me 1,600 volumes." He would be imprisoned in Marrakesh for two years. Other intellectuals dispersed to the Volta River basin, Ghana, and northern Côte d'Ivoire—ending Timbuktu's days as a world capital of scholasticism.

Yet the city's devotion to scholarship never disappeared. After the Moroccan Empire abandoned direct rule over Timbuktu in 1660, control of the city initially fell to the Tuaregs, the Berber tribe that dominated the Sahara. Tall, light-skinned raiders swathed in indigo robes, their faces covered with a five-foot length of blue or white cotton wound around their heads so that only their eyes were exposed, they "are all wanderers in the Sahara, nomads with no settled dwelling," observed the author of the *Tariq Al Sudan* in the mid-seventeenth century. They also were a literate people, and some manuscripts of Timbuktu are written in Tifinagh, a two-thousand-year-old script developed by the Berbers that spread through the Sahara; one group of Tuareg *marabouts*, or knowledge men, the Kel Al Süq, maintained the city's scholarly traditions during the centuries of decline that followed the Moroccan occupation.

In the early and mid-nineteenth century, Sufi reformers from the Inland Niger River Delta led a "jihad of the sword" that reached as far as Timbuktu. The jihadis killed pagan chieftains, banned tobacco, alcohol, and music, opened madrassahs, or Koranic schools, required the full segregation of women and men in school and public life, forced the closure of the Great Mud Mosque of Djenné based on a strict interpretation of Islamic prohibitions against ostentation, and tracked down and destroyed manuscripts considered to be a distraction from the pure worship of God. The extremists pillaged Timbuktu's libraries and raided private homes for books as well.

The jihadis made the city's bibliophiles more careful, but didn't dissuade them from trading and collecting manuscripts. The German explorer Heinrich Barth reached Timbuktu in 1853, following an arduous Saharan crossing. "All these people, who possess a small degree of learning, and pride themselves in writing a few phrases from the Koran, were extremely anxious to obtain some scraps of paper, and I was glad to be still enabled . . . to give away some trifling presents of this kind," Barth wrote. The jihadis had depleted the manuscript collections, but the German admired a dog-eared copy of an Arabic translation of the works of Hippocrates and found a copy of the *Tariq Al Sudan*, the prized history of the Songhai Empire written in the 1650s. "I was so successful as to have an opportunity of perusing a complete history of the kingdom of Songhai, from the very dawn of historical records down to the year 1640 of our era," he wrote in his memoir, *Travels and Discoveries in North and Central Africa*.

Then, in 1879 French Sudan's governor, Louis Faidherbe, proclaimed that the territory encompassing the Senegal and Niger Rivers would be "the foundations of a new India" that would stretch as far as the Red Sea. The French occupied Bamako, then a bustling slave-trading entrepôt, in 1883. On the 12th of February 1894, after a brutal desert march of five hundred miles and forty-nine days, a column led by Colonel Joseph Césaire Joffre occupied Timbuktu, built a fort, and ushered in the French colonial era in the Malian Sahara.

Félix Dubois, a French journalist who showed up just after the military conquest, found it nearly impossible to persuade the city's bibliophiles to show him their book collections. "They were afraid that I should practice the nefarious customs of the [jihadis]," he wrote in *Timbuctoo the Mysterious*. As he visited the homes of Timbuktu's intelligentsia, his hosts gradually opened up. "Poetry and works of imagination are not lacking, nor compositions of a kind peculiar to Arabian literature," he observed. "The historical and geographical works of Morocco, Tunis, and Egypt were well known in Timbuctoo (Ibn Batuta being often quoted), and the pure sciences were represented by books on astronomy and medicine." Timbuktu's bibliophiles remained committed to "searching with a real passion for volumes they did not possess, and making copies when they were too poor to buy what they wanted," Dubois observed. "They would . . . collect from seven hundred to two thousand volumes; and . . . these bibliophiles experienced a real joy in sharing their most precious manuscripts."

However, as the French consolidated their control over the north, the days of open commerce and book exchanges ended. Soldiers and visiting scholars made off with manuscripts and took them home to France, where they ended up on display in university and government collections, including the Bibliothèque Nationale in Paris. Three copies of the *Tariq Al Sudan* seized in Timbuktu were carted off to Paris, translated by Octave Houdas, and published in French editions in 1900. People hid manuscripts all over Mali. They placed them inside leather bags and buried them in holes in their courtyards and gardens, stashed them in abandoned caves in the desert, and sealed the doors of their libraries with mud to hide the treasures inside. Under the new colonial rulers, French became the primary language taught in Mali's schools. As a result, several generations in Timbuktu and other towns in the region grew up without learning to speak Arabic, which doomed the works to irrelevance.

The volumes of history, poetry, medicine, and astronomy once proudly displayed in libraries, markets, and homes became rare and then disappeared. The great writing tradition was almost completely

3

Abdel Kader Haidara signed on as a prospector for the Ahmed Baba Institute in the fall of 1984. Mahmoud Zouber, the director, showed Haidara how to approach the manuscript owners, and how to encourage them. The most important thing, Zouber said, was to avoid mentioning the Ahmed Baba Institute at first, because, after the trauma of the French occupation, people were still deeply afraid of organizations affiliated with the government. "Say you're the son of Mamma Haidara, the illustrious scholar," Zouber advised. "You have to bring up the manuscripts gradually," he went on. "Don't get them angry, don't make them nervous. Use patience. You may have to go back several times."

One of Zouber's longtime friends was John O. Hunwick, the world's leading expert on Timbuktu's literary heritage, as well as a scholar of the manuscript tradition in Egypt, Nigeria, and Ghana. At Zouber's invitation, Hunwick set up camp in Timbuktu for a

forgotten. "Perhaps in the future, there will be some African history
to teach. But at present there is none," the British historian Hugh
Trevor-Roper proclaimed in an interview with the BBC in 1963.
"There is only the history of Europeans in Africa. The rest is darkness."

month and gave Haidara a crash course in manuscript history.

Born in Somerset, England, in 1936, Hunwick had served with the British Army in Kenya during the Mau-Mau rebellion and with the Somaliland Scouts in Hargeisa, then mastered Arabic at the University of London's School of Oriental and African Studies. He had first encountered Timbuktu's manuscripts while teaching in the mid-1960s at the University of Ibadan in Nigeria, translated original manuscripts recounting the history of the Songhai Empire, and spent the next quarter century gathering information about the titles and locations of tens of thousands of Arabic manuscripts from Mali, Senegal, Guinea, Ghana, the Ivory Coast, Burkina Faso, and Niger. Hunwick also created the Institute for the Study of Islamic Thought in Africa at Northwestern University in Chicago, widely regarded as the foremost academic institution for Arabic manuscript study in the world.

In Timbuktu, Hunwick and Haidara sat together for hours each day at the home of Zouber and in a conference room at the institute, discussing the provenances of manuscripts, preservation methods, and the best areas of Mali to prospect for the books. After his tutelage from Hunwick, Haidara attended UNESCO conservation workshops in Rabat, the Moroccan capital, and Bamako, and learned to assess the value of manuscripts by age, authorship, and design. The training course went on for eight months.

Haidara began his search by knocking on the doors of the twelve most prominent families in Timbuktu, who had dominated book collecting in the region for centuries. Haidara introduced himself, made small talk, sometimes going back two or three times before gently broaching the subject of the manuscripts. The reaction was always the same. "You?" the owners responded dismissively, waving Haidara away. "Who do you think you are, *mon petit*?" they would say, mocking him for his youth and his inexperience and the less exalted position of his family in Timbuktu's social hierarchy. "You have the nerve to talk to me about the manuscripts?" After a few weeks he gave up, having failed to persuade them to turn over more than a handful of manuscripts.

Then he expanded his territory. On his maiden voyage beyond the city, Haidara headed down the Niger in a pinasse, a motorized and covered wooden longboat that was used to carry passengers and cargo. His destination was a town one hundred miles downriver, or east, from Timbuktu, called Gourma Rharous, an intellectual center at the height of the Songhai Empire. Haidara had met many people who spoke about the town in wondrous terms, as a meeting place for poets, scientists, and *marabouts*. The hereditary chief, Mohammed Al Hanafi, had been a friend of his father, and Haidara knew that the town had been a repository for manuscripts for centuries.

The previous prospecting teams had roared into villages in two or three government Land Cruisers—an army of eight people carrying cameras, microfiche machines, and generators. Realizing that the onslaught intimidated villagers, Haidara traveled by himself, dressed humbly, and carried nothing but a small satchel. He had several thousand dollars hidden inside the bag for purchasing manuscripts, but reasoned—rightly, as it turned out—that his modest appearance would prevent him from becoming a target of bandits.

The boatman motored the craft past beaches and low dunes, devoid of vegetation except for patches of desiccated grass and the occasional acacia tree—typical of the landscape along this stretch of the Niger River as it curved and flowed eastward through the semidesert of central Mali. Protected from the sun by a canvas roof mounted on the gunnels, Haidara passed the dugout canoes of Sorhai fishermen, known as Bozos, who dwelled in boxlike mud huts lined up against the olive-green water. "They form the sole population of these settlements and occupy distinct quarters in the towns and cities, thus emphasizing . . . that the Bosos still belong exclusively to the river," wrote Félix Dubois, the French journalist and historian who traveled throught the area at the time of the French conquest, and who observed the riverine subculture during a 300-mile journey downstream from the colonial town of Ségou to Timbuktu in 1895. The scene witnessed by Dubois had changed little by the time Haidara made the journey. "I have seen them set out to the capture of their great prey (the alligator and the sea-cow)," Dubois went on. "Silently, almost without movement, they advance until the watchful eye in the bow discerns some alligator asleep on the tide, or some great bearded fish dozing betwixt wind and water. Then the nude silhouette in the bow is strained by a beautiful movement of the free body, the right arm is poised, and the harpoon flung, striking the great beast unawares."

Arriving in Gourma Rharous after a journey of two days and one night, Haidara clambered onto the riverbank and searched through the sandy alleys for the hereditary chief. Haidara introduced himself as Mamma Haidara's son to Al Hanafi. They drank tea together and he spent the night at Al Hanafi's house. The following morning, over further cups of tea, he announced the real reason for his mission.

Haidara assured Al Hanafi that the Ahmed Baba Institute would register all manuscripts, so that nobody would lose track of his contributions. He emphasized that he was willing to compensate the owners generously. The chief said that he had no manuscripts himself, but offered to do what he could to help. "Stay here, don't go into town," Al Hanafi said. "I'll go to the mosque, and I will speak to all of the owners there."

Villagers trickled in, bearing books. Some were in good condition, while others fell apart in Haidara's hands. Silently and carefully he turned the pages, assessing their value with expert eye, noting their age, their place of origin, the decorations in the margins, the amount of gold leaf. He purchased 250 manuscripts, loaded them into a pinasse, and sailed back upriver to Timbuktu.

Over the coming months, Haidara returned two more times to Gourma Rharous and bought 250 more works. He was becoming increasingly confident about his persuasive powers and his ability to assess a manuscript's value. Then, on the fourth voyage, without explanation, the sellers stopped coming.

"Nobody's talking to me. People are avoiding me. What's going on?" he asked the chief.

"I've got no idea," Al Hanafi replied.

Another week went by. When he greeted people on the street, they turned away. At last, an acquaintance approached him in the market. One of Gourma Rharous's officials, a man whose responsibilities included safeguarding the town's cultural patrimony, was looking for Haidara, he said. "He's very angry."

Haidara sought out the man, and introduced himself. The official refused to shake his hand. "You've created a lot of problems for us. Everybody thinks you're trafficking in manuscripts for profit. Nobody is happy with what you are doing."

Haidara tried to explain the nature of his mission, but it was no use. The official, a highly influential figure, had begun actively dissuading everyone in the town from cooperating. "Pay attention, you have to keep hold of your manuscripts, ignore this fellow," the official advised. "We don't have any idea who he is. We don't know where he's going." Haidara stayed a few more days. Unlike the previous three visits, when he had collected a total of five hundred volumes, he left empty-handed and discouraged. It had taken a single skeptic to undermine Haidara's efforts to win over the population.

The skeptics were everywhere. He journeyed down the river to his ancestral home of Bamba, and east along the Niger as far as Gao, the ancient capital of the Songhai Empire, located two hundred miles east of Timbuktu. There he sought out the Islamic judge, or *qadi*, one of the city's foremost intellectuals. He greeted Haidara cordially, invited him to sit down, and they talked about the manuscripts and the patrimony of Mali. Haidara gently broached the subject of the Ahmed Baba Institute and said he had come to encourage the *qadi* to contribute his manuscripts to the collection. Abruptly, the *qadi*'s attitude changed.

"Who led you here?" the *qadi* demanded.

"I read a lot, and I learned that your family comes from a long line of scholars and intellectuals, and has a collection of ancient manuscripts."

"No, no, no," the *qadi* said. Haidara knew that he was lying—he had heard from a reliable source that the *qadi* stored his treasures in a secret chamber in his house—but there was nothing he could do. The *qadi* called Haidara a "bandit" to his face, and threw him out of his house.

He journeyed by camel for five days to the onetime salt-trading entrepôt of Araouan, deep in the Sahara, 150 miles north along a historic caravan route. Five hundred years ago Araouan, the birthplace of Ahmed Baba, had been a center of Islamic scholarship as well as salt commerce, and he had heard through his Saharan sources that many illustrious works were hidden there—including those collected by the Scottish explorer Laing and stolen by Arab nomads after his murder. Haidara was not used to traveling by camel. He held on tightly to the saddle as the beast mounted sixty-foot-high dunes covered with grass, then, knees buckling, plunged sharply down the other side. He rode jarringly through valleys filled with a sea of spiny bushes that thinned out as they journeyed further north. Then the great waves of sand gradually disappeared, replaced by soft undulations furrowing a barren desert plateau. Nearby were the ruins of the legendary city of Taghaza, which had inspired medieval travelers to fantastic flights of imagination. "The ramparts of the city were of salt as also all its walls, pillars, and roofs," the medieval Persian cartographer Al Qazwini wrote of Taghaza, basing his account on the fanciful testimony of an eyewitness who had recently visited the oasis. "The doors, too, were made of slabs of salt covered with leather so that the edges might not crack . . . all the land around the town is a salt pan . . . if an animal dies there it is thrown into the desert and turns to salt." Araouan, a crumbling village where it hadn't rained in forty years, hadn't turned to salt, but it had fallen on hard times. The population of two hundred subsisted on a diet of fried locusts, and regarded outsiders with hostility. "He's dangerous. What does he want with these manuscripts?" people said about him. "Maybe he wants to destroy them. Maybe he wants to bring us a new religion."

Promising leads turned into crushing disappointments. In Majakoy, on the Niger River, villagers led to him to a man who, they said, had a valuable collection. Haidara found him guarding a locked trunk. He refused to open it.

"It's for the town's orphans, it's not for me. I can't even touch it."

"Can I at least see it?" Haidara pleaded.

"That's not possible."

The dialogue went on for four days, until the man threw open the chest. Haidara eagerly peered inside—then recoiled in dismay. Termites scuttled in every direction. They had been devouring the last shreds of the manuscripts. Ninety percent had been reduced to dust. The owner looked at the seven volumes that were left—and wept. He hadn't opened the trunk, he admitted, in twenty years.

But Haidara was patient. Over the course of his journeys he constantly refined his approach to manuscript hunting, and achieved better and better results. "My predecessors made a number of errors that I tried to correct," Haidara recalled years later. "I avoided everything that didn't work for them, and I introduced my own strategies." He never traveled by motor vehicle, believing that it would cause the manuscript owners in poor villages to think that he had vast wealth, and prompt them to inflate their asking price. Instead, when he journeyed away from the river, he rented camels or donkeys. Traveling with pack animals instead of in a motorized vehicle extended his journeys by days, sometimes weeks, but Haidara was convinced that it earned him villagers' trust. Often, when Haidara talked with the head of a family about "buying" the manuscripts, he was immediately shown the door. "Get out. Get out!" the owner would say. He soon realized that the word had a distasteful connotation for many manuscript owners, equating a treasure passed down through generations with cold cash. From that point, he used only the word "exchange." He acquired manuscripts in return for building the village a school, and, more often, in a trade for livestock. "I gave out a lot of cows," he said.

Many times he arranged to trade the manuscripts for printed books, a highly sought after commodity in remote villages. Haidara reached out to booksellers across the Maghreb—Tunisia, Morocco, Algeria, and Libya—and received shipments in the mail of Arabic literature, history, and poetry, then returned to the villages bearing the books. The process could take six months, but it was almost always worth the trouble. "Take whatever you want," the owners exclaimed joyfully, running their hands over the bound and printed volumes. Over time, as well, word spread up and down the Niger and through the desert about the conservation work being done by the Ahmed Baba Institute, and some manuscript owners traveled to Timbuktu and saw the care with which their precious heirlooms were being treated. Faith in Haidara grew.

Haidara was developing an acute sense of each book's worth, and was becoming a skilled negotiator. If the manuscript was complete, which was not that common, it would elevate its value. If Timbuktu's scribes had made many copies of a single work it would diminish the price. He valued manuscripts written by Timbuktu's most illustrious calligraphers—a handful of artistic geniuses identified by the colophons at the end of each volume—far more highly than the work of lesser scribes. Subject matter was another key criterion. Haidara highly esteemed works on conflict resolution, contemporary politics, geography—particularly those with detailed and colorful maps—and government corruption, because few such studies existed, and he also placed a high value on medical manuscripts, because the knowledge they imparted was often applicable today.

Haidara took into account damage from termites, dust, or bacteria, but weighed the extent of the destruction against the rarity and beauty of the work, and often bought it anyway, figuring that he would restore it when he brought it back to Timbuktu. And he was prepared to pay huge prices if something captured his imagination. In Sikasso, a town southeast of Bamako near the border with Burkina Faso, he once came across a large trunk containing several hundred manuscripts—poetry written by the great *ulemas*, or Islamic scholars, from the Peul tribe of Massina in the eighteenth century; manuscripts that described the arrival of French troops in the country in the mid-nineteenth century and debated the implications of the foreigners' presence; manuscripts about jurisprudence written in a variety of Malian languages, including Peul, Bambara, and Soninké, and transliterated into Arabic; and works that delved deeply into herbal medicines and other esoteric remedies. Haidara acquired the trunkful of manuscripts in exchange for constructing a new mosque for the village as well as a primary school, paying "many thousands of dollars" for the collection. It was the most expensive transaction he made in fifteen years of manuscript prospecting.

People also sensed that Haidara was playing fair. After nearly being run out of Gourma Rharous, the first town he had visited, Haidara returned there a year later. On his first afternoon back in town, a Tuareg nomad in his forties, a gaunt man in a ragged turban with half a dozen children playing around him in the sand, called out to him in greeting as he passed by his tent.

"Come inside," he cried.

Haidara entered the traditional dwelling, stitched together from goatskins, and sat on the ground in the semidarkness. He noticed a metal chest at the rear of the tent, the type normally used to hold manuscripts.

"You come from where?" said the Tuareg.

"I'm from Timbuktu," replied Haidara in Tamasheq, the language of the Tuaregs. In addition to his native Songhoy, he was conversant in Peul and Tamasheq, the two other main languages of Mali's north, as well as French, and thus had no problem negotiating with manuscript owners across the region.

Haidara made small talk, and, seeing that the Tuareg was too poor even to offer his visitor a cup of tea, he offered to purchase some food and drink for him and his family. Haidara ran out to the market, and returned with half a slaughtered lamb and a kilogram bag of tea. The Tuareg grilled the lamb outside the tent and, as they sat eating in the sand with the man's family, Haidara gently broached the subject of manuscripts.

"I don't have any of those," the Tuareg said. "I only have printed books."

"Can I take a look?" asked Haidara.

"Why not?"

Haidara opened the trunk and pored through the volumes. Buried among the printed material was one work that caught his eye: a Koran from the seventeenth century. He looked through it carefully, noting the delicate Maghrebi letters, the fragile gilt that caught the late afternoon light filtering through the tent flap. It was, Haidara realized, a masterpiece.

"How much do you want for this?" asked Haidara.

"Whatever you want to give me," the owner said, shrugging.

"You have to name your price."

"Give me five thousand CFA," or about ten dollars, the nomad said. It was a pitifully low sum. Haidara could not accept it. They bargained—but this time the buyer was bidding up the price.

"No, no. This treasure has a huge value," he replied.

"Ten thousand CFA."

"No," said Haidara.

"Twenty thousand."

Haidara gave him one hundred thousand CFA. The man received the money, wide-eyed. "If I've got more books like that will you pay for them?" he asked.

"Of course."

At five o'clock the morning after that, in total darkness, Haidara heard a knock on his door.

"Who's that?" Haidara said.

The Tuareg entered his room, carrying a large camel-skin sack. Wordlessly he dumped a pile of manuscripts on the ground. In the murkiness before dawn, Haidara could barely see what was lying there. But at six o'clock, golden light filtered through his window, illuminating magnificent treasure. When Haidara stepped outside the hut later that morning he stared in astonishment. Tuaregs from across the region had formed a long line in front of his door, bearing camel and sheepskin sacks stuffed with manuscripts. Many had been hidden in caves or holes in the sand for decades. Haidara handed out the equivalent of thousands of dollars—Kuwait and Saudi Arabia had subsidized the effort—and left with more than a thousand manuscripts. He had paid the sellers everything that they had demanded, and even more. He had taken everything they had.

Haidara headed back upriver to Timbuktu, his boat riding low in the water, weighed down with footlockers and piles of camel-skin sacks.

In Timbuktu, Mahmoud Zouber looked on with astonishment. "You found all that?" he said.

In his first year of work at the Ahmed Baba Institute, Haidara managed to acquire as many manuscripts as the previous team of eight prospectors had collected in a decade.

Haidara's obsession was growing. He was spending an average of three weeks a month on the road, mostly traveling by pinasse and dugout canoe along the Niger, then returning to Timbuktu to catalogue his works and rest before heading out on the road again. Serendipitous discoveries kept him craving more. Once, in a village near Timbuktu, Haidara acquired a fifty-page fragment of a biography of Islamic saints that he found pleasing, then, on a hunch, traveled up and down the Niger looking for the rest. After two years of assiduous searching he located a similar fragment in a storage room in a village near Gao, 250 miles from the site of the first acquisition. In Timbuktu, he assembled the two parts—and discovered that he now held a complete work by the great Ahmed Baba written during the savant's captivity. On the last-page colophon Baba had written his name; the date, "991," according to the Islamic calendar, equivalent to 1593: and the place of its creation, "Marrakesh." The biography, in two pieces, had made its way back across the desert centuries later to Mali.

Haidara had become consumed by the urge to discover the provenances of the manuscripts, tracing the often circuitous journeys that they made over the centuries. "When I was at the Ahmed Baba Institute, I had an office filled with manuscripts," he would recall decades later. "When I was home, manuscripts surrounded me. My friends told me 'you have gone crazy. You can't talk about anything else.' I said, 'leave me alone.' The manuscripts had a certain smell, and they said 'you are smelling of manuscripts, Abdel Kader.'"

In 1992, Zouber confronted Haidara at the headquarters of the
Ahmed Baba Institute. The director, who had taken a paternal interest in his young prospector, was concerned about his personal life.
"What's the matter with you?" he asked. "Why haven't you gotten
married yet? What are you waiting for?"

"Look," Haidara said, not wanting to feel pressured. "I don't
even have a house to call my own." Haidara was content sharing
with his siblings the spacious home in Sankoré that had been be-
queathed to them by their parents. And though he hadn't yet found
a mate, he felt no need to hurry. He had an active social life, plenty
of friends in Timbuktu, and remained close to many of his siblings,
including a couple of far-flung elder brothers who had become
traders in Cameroon and Senegal. Zouber, however, insisted that
Haidara settle down.

"Okay," said Zouber, "I owe you a lot of money for the last mission you undertook for us. I'm going to write you a check, and I
want you to buy some property with it." With his earnings, Haidara
heeded Zouber's wish and purchased a plot of land owned by an
uncle in Bella Farandja, a newer neighborhood on the eastern edge
of Timbuktu, facing the desert. Later, he built on the property a traditional house of limestone blocks, a large vestibule, and an inner
courtyard, much like the one in which he had grown up. Months
afterward, Haidara met a young woman, a university student in Bamako and the daughter of a traditional Sorhai chief from Timbuktu's Djingareyber quarter. They initiated a courtship and continued
to see each other whenever she returned to Timbuktu.

One day Haidara set forth from Timbuktu toward Mali's border
with the Sahel nation of Burkina Faso, five hundred miles to the
southeast. He had heard that a family in a remote village had accumulated the finest collection of manuscripts in the region. He

traveled by truck toward Gao, skirting a vast lake the color of café au lait, where longhorn cattle grazed along the barren brown shore and the skeletal remains of drowned acacia trees protruded from the shallows. The lake, near the town of Gossi, was also known for the large herds of desert elephants, among the last in the Sahel, that cluster around its banks during Mali's dry season. Just beyond the lake rose the strange quartz-and-sandstone outcropping called Fatimah's Hand, named after the daughter of the Prophet and his wife Khadijah, three fingerlike pillars almost the color of human flesh, tilting slightly backward and extending two thousand feet from the desert floor toward the sky.

In Gossi, the site of the region's biggest cattle market, he hitched another ride on a truck to a smaller village. There he joined a fifty-camel caravan, bringing bars of salt from the Taoudenni mines in the northern Sahara to Burkina Faso. Haidara mounted a camel at two o'clock the first afternoon, but after half a mile, he begged to get off.

"What's the problem?" the camel driver asked.

"I'm in pain. I need to walk."

They trudged through the sand for eleven hours, and at one o'clock in the morning they found a suitable place to camp. His companion prepared a meal, but when Haidara saw what he was eating—gristly, rotten-looking antelope—he felt sick, and preferred to go hungry. At six a.m. they resumed their journey, heading east for another twelve hours and camping in the sand. They left early again the following morning, and crossed a shallow lake near the Burkina Faso–Mali frontier. "We're going to go our separate ways here, and you have to continue on your own," the camel driver said upon reaching the other side. With his small sack on his back, Haidara began walking. "It's very close," the man shouted after him. "Just follow the lake. Don't leave it behind."

Haidara trudged along the lake beneath a broiling sun, with

temperatures approaching one hundred degrees, sipping from the half-liter flask of water that he had brought with him, managing to cool himself off by splashing himself from time to time in the tepid, muddy waters of the lake. He was carrying thousands of dollars of cash in his satchel, but, as always, he was dressed humbly, and was confident that he would strike nobody as being a promising target for robbery. Eight hours after starting out, nearing sundown, parched and exhausted, he arrived at the village. The manuscript owner was gone. He recuperated from his exhausting walk, and waited two days until the man returned. Haidara introduced himself and announced that had come to see his manuscripts.

"Who told you about that?" the man demanded.

"Everybody knows about it. Your father was a friend of my father."

"What do you want? You want to copy them? You want me to lend them to you?"

"No, no, I want to exchange them with you."

"I can't even talk about this with you. This is our history, there is no price."

"Well I want to see them anyway."

The man brought out sacks filled with manuscripts. Most were in terrible condition—bloated from water damage or gouged by termites—and were beyond repair. Some had torn pages and mold growing on them, but Haidara was confident that he could restore them. Others were in mint condition, and included some of the finest works that he had ever seen. There were theological treatises from the fifteenth and sixteenth centuries, leafed in gold, and adorned with the handwritten commentaries of generations of scholars. The greatest treasure was a Koran from the eleventh century, written in Egypt one hundred years before Timbuktu came into being.

Haidara knew that he had to have them—at any cost.

"I'm not selling them," the man insisted. "The manuscripts don't leave our presence."

"I want to take them to Timbuktu," Haidara explained. "An institute there will conserve them, display them, and restore them to good condition. They will be there for the whole world to share and see—including you and your children."

"This is not just for me," the man replied. "It is for for my older brother, who lives in a village not far from me." A search party went out looking for the brother. He showed up the following night. Haidara could sense that he was open to negotiation.

"I'm ready to give you goats, sheep, cows, whatever you want."

Haidara and the older brother crossed the marsh in a pirogue and then walked another two days to a market town across the Burkina Faso border. In this remote and sparsely populated corner of the Sahel, the frontier was not clearly marked or policed, and people moved back and forth freely. The man brought out a shopping list: fifty goats, two mules, a huge quantity of rice, millet, and fabrics. Haidara spent $10,000—an unheard of sum. Mules brought the goods back to the village. Haidara loaded the sacks of manuscripts onto the backs of three camels, and then, after handshakes all around, headed back to Timbuktu.

By now he had spent almost all of his money. His guide brought him to a village, where he waited five days before renting a four-wheel-drive that carried him to Gao, and from Gao he hitched a ride on a truck back to Timbuktu. It had been a four-week journey to retrieve these manuscripts, the longest, most difficult voyage that Haidara had ever made. When he finally arrived, after all the grueling days of trekking through the bush there and back, he was gaunt, broke, thirsty, and physically spent. But he never regretted making the trip.

Nor did Haidara have second thoughts about the life that he had chosen. "I was well paid for this work. They let me do whatever

I wanted, and I did it well," he recalled three decades later. "I had my freedom. And I had a great responsibility. I had to convince people not to lie. I had to convince them to hand over their manuscripts. They gave me this responsibility with confidence, and I had to fulfill it. And when I started reading these manuscripts, I discovered amazing things, and I couldn't leave them alone. I couldn't stop reading." He steeped himself in the lives of kings and savants, in the wondrous encounters of Timbuktu's intellectuals with the city's first Western visitors, in the divisions within Sufism over *fikh*, or Islamic law, and in the ethical arguments of Ahmed Baba and other polemicists.

He was particularly interested in manuscripts that contradicted Western stereotypes of Islam as a religion of intolerance—pointing with pride to Ahmed Baba's denunciations of slavery, and to the strident correspondence between the jihadi sultan of Massina and Sheikh Ahmed Al Bakkay Al Kounti, a mid-nineteenth-century Islamic scholar in Timbuktu known for his moderation and acceptance of Jews and Christians. As time passed he became something of a savant himself, revered by many peers in Timbuktu for his knowledge of the region's history and religion, sought after by parents to offer their children guidance.

Soon after returning to Timbuktu with his prized acquisitions from the Burkina Faso border, he went back on the road. The pace was unrelenting. He traveled for hundreds of miles along the Niger, paddling canoes and riding in motorized longboats, heading upstream and downstream, stopping at nearly every village and town en route—Diré, Tonka, Goundam, Niafounké, Gourma Rharous, Bourem Inali, Gao. He made repeated trips in camel caravans north to the barren desert along the Algerian border, and sometimes crossed the frontier into Algeria and Morocco. Haidara was single, and could be gone for long periods, but he found the journeys exhausting—and sometimes dangerous. He fell off a camel. He suffered from exposure, burned beneath the desert sun, and seared himself in the desert wind.

Near Gao, an eighteen-wheeler he was riding in overturned while trying to surmount a huge sand dune. Dozens of passengers, including women and children, were sandwiched between large burlap sacks of grain and other goods carried with them in the back, and several were badly injured. Haidara leapt free of the huge vehicle moments before it toppled over, and came out of it with only a few scratches. Three times his pirogue overturned in rough waters in the Niger, sending satchels and other belongings to the bottom of the river. By an astonishing stroke of fortune, each accident occurred while he was on the way to a village from Timbuktu on a buying expedition. Each time, he was able to salvage the money he had brought with him, carefully wrapped, inside his gown. And he never lost a single manuscript.

4

In 1993, Haidara considered moving on. He had worked at the Ahmed Baba Institute for nine years, surviving road accidents and canoe capsizings, losing his way in the Sahara. He had acquired 16,500 manuscripts, creating one of the largest public collections of Arabic handwritten books in the world. Haidara had become engaged to the university student in Bamako and was ready to settle down and start a family; they would be married in 1995. And he had become focused on the future of the Mamma Haidara collection, languishing in tin crates in storage rooms in Timbuktu and his ancestral village, Bamba. One day he approached the director, Zouber, by now one of his closest confidants. Haidara would name his eldest son after him.

"You know I have a problem," he said. "I've been working for the Ahmed Baba Institute, collecting and preserving the manuscripts of Timbuktu, for quite a while now, but I've never done this for the manuscripts of my own family."

"Why not?" Zouber asked.

"Because I don't want to bring them here."

"You have to bring them here."

"But I can't," said Haidara, explaining that he had made a vow when he was seventeen never to part with any of the works from the collection.

"What do you want then?"

"I want to create a private manuscript library."

"It's a fine idea," the director said. "You have to do it."

Haidara, pleased by Zouber's support, kept his office at the center while embarking on a search for funding. He pored through newspapers and magazines, tracked down the addresses of foundations and research centers, and sent out a hundred letters to addresses in Turkey, Iraq, Iran, Kuwait, Saudi Arabia, Egypt, Libya, Syria, and Lebanon, as well as Western Europe and the United States. Most institutions didn't respond. A few expressed interest, but those demanded a full catalogue of Haidara's manuscripts. Haidara couldn't do it. Nobody had ever attempted to itemize the thousands of works in the Mamma Haidara collection; even he had no idea what it contained. If he sent them a sample of just a few hundred, he reasoned, they would dismiss the archive as small and insignificant, and refuse to fund him. He reached out to the minister of culture in Bamako, who informed him that private libraries didn't exist in Mali.

That same year, Haidara hosted in Timbuktu a Malian student who was writing his doctoral dissertation in Libya on Saharan manuscripts. Haidara gave him a tour of the Ahmed Baba Institute, allowed him a peek at his own collection, and permitted him to take photographs. News of Haidara's collection eventually reached the Libyan government, which contacted him in early 1996.

"We're going to help you," an official close to Muammar Al Qaddafi said. Five Libyan historians and archivists arrived from Tripoli in a government plane and came directly to Haidara's house from the Timbuktu airport. The men looked through the manuscripts, then conferred.

"We have a proposition for you," they said.

"I'm listening," Haidara replied.

"We want to buy everything we see here." They opened a brief-case, and showed Haidara stacks of bills in various currencies. "You name the price."

Haidara had little affection for Muammar Al Qaddafi or his politics. The Libyan dictator had often expressed his devotion to Saharan culture and Timbuktu—he would call it "my favorite city" and spend millions of dollars buying real estate and refilling the canal where Haidara had swum as a child—but Haidara regarded him as a power-hungry megalomaniac who had sowed mischief across the region. It was widely known that the Libyan leader was playing a double game—supporting the Malian government with generous outlays of money for development projects while keeping the Tuareg insurgency in the north alive by harboring rebel leaders, training young Tuaregs as mercenaries, and funneling cash to the movement. Qaddafi had numerous hidden agendas, and he seemed to believe that everybody had a price.

"I understood their politics, and they weren't mine," Haidara would tell me years later. "I'm not rich, but it wasn't money that I was looking for."

"Thanks, but no thanks," he told the Libyans. "You never said that you were coming here to attempt to purchase the manuscripts."

"What do you mean? We will pay you in any currency you want."

"It's not for sale."

"Why not?"

"Because this isn't for me. This is the heritage of Mali. It belongs to a great nation."

"But we can make you comfortable for the rest of your life."

"No," he said.

At about the same time that Haidara was fending off the interest of Qaddafi and his representatives, Henry Louis "Skip" Gates, the American literary scholar, filmmaker, professor, and director of the Hutchins Center for African and African American Research at Harvard University, was contemplating a visit to Mali. Born in Keyser, West Virginia, Gates had earned a summa cum laude degree in history at Harvard in 1972, and became the first African-American to win an Andrew W. Mellon Foundation Fellowship, which funded his PhD research at Cambridge University. After being wooed by several Ivy League universities, he accepted a tenured position in Harvard's English department in 1991. From that prestigious perch, Gates became the country's most prominent critic of the Eurocentric literary canon and, in books such as *The Signifying Monkey*, a 1989 American Book Award winner, promoted the recognition of African and African-American literature and history.

In 1960, *Ripley's—Believe It or Not!,* the popular syndicated comic strip that appeared in many American newspapers and features oddities and bizarre events—a meteor strike on a ship in the Pacific, a two-foot-long bug in Borneo, thieves who stole "an entire beach" in Jamaica by removing the sand—highlighted a curiosity from Africa that enthralled the ten-year-old Gates. The single-panel drawing, appearing in Gates's local newspaper, showed men in gowns and turbans holding books and strolling through a great university library in Timbuktu in the sixteenth century. For the young Gates, raised with traditional conceptions of Africa as a continent of savages in the bush, the comic strip was a revelation. "It blew my mind, and the image stuck with me ever since," Gates said.

The newspaper comic contradicted the long-accepted "truth" about Africans presented by some of the greatest historians and philosophers of the Western world. In a 1754 essay called "Of National

Characters," David Hume had declared, "I am apt to suspect the Negroes . . . to be naturally inferior to the whites. . . . No ingenious manufactures among them, no arts, no sciences." Immanuel Kant, in his work on aesthetics, *Observations on the Feeling of the Beautiful and Sublime*, published in 1764, contended, "The Negroes of Africa have by nature no feeling that rises above the trifling . . . not a single one was ever found who presented anything great in art or science or any other praiseworthy quality." Georg Wilhelm Friedrich Hegel, in the 1837 *Philosophy of History*, argued that Africa had no indigenous system of writing, no historical memory, and no civilization. "It is no historical part of the World; it has no movement or development to exhibit," he declared. "What we properly understand by Africa is the Unhistorical, Undeveloped Spirit." The arguments of these Enlightenment philosophers had frequently been cited as a justification for the slave trade. The supposed absence of books in Africa, the argument went, provided confirmation of the subhuman position of blacks in the Great Chain of Being—a Platonic concept that had developed in the Middle Ages and persisted in the Age of Enlightenment, linking all life in a strict hierarchy of obedience with God at the top, followed by angels, nobles, men, wild animals, domesticated animals, vegetables, and inanimate matter.

Thirty-seven years after being inspired by the *Ripley's—Believe It or Not!* cartoon, Gates received funding for a six-part documentary series about African history for the BBC and PBS. He decided to devote an hour-long segment to "The Road to Timbuktu," which would examine the rise and achievements of the Malian and Songhai Empires. "I wanted to see the Great Mosque in Djenné, and go to Timbuktu, and investigate myself the truth of the university's presence and its so-called library," Gates recalled. Gates and his film crew arrived in Bamako in the spring of 1997, and traveled for a week by pinasse down the Niger. Arriving at the port near Timbuktu, they planned to film at the Ahmed Baba Institute, and the

Sankoré and Djingareyber Mosques, where informal universities had flourished during Timbuktu's Golden Age.

But when they reached their hotel, their translator-guide, an acquaintance of Haidara, approached them with a different proposal. "If you want to see a real library," he said, "these books are held mostly in private hands, and there is a man I know who might be willing to show you his collection." Gates, intrigued, changed his itinerary, and he and his film crew followed his guide through the back alleys to Haidara's house.

Haidara meanwhile, was growing despondent. The library he had dreamed of creating for five years was going nowhere. More than one hundred foundations had turned down his proposal, and he had run out of ideas.

"A big delegation of Americans is here in Timbuktu," Gates's guide informed Haidara on the morning of the Harvard professor's arrival. "They want to visit you. They want to see your manuscripts, so be ready."

Haidara sensed that the visit could be an opportunity for him. "Fine," he replied. "I'll prepare something for them." Haidara laid down a carpet, and gathered the best manuscripts in his Timbuktu collection. Gates and the film crew arrived later that day. As the crew filmed, Gates leafed through a treatise on astronomy, a ledger book that recorded slave transactions, and other works.

"These are books written by black people?" Gates asks Haidara in a scene captured on camera. Haidara, a bushy-haired and youthful thirty-three-year-old, nods. "When I was growing up," Gates replies, shaking his head in amazement, "the schoolbooks said that Africans couldn't read and write, and didn't have any books." For hours, Haidara gave Gates a tutorial on Timbuktu's literary heritage, describing the rise of the University of Sankoré and its illustrious roster of biographers, jurists, and historians; enumerating the twelve important families that had accumulated most of Timbuktu's manuscripts during its Golden Age; chronicling the invasion by Morocco that drove most of these volumes underground; and explaining the role played by descendants of Timbuktu's collectors, who had protected the works for four hundred years. "It was one of the most moving days of my life," Gates recalled. "I was so emotional, holding these books in my hands."

Not a word was spoken about Haidara's stymied plans to build a library, but Gates left his encounter convinced he had to do something to preserve the manuscripts. Unprotected in neglected storage rooms, many were turning to dust or being devoured by termites, and some had already been lost. "It was a bone-dry climate in Timbuktu, so he was lucky," Gates said. "If they'd been stored in the humidity of Nigeria, they would have turned to mush long ago."

When he returned to the United States, Gates informed the project director at the Andrew W. Mellon Foundation in New York City of the "amazing discovery" he had made in Timbuktu. "All of these books still exist, this guy has them, and they're not even in a library," he said. Three months later, on the strength of Gates's recommendation, the Mellon Foundation awarded Haidara a grant of nearly $100,000 for the creation of a new manuscript center in Timbuktu. The money came with strings attached: Mellon required the collector to create a digital archive before moving ahead with the physical construction. "I know you want to build a library, but the cataloguing and digitization have to come first," Gates emphasized. Haidara expressed his gratitude. Then he hired an architect and construction crew and built the library anyway.

"What?" Gates said, when Haidara informed him several months later that the library was complete. "I told you that you needed to catalogue first."

"We can't do that without first having a building," Haidara replied. He argued that the manuscripts had been exposed to the elements and imperiled in their dusty storage rooms, and that his first priority was to protect them.

Exasperated, and fearing a scandal, Gates reported the misuse of the grant money to the Mellon Foundation. They grumbled about it, but the attitude, says Gates, was "what's done is done."

A few months later, Haidara again called Gates at Harvard.

"What is it?" asked Gates, still annoyed by Haidara's high-handedness.

"I need another grant to build another library," Haidara said.

"What?" Gates exclaimed once more. "It's amazing that you got a grant to begin with."

"I know," Haidara said, "but there was a slight miscalculation."

"What are you talking about?"

"We built it in the floodplain. We have to rebuild it." As Haidara explained it, after many years of little or no rainfall in Timbuktu, he and his construction team had taken for granted that the building site was secure. But that year a once-in-a-generation series of rainstorms had struck the region. Rainwater had deluged the rooms, cracked the cement, and caused the roof to collapse.

"Everything is filled with water," he told Gates. Luckily, Haidara hadn't yet started moving his manuscripts into the new library, and they had all been spared.

Gates, mortified, went back to the Mellon Foundation. "You remember that library in Timbuktu that was built without your authorization with your money?" he asked the program officer.

"Yes," he replied.

"Well . . . we've got to build it again."

The program director just laughed. The whole situation was so "absurd," said Gates, and Haidara's demand for more money so audacious, that it evoked more amusement than outrage. The Mellon Foundation decided to come through with the extra funding, and the Ford Foundation contributed money as well. A new building soon rose on the site, this one built with reinforced concrete and with its foundation raised several feet off the ground. On January 13, 2000, in a ceremony attended by many luminaries, including the ministers of culture of Mali and Morocco, and the first lady of Mali—Henry Louis Gates had conflicting engagements and couldn't make the trip, and the Mellon Foundation sent a representative months later—the Mamma Haidara Commemorative Library officially opened its doors to the world.

5

In March 2006, after reading a newspaper article about Timbuktu's reemerging manuscripts, I obtained an assignment from *Smithsonian* magazine to travel to Mali to write about the literary salvaging operation in the Sahara. I flew up from Bamako on a new private airline, Mali Air Express, to meet Abdel Kader Haidara for the first time.

Timbuktu's campaign of literary rescue had dovetailed with a musical flowering in the Sahara. A phenomenon called the Festival in the Desert, three days of camel races and performances by some of Mali's most popular musicians, including the great bluesman Ali Farka Touré, who grew up in the Niger River town of Niafounké near Timbuktu, and a band of Tuareg ex-rebels known as Tinariwen, or "People of the Desert," had started in January 2001 and was now drawing thousands of aficionados from across the globe each January to a dune-filled oasis called Essakane, forty miles down a desert track due west of Timbuktu. Both awakenings—one sober and scholarly, the other exuberant and sometimes garishly commercial—had turned Timbuktu into a cultural hub, as it had been during the sixteenth-century Golden Age. Thanks as well to the rise of the Internet and the growing ease of international travel, the isolated town of Haidara's youth was opening to the world.

The changes in Timbuktu since my last visit, in 1995, were extraordinary. Back then, two fellow correspondents and I had chartered a small plane from Bamako and toured the town for two rushed hours while the pilot waited at the airport, his meter running. In a piece I wrote for *The New Republic* about Timbuktu, called "Still Here," I described the "suffocating remoteness" of a place hurting from the effects of a Tuareg rebellion that had sputtered on despite the signing of a peace deal in 1992. The Saharan nomads had resisted the French colonial army in the late nineteenth and early twentieth centuries with swords and spears, then the Malian government with AK-47s, attacking army camps and provoking fierce retaliation against civilians. "Sweeping out of the Sahara on camels and four-wheel-drive Toyotas, the Tuaregs stopped road traffic dead, cut off supplies, and wiped out the tourist trade," I wrote back then. "Tensions between Tuaregs and blacks grew, and black vigilantes, supplied with weapons by the Malian military, burned down Tuareg encampments in retaliation for rebel raids." Tens of thousands of people fled across Mali's western border into Mauritania, and Timbuktu, always tenuously connected to the rest of the world, slid deeper into isolation.

In 1995, the town had no newspapers, one radio station, and two phone lines. At the Hotel Bouctou, one of Timbuktu's two tourist establishments, I sipped tea with owner Boubacar Touré in a sand-filled lobby decorated with decade-old Mali tourist posters. "The next Air Mali flight from Bamako was three days away, and Touré hoped it would bring some business," I wrote back then. " 'We had no Westerners this week, and none the week before, but maybe we'll get lucky," he said. Of his twenty-nine rooms, only four were occupied, all by Malian traders."

But the year after my brief visit to Timbuktu, the last rebels of the Tuareg uprising that had devastated the north for half a decade agreed to lay down their weapons, and the nomadic warriors surrendered thousands of Kalashnikov rifles to the government. The weapons were buried in the concrete pedestal of a "Monument of Peace" that sits on a rise on Timbuktu's outskirts—an assemblage of interlocking archways surrounded by colorful murals of Malian government soldiers and Tuareg rebels shaking hands and burning their weapons.

Now, a decade after the Tuaregs gave up their guns, the fruits of peace were apparent: a fleet of four-wheel-drive taxis waited to ferry tourists down a new asphalt road between the airport and the town. Five hotels had just opened to cater to the fast-growing number of visitors. Ikatel, a private cellular phone network, had set up shop. Three Internet cafés had opened. Hammering and bricklaying were going on all over town. A delegation of imams from Morocco, three researchers from Paris, a team of preservationists from the University of Oslo, and a pair of radio reporters from Germany were on hand to look at the manuscripts.

Tall and ebullient, with a Falstaffian goatee and tufts of curly hair framing a balding pate, Haidara met me at his home in the Bella Farandja neighborhood on the eastern edge of the city, a short stroll from the Sankoré Mosque. Rambunctious children spilled through the two-story limestone house and into the tiled courtyard, dominated by potted plants and colorful flower arrangements put together by Haidara's wife. The brood included Haidara's daughters, ages eleven, nine, and five, and his sons, ages seven and two. Haidara's home felt warm, cozy, and bursting with life. From the rooftop, the family could look over the sand dunes and azure skies of the Sahara.

To preserve the region's literary treasures Haidara had organized twenty Timbuktu families with manuscript collections into
an association, known by the unwieldy acronym Savama-DCI, the
Association for Manuscript Preservation and Valorization for the
Defense of Islamic Culture. "I said, 'You have to open your own libraries, and undertake the work of restoring the manuscripts.' And
everybody was in favor of the idea," he recalled. The group had lob-
bied for, and begun receiving, financial assistance from around the
world. The Ford Foundation had given $600,000 as seed money to
help develop three libraries, including Haidara's own. Haidara used
some of the funds to merge the forty-thousand-volume collection
from Bamba, with the five thousand volumes in Timbuktu, and his
Mamma Haidara Library was now drawing two hundred visitors
a day. Financial support was pouring into Timbuktu as well from
the Al-Furqán Islamic Heritage Foundation in Great Britain, run
by a Saudi ex-oil minister, the Juma Al-Majid Center for Culture
and Heritage in Dubai, Lyon's Ecole Normale Supérieure, the Gerda
Henkel Foundation in Germany, the Prince Claus Fund for Culture
and Development in the Netherlands, the princess of Luxembourg,
and other benefactors. Donors allocated millions of dollars for
building supplies, conservation materials, cataloguing, and computers, scanners, and other equipment.

Even Qaddafi had become involved. Deprived of the opportunity to appropriate Haidara's collection, he began constructing
his own library and center for conservation in Timbuktu. Qaddafi
would spend five years buying land, dispatching engineers, and
erecting a building, only to see it come to nothing with the out-
break of the Libyan revolution of 2011 and his downfall. The Libyan
leader announced the creation of the "Qaddafi Prize for Human
Rights," and awarded it to Haidara and a handful of his librarian
colleagues for their work rescuing Timbuktu's literary patrimony.

Haidara had, almost singlehandedly, transformed Timbuktu

from a depressed backwater into a Mecca for researchers, diplomats, and tourists from around the world. "Really, we are doing good work, we have received a lot of money from the international community," Haidara told me. "There is a great opening here in Timbuktu, a reawakening of the cultural life of the city."

And the manuscripts were beginning to find their way into the wider world. Haidara had recently flown to Washington, D.C., to help oversee a Library of Congress exhibit of samples from the Mamma Haidara collection and had arranged a tour of the works through Jackson, Mississippi; New York; Chicago; Hartford, Connecticut; and Buffalo. American museum-goers for the first time could grasp the breadth of the intellectual inquiry led by the savants of Timbuktu. *The Important Stars Among the Multitude of the Heavens*, written by a Timbuktu astronomer in 1733—during a second period of scholastic flowering that followed Timbuktu's sixteenth-century Golden Age—explored the movement of the stars and their relationship to the seasons. *Curing Diseases and Defects Both Apparent and Hidden* was a seamless blend of the religious and the scientific, describing animals, plants, and minerals that could be used as medications, as well as Islamic prayers and Koranic verses that were believed to be helpful in treating the sick. *The Book Describing the Blessed Merits of Crafts and Agriculture* discussed the social benefits of the working life. *Letter to the Warring Tribes* quoted from the Koran and the Hadith to urge two feuding factions to live in peace and tolerance.

A new crop of librarians was emerging in Timbuktu, almost all of them the descendants of the great scholars and manuscript collectors from centuries ago. Sidi Yayia Al Wangari, who had taught Arabic literature in Fez, and served as a UNESCO consultant in Dakar, Senegal, was one of Haidara's most successful protégés. In the mid-sixteenth century, his ancestor, Mohammed abu Bakr Al Wangari, became a teacher at the Sankoré Mosque, and amassed handwritten books on subjects ranging from history to poetry to astronomy. "He had enormous patience in teaching throughout the day, and was able to get his matter across to even the dull-witted, never feeling bored or tired," wrote one of his favorite students, Ahmed Baba As Sudani, the exiled sage known as the "The Unique Pearl of His Time." After the scholar's death in 1594, the books dispersed to an ever-widening circle of family members. "Nobody in the family had thought about collecting them or preserving them," Al Wangari told me, as I knelt beside an old wooden chest in his dank storage room, leafing through yellowing pages and gazing at elegant Arabic calligraphy and intricate geometric designs. Turquoise and red dyes were still visible inside grooved diamonds and polygons that decorated the cover of a sixteenth-century Koran, but the costs of centuries of neglect were apparent. As I admired the book, the brittle leather broke apart in my hands. Centuries-old pages fluttered from the broken binding and crumbled into fragments. I pored through more volumes in the footlocker, some bloated by moisture; others covered by white or yellow mold. I opened a manuscript on astrology, with annotations carefully handwritten in minute letters in the margins: the ink on most pages had blurred into illegibility. "This one is rotten," Al Wangari muttered, tossing aside a book of Hadith. "I am afraid it is destroyed completely."

With Haidara's endorsement, he had secured a $200,000 grant from the Ford Foundation to construct the Al Wangari Library and protect the collection before it was too late. Laborers were mortaring concrete-block walls and laying bricks to dry in the sun outside the half-finished structure.

Another emerging Timbuktu collector, Ismail Diadjié Haidara (no relation to Abdel Kader), was the direct descendant of a famed Moorish scholar who had fled Toledo in Spain with his entire library in 1469, married the elder sister of King Askia Mohammed, and established the first library in Gao. "It was a lending library,

like modern ones, with margin notes declaring that 'Mr. X has borrowed this book,'" Ismail Diadjié Haidara recalled. Haidara initiated
a search to track down the volumes, and raised funds from Spain to
create Timbuktu's Bibliothèque Fondo Kati. The 7,028 manuscripts
included accounts of the lives of Christians and Jews in the Songhai Empire; the buying and selling of slaves; and the commerce of
books, salt, gold, fabrics, spices, and cola nuts. There were books
that originated along the Niger annotated by the learned men of
Timbuktu and Djenné. Others had come to Mali from across the
Middle East, margins filled with the musings of sages of Córdoba,
Granada, Fez, Marrakesh, Tripoli, Cairo, and Baghdad. Ismail Diadjié Haidara was especially proud of two illuminated Korans, one
copied in Turkey in 1420, the other on sheepskin in Ceuta, Andalusia, in 1198, and kept hidden for centuries in a family chest in
Kirshamba village, a hundred miles from Timbuktu.

I visited the Ahmed Baba Institute, located in the complex
where Abdel Kader Haidara had been employed for years. It was
still receiving funding from wealthy Middle Eastern governments,
as well as from Norway and South Africa, and remained the most
prestigious, best endowed, most modern, and largest library in
Timbuktu. Engraved on the lintel above the Moorish-style arched
entrance was the lamentation of the eponymous savant who had
been taken in chains to Marrakesh: "O friend, when you go to Gao
make a detour by Timbuktu and murmur my name to my friends," it
read, "and bring them a greeting perfumed with an exile that yearns
after the soil where its friends, family, and neighbors reside." In an
atelier fourteen workers were making storage boxes and carefully
wrapping crumbling manuscript pages in Kitakata, a thin, strong
Japanese paper made from the woven fibers of the kozo plant, considered ideal for repairing the tears or reinforcing the backs of fragile manuscript pages, which typically contained writing only on one
side. "This will protect them for at least a hundred years," Mohamed

Gallah Dicko, the Ahmed Baba Institute's director, who had replaced Mahmoud Zouber after his retirement, told me. (Zouber
would later go on to become Mali's ambassador to Saudi Arabia.)

Dicko's technicians had "dedusted" 6,538 manuscripts, wrapping each page of the unbound volumes in acid-free paper and
placing them in boxes; there were another 19,000 to go. South Africa's National Archives had flown dozens of employees to workshops
in Cape Town and Pretoria, part of a program initiated by President
Thabo Mbeki after a state visit to Mali in November 2001. Taken
on a tour of Timbuktu by his Malian counterpart, President Alpha
Konaré, Mbeki had been so moved by the Ahmed Baba Institute's
manuscript collection that he had pledged to assist the Malians in
their preservation efforts, and the National Archives had begun
training Malian conservators in 2003. In a sunlit room across the
courtyard, a dozen archivists huddled over Epson and Canon scanners, creating digital images of the works. "We're expanding our
search to the northwest and the northeast," Dicko told me. "There
are hundreds of thousands of manuscripts still out there."

Haidara's organization was also exporting its cultural renaissance far beyond the city. In 2004, the group had opened a library
opposite Djenné's Great Mud Mosque—a towering multipinnacled
structure, built originally in the fourteenth century and recon-
structed many times since, that is one of Mali's most recognizable
landmarks. Savama-DCI renovated a library in Gao, launched another in the southern Niger River town of Ségou, and even ventured
into a handful of remote Saharan settlements where Islamic scholars had begun tracking down lost and buried manuscripts in the
desert and building their own crude libraries.

Abdel Kader Haidara arranged for me to visit one of these communities: the Tuareg village of Ber, forty miles east of Timbuktu. The
sun was just rising when Ber's library curator, a gaunt man in his fifties with wispy side burns named Fida Ag Mohammed; my driver,

Baba; and I departed Timbuktu, and a chill wind whipped through the open windows of our battered Land Cruiser. Baba steered the vehicle over a rolling sand track into the heart of the Sahara, fishtailing past dunes and thorn trees. Ber, a shadeless collection of mud-brick huts and tents scattered across a saddle between two low desert ridges, once had fifteen thousand manuscripts dating as far back as the fifteenth century. But during the 1990 Tuareg rebellion, government troops and mercenaries from Arab tribes attacked, looted, and burned many Tuareg villages in the area, and Ber's inhabitants, as a precautionary move, dispersed all but a few hundred manuscripts to family members living in settlements deeper in the Sahara, or buried them in the sand. It was a modern-day version of a story that has played out in Mali for centuries, a story of war, hiding places, and loss.

We crossed a sandy field and entered a tin-roofed shack, Mohammed's Centre de Recherche. Mohammed opened a trunk at my feet and took out dozens of volumes that he had recovered from the desert. He touched them reverently. "Dust is the enemy of these manuscripts," he murmured, shaking his head. "Dust eats away at them and destroys them over time." I picked up a miniature Koran from the fifteenth century, thumbed through it and stared in amazement at an illustration of the Great Mosque of Medina: a minutely rendered, pen-and-ink depiction by an anonymous artist of Saudi Arabia's stone-walled fortress, two pencil-thin minarets rising over the central golden dome, date palm trees at the fringes of the mosque, and desert mountains in the distance. "You are one of the first outsiders to see this," he told me.

After I returned to Timbuktu, Abdel Kader Haidara led me down sandy alleys crisscrossed by a tangle of phone wires, past teetering, two- and three-story structures of mud brick and limestone, everything the same oppressive beige. The few splashes of color that brightened the landscape came from the fiery red jerseys of a soccer team practicing in a sandy field, the lime green facade of a grocery store, and the peacock blue boubous, or flowing Malian gowns, of the local Tuareg and Sorhai men.

We entered the tiled and acacia-shaded courtyard of the Mamma Haidara Library. Haidara led me through traditional Moorish wooden doors, inlaid with dozens of ornamental silver knobs. Inside the sun-splashed exhibition hall, financed by the Ford Foundation, the best of Haidara's archive was neatly arranged in vacuum-sealed glass cases: he showed me a fourteenth-century Koran, a work of astronomy opened to a chart of the heavens, and an 1853 epistle by spiritual leader Sheikh Ahmed Al Bakkay Al Kounti, in which he asks the sultan of Massina to spare the life of the German explorer Heinrich Barth. Non-Muslims were barred from entering the city under the sultan's harsh Islamic rule, but Al Bakkay argued that religious law forbade Barth's execution. "It is forbidden to be unjust against an infidel whoever he may be, fighter or nonfighter, who has entered the lands of Islam with a safe conduct given to him by a Muslim," Al Bakkay wrote. Barth remained under the protection of Al Bakkay and made it back to Europe unharmed. "The manuscripts show that Islam is a religion of tolerance," said Haidara. "We need to show the West the truth."

However, it was not the only truth in Timbuktu. On the northeast edge of town, a short drive down a sand track from Haidara's home, a new construction project was rising in the dunes: a large, butterscotch-and-peach-painted concrete mosque. Wealthy members of the fundamentalist Wahhabi sect from Saudi Arabia had built the multimillion-dollar edifice. It had Moorish archways, a green-copper dome topped by a crescent moon, a forty-foot-high minaret, and five loudspeakers that blared the Koran in all directions. Without yet attracting much attention from the outside world, the Wahhabis were trying to export their hard-line Islam to the Sahara.

One hundred years earlier, the French journalist and historian Félix Dubois had cited "the influence of the Arabian Mussulman" on the two waves of Malian jihadis who had imposed Shariah law on Timbuktu in the early and mid-nineteenth century. Muhammad Abd Al Wahhab, an eighteenth-century preacher from the desert interior of what is now Saudi Arabia, had urged a return to the austere Islamic society created by the Prophet following the Hejira, his migration to Medina from Mecca in 622 CE. Al Wahhab's followers rejected modernism and secularism, supported the imposition of Shariah, called for a restricted role for women, and aspired to create an Islamic caliphate modeled after the seventh-century religious state ruled by the Prophet and his successors. Al Wahhab declared holy war on Shi'ism, Sufism, and Greek philosophy. He formulated the doctrine known as *takfir*, by which he and his followers could designate as an infidel, and punish with death, any Muslim who refused to pledge allegiance to the caliph, the leader of the Sunni Islamic world, or who venerated any entity other than God. In the nineteenth century Malian Sufis had come into contact with these Arabian zealots during the hajj, the pilgrimage to Mecca, and grafted their rigid ideology and culture of intolerance onto Niger River cultures raised on Sufism, animism, and a syncretic blend of the two. With these Malian jihadis, dedicated to the "purification" of Islam through the implementation of Shariah law, the two interpretations of the religion came into violent conflict. Now, more than a century and a half later, history was seeking to repeat itself.

That evening, I sat at the outdoor bar of the Hotel Bouctou, Timbuktu's oldest tourist lodge, at the edge of the Sahara. Tuareg nomads draped in boubous; Westernized locals in jeans and college T-shirts; and foreign tourists swayed to the recorded music of Ali Farka Touré. In the fading light, almost nobody seemed to notice the five young Americans with close-cropped hair and trim physiques nursing Castel beers at a table in the corner. The men were

U.S. Special Forces instructors dispatched to Mali to train the country's ill-equipped army to confront a growing terrorist threat in the
desert. "They've taken over a block of the Hotel Bouctou, and they
keep to themselves," Azima Ali, a Tuareg tour guide, whispered to
me as the call of the muezzin from Timbuktu's dozens of mosques
rose over the alleys in the darkness.

In recent months Western and Malian officials had detected a
surge of Islamist recruitment efforts in the Malian Sahara. The Malian government had closely followed the travels of several itinerant imams from Pakistan who proselytized throughout the north.
"They've let the Pakistanis know they're not welcome," one American official had told me in Bamako. Salafis from Saudi Arabia—
fundamentalist Muslims who extol a return to the Islam practiced
by the Prophet and his original followers, the Salaf, or ancestors—
had constructed Wahhabi mosques both in Timbuktu and other
desert communities, founded orphanages, and lavished cash on
local charities. "The north is huge and impoverished, with lots of
unemployed and angry young men," the American diplomat in Bamako had told me. "The potential for the exploitation of disenfran-
chised youth definitely exists."

The imam of the new Wahhabi mosque in Timbuktu, a member of the local Sorhai tribe, had succeeded in attracting two dozen
residents of Timbuktu to Friday prayers, my driver, Baba, told me,
including some young men who had proudly displayed Osama bin
Laden T-shirts after the attacks of September 11. But Azima Ali, the
Tuareg tourist guide, insisted that the imam's message was still un-
popular in Timbuktu. "The people here are not extremists," he said.
"The kind of Islam that we practice is generous and kind. We don't
believe in spreading the religion through violence. If you are not a
Muslim, nobody can force you to be one."

After our visit to the Saudi-built mosque, Baba and I drove
through the center of town. We passed Timbuktu's renowned

Djingareyber Mosque, the imposing fourteenth-century mud fortress. "As long as this mosque rises over the city," Baba told me, "the Wahhabis can never be strong." But a few moments later, a jeepload of Malian soldiers roared past, kicking up clouds of dust, back from a military exercise in the Sahara with U.S. trainers. Baba watched them somberly. "We are glad to have the Americans here," he murmured. "Who knows what is happening in the desert?"

6

General Charles F. "Chuck" Wald, the deputy commander of the United States European Command, based in Vaihingen, Germany, on the eastern outskirts of Stuttgart, was a burly ex-college football star from North Dakota with a hard-charging manner that both inspired and intimidated his underlings. After being selected in the fourteenth round of the NFL draft as a wide receiver by the Atlanta Falcons in 1969, Wald had opted instead for a career as a pilot in the Air Force. He had flown or directed combat missions in every U.S. military campaign since the late 1960s, a distinction that had prompted one defense expert to call him "the Zelig of airpower"—referring to the Woody Allen character with a knack for being present at one momentous event after another during the 1920s and 1930s. Wald flew light aircraft into combat over Vietnam, Laos, and Cambodia; and directed aerial raids on Muammar Al Qaddafi's compound in Tripoli in 1986 following a Libyan terrorist attack on a Berlin nightclub that killed two U.S. soldiers. A decade later, at the end of the Bosnian war, he bombed Serb ammunitions depots in Bosnia-Herzegovina from an F-16. He had been the Air Force point man in Afghanistan, overseeing 35,000 men and 350 aircraft in the campaign to destroy the Taliban.

At the time that Wald arrived in Vaihingen, in 2002, responsibility for conducting U.S. military operations in Africa was divided among three Unified Commands, with the European Command in charge of West Africa. (Five years later Secretary of Defense Donald Rumsfeld would create the Africa Command, basing it in Stuttgart after no African government would accept a permanent U.S. military presence on its soil, and placing the entire continent under its supervision.) Wald spent much of his time monitoring a worsening crisis in the oil-rich Niger Delta of Nigeria, where rebel groups and criminals were kidnapping American oil workers and holding them for multimillion-dollar ransoms. Wald also spotted the potential for trouble in what he called the "vast, ungoverned spaces" of the Sahara. Arab racketeers were making tens of millions of dollars a year running cigarettes, drugs, weapons, and illegal immigrants from Mali and Niger to North Africa and across the Mediterranean to Europe. Some smugglers had links to the Islamist rebel groups that had waged a brutal civil war against the Algerian regime in the 1990s in which tens of thousands of civilians had been killed. The nexus of money, weapons, crime, and radical Islam was worrying the Algerians, and the Americans, who passed on intelligence to them and helped them with border surveillance, shared their concern.

In the wake of the 9/11 attacks, and the George W. Bush administration's war against the Taliban and Al Qaeda, Wald believed that the Sahel region was fertile ground for jihadism. The U.S. military had driven Al Qaeda and its Taliban protectors out of Afghanistan, depriving it of its main safe haven; the Islamist government of Sudan, which had protected bin Laden for five years during the 1990s, had expelled him under U.S. and Saudi pressure in 1996, and made it clear that the terrorist group was no longer welcome there. That left the radicals with reliable refuges only in Yemen, where a weak regime had ceded control of the mountains east of the port of Aden to the jihadis, and the "Wild West" of the Sahara—especially Mali. As a part of the peace deal signed with the Tuareg rebels in 1996, Malian authorities had agreed to draw down their military presence in the region north of Timbuktu, and there was also a tacit understanding that they would not interfere with the Tuaregs' traditional source of income, the smuggling of contraband across the porous desert borders, often in league with Arab tribesmen. After the Malian army retreated in the mid-1990s, the area became an ever-wilder no-man's-land, and extremist elements had moved into the vacuum. Mali was a forerunner of other collapsing states such as Syria, where the loss of power of the beleaguered regime of Bashar Al Assad in 2012 and 2013 allowed the radical group the Islamic State of Iraq and Syria to gain supremacy over a large swath of ungovernable territory.

In early 2003, U.S. intelligence services delivered to Wald a set of grainy photographs taken by a "spy in the sky" satellite. The images showed dozens of armed men lined up in neat rows at a desert training camp north of Timbuktu. In a safe room in the headquarters of the European Command—a leafy complex of beige-concrete buildings, built for the Nazi war machine in 1936, and occupied by the United States Third Army after World War II—Wald held the photos up to the light. He scrutinized the elements: semiautomatics, a remote desert setting, men who appeared to be Islamist fighters, some of them on horseback. The images looked almost exactly like the surveillance photos that he had often analyzed of Taliban fighters in Afghanistan. *It's a military formation*, he thought. *It looks like terrorist training.* The photos were too grainy to make out individual faces. But intercepts of satellite phone calls and other intelligence, Wald told me years later, suggested that the commander of the group was the Sahara's most notorious outlaw, an individual destined to become a leader of Al Qaeda in the Islamic Maghreb in Mali: Mokhtar Belmokhtar.

Belmokhtar, thirty, was born and grew up in Ghardaïa, a dusty town of high unemployment and smoldering antigovernment resentments, in the M'Zab Valley in the Algerian Sahara, 370 miles south of Algiers. "It's too bad that there's no ocean here," runs a typical youthful lament in the valley. "Then we could have fled this country where there is no place for us." During his adolescence, many young men in Ghardaïa were being drawn to Salafism, and Belmokhtar became one of its most zealous devotees. Stirred in secondary school by the jihad against the Soviet Union in Afghanistan, he listened ardently to cassettes and read the sermons of a Palestinian idealogue, Abdullah Yusuf Azzam, a mentor of Osama bin Laden and cofounder of the Pakistani terrorist group Lashkar-e-Taiba.

Azzam died in a car bomb explosion in Peshawar in 1989, a decisive event in young Belmokhtar's life. One year later, Belmokhtar traveled to Mecca for the *umrah*, a secondary pilgrimage typically carried out during Ramadan. The following year, he and three other teenagers from Ghardaïa made their way to Afghanistan to join the jihad. They were motivated, in part, by a desire to avenge Azzam's murder, though it was never clear who the culprits had been; the suspects ranged from the Mossad, Israel's covert operations and counterterrorism unit, to rivals within the recently formed Al Qaeda. The Soviet Union had withdrawn from Afghanistan in February 1989. Belmokhtar fell in with Hezb-i-Islami, an Islamist guerrilla group fighting to bring down a secular regime in Kabul. Comprised of thousands of international recruits, the Islamist rebels were based in the tribal areas of Pakistan and were led by Gulbuddin Hekmatyar, a virulently anti-Western mujahideen leader to whom the Central Intelligence Agency had funneled at least $600 million to wage war against the Soviets during the 1980s.

Later Belmokhtar found his way to an Al Qaeda camp in Jalalabad, a city in eastern Afghanistan, about a hundred miles from Kabul, and there forged connections with radical Islamists from across the Middle East. They included Abu Qatada, a Bethlehem-born jihadi who would later become known as "Osama bin Laden's Ambassador man in Europe" and who called for attacks on American citizens "wherever they are." Another acquaintance was Abu Mohammed Al Maqdisi, a Nablus-born ideologue who would become the spiritual mentor to the murderous commander of Al Qaeda in Iraq, Abu Muṣab Al Zarqawi—whom Belmokhtar also claimed to have met, briefly, in Jalalabad.

Belmokhtar lost his left eye when explosives he was handling during a training exercise blew up in his face, according to an interview he gave to a jihadi website years later. In late 1992—just before the government of Pakistan, under international pressure for harboring potential terrorists, expelled many foreign mujahideen, or holy warriors—Belmokhtar returned to Algeria. Earlier that year the Algerian military had nullified the election victory of a popular Islamist party called the Islamic Salvation Front (FIS), and plunged the country into one of the bloodiest civil wars of the twentieth century. Belmokhtar, whose Islamist views had been hardened by his years in Afghanistan, joined the Armed Islamic Group of Algeria (GIA), a brutal militia fighting to overthrow a newly established military regime and replace it with an Islamist state.

By the mid-1990s, according to a 2004 human rights report by the Justice Commission for Algeria, the GIA was engaging in horrific killings of civilians suspected of collaboration with Algerian security forces, or simply for behavior deemed un-Islamic. "The GIA attacked families, young people and imposed taboos," recalled one survivor near Algiers. "Every other day we discovered bodies, including of young girls. They were sometimes hung to a post or tied up with metal wires, sliced to pieces or beheaded. There seemed to be no limit to horror." The GIA set up roadbocks, stopped buses, searched for "suspects"—including anyone who had done military service—and executed them on the spot. Soon the GIA gravitated from shootings to bombings of buses, markets, trains, schools, administration buildings, and factories. Large-scale civilian massacres, carried out by both Islamic extremists and the Algerian army, swept the country. "The sound of gunfire and bomb explosions, the screams of the victims, and the flames and smoke of the houses on fire are audible and visible from a distance," an Amnesty International report noted at the end of 1997, at the height of the killings.

The civil war began to wind down in 1999. President Abdelaziz Bouteflika pardoned both Islamist fighters and government torturers and execution squads. By then, the army and the Islamist rebels had killed 100,000 civilians. "The weaker brethren of the Islamist revolt went home while the hard, unforgiving men emigrated into the deserts and across the Algerian border," wrote the journalist Robert Fisk in *The Independent*. A new phase of the jihad was taking shape—one that would target French and American citizens in North Africa, draw fighters from across the Islamic world, seize swaths of lightly patrolled territory, and lay the groundwork for a caliphate in the Sahara. "Belmokhtar inherited a 'cleansed' Al Qa'ida qatiba [brigade]—and a new version of Bin Laden's battle," Fisk wrote.

Belmokhtar had always been a reluctant participant in some of the GIA's more cold-blooded crimes. Though he killed Algerian soldiers and customs officers with cool efficiency—the Algerian government sentenced him to death twice in absentia for these murders—he had also argued that murdering noncombatants tarnished the jihadis' image and cost them popular support. Around 1998, while the GIA was still carrying out near-daily massacres in the suburbs of Algiers, Belmokhtar quit the group and retreated to Tamanrasset, an oasis town in the Ahaggar Mountains north of the Mali-Algeria border, and the principal city of the Algerian Tuareg tribe.

Here, Belmokhtar moved from Islamic jihad to self-enrichment. Ingratiating himself with elders in Arab and Tuareg villages on both sides of the border—the two ethnic groups maintained an uneasy coexistence in the Sahara—the former mujahid spread around cash and livestock, took four Tuareg and Arab brides, including pubescent girls, established deep roots in the communities, and became the dominant player in the smuggling of tobacco across West and North Africa. Belmokhtar traded in both counterfeits produced in China and Vietnam and genuine Western brands, which typically entered West Africa from the United States and Europe through Ghana, Benin, Togo, and Guinea, and reached Mali by road or by boat along the Niger. Belmokhtar and his colleagues charged a tax for safe passage of the cigarettes or smuggled the product themselves through the Sahara along established salt-trading routes by SUVs, trucks, and motorcycles. The final destinations were Algeria, Egypt, Libya, Morocco, and Tunisia, which together consume nearly half of Africa's cigarettes, much of them purchased on the black market.

Belmokhtar was, by all accounts, a cunning, energetic, and resourceful gangster. Within a couple of years, by building an entrenched network of support through the desert, and intimidating would-be competitors, he gained so great a share of the trans-Saharan contraband business that he became known in the region as "Mr. Marlboro." (Others called him "One Eye.") His success moving cigarettes illegally across borders caught the attention of a breakaway Islamist movement in Algeria, the Salafi Group for Preaching and Combat (GSPC), which had split from the GIA in the waning days of the civil conflict and declared war against

Algeria's secular regime. The group's leaders, hidden in the mountains, recruited Belmokhtar in 1998 and named him "emir" of its southwest Saharan zone. His main responsibility was smuggling weapons and ammunition to GSPC cadres. In 2002, Algeria's intelligence service claimed to have evidence that the group was seeking ties to international terror networks, and that it had the official sanction of Osama bin Laden.

Other violent figures, who would eventually join Belmokhtar in forming the leadership of Al Qaeda in the Islamic Maghreb in Mali, were showing up on the Americans' radar screen. One was Abdelhamid Abou Zeid, born in December 1965 to a penniless family of Bedouins in a tented camp outside Zaouia El-Abidia, an oasis town with a single paved street in the Algerian Sahara. As a boy, Abou Zeid (born Abed Hamamou) had known only poverty, desperation, and ridicule. His father, an itinerant laborer, moved the family to Bougaa, set on a windswept four-thousand-foot-high plateau in the northeast corner of the country, 190 miles east of Algiers, where he found work on a farm. Later the family picked up stakes again and settled in Sétif, another high-altitude town, infamous for the slaughter of 104 *pieds-noirs*—European settlers in Algeria—by Algerian freedom fighters at the end of World War II, and the subsequent massacre of thousands of civilians by French colonial forces in retaliation. In this landscape of snow-covered plains and frigid winters, he was mercilessly teased at school because of his dark skin, his short stature, and a case of rickets—a deficiency of vitamin D that weakens the bone structure and causes stooped posture and bowleggedness. He dropped out of secondary school, and shortly after that, his father, again chasing work, moved the family back south to Zaouia El-Abidia, where many of the 22,000 inhabitants scratched out a living cultivating date palm trees.

The boy and his family lived in a modest house of dried mud brick on a sandy alley in the poorest quarter of the town, with an inscription on the iron front door that read, "Dar Es Salaam," or "House of Peace" in Arabic. "It was Abed who painted that by his own hand," his mother recalled to a visiting journalist years later. The teenager worked on a farm, then became a mason—a job that provided him with a nickname, "Mouallem," or "Teacher," because knowing the craft of masonry was considered a form of scholarship in that corner of Algeria.

He swiftly moved from construction to contraband. In the early 1980s Abou Zeid tapped into Saharan smuggling networks and brought bulk quantities of tea, electronics, and cigarettes from Libya across the poorly patrolled border into Algeria, selling them on the black market in Zaouia El-Abidia. But Abou Zeid was no Belmokhtar. Arrested for the first time for smuggling by the Algerian gendarmerie in 1984, he shuttled in and out of jail cells during his twenties, where the mistreatment and bullying he had suffered as a teenager continued. "He was manhandled [by the police] many times," a member of the Algerian police told a *Paris Match* reporter for a 2010 profile. Mohamed Mokeddem, the director of the Algiers newspaper *Ennahar* and an expert on Sahel Terrorism, declared that "His hatred of the Algerian government became deeply anchored in his personality."

Filled with resentments, destabilized by the death of his father in 1989, Abou Zeid drifted toward radical Islam. "Before [his father died] he had always been very open, he liked to laugh," said a close friend from Zaouia El-Abidia, where the Bedouin population is well known for their festivals and fondness for drinking palm wine, despite its interdiction by the Koran. Abou Zeid attended clandestine meetings of the Algerian Muslim Brotherhood in Zaouia El-Abidia, smuggling weapons from Libya to Islamist groups, and preparing, say security officials and journalists, for a coming jihad against the Algerian regime. At the beginning of the 1990s, he purchased a small date palm farm just outside the city. "He asked me to prepare semolina for forty people, saying that they were workers at his farm," his mother remembered. "In fact they were Islamists, but I could not refuse them."

In 1991, the Islamic Salvation Front seemed on the verge of a landslide victory in Algeria's legislative elections, prompting the military to annul the second round of voting. Abou Zeid at the time was a member of the Islamic party's bureau in Touggourt, a large town not far from Zaouia El-Abidia, and he, like many of his comrades in the organization, vowed to take revenge.

Some time afterward, the Algerian army ambushed an armed group of Islamists outside Zaouia El-Abidia, and killed Abou Zeid's beloved older brother, Bachir. Immediately after the killing, he joined the Armed Islamic Group of Algeria, the most violent terrorist band fighting the state, and may have participated in a series of massacres of civilians accused of being collaborators with the Algerian military. In 1998, he joined the Salafi Group for Preaching and Combat. Abou Zeid was an ordinary foot soldier, under the command of Amari Saifi, a former Algerian army paratrooper and ex-bodyguard of the Algerian defense minister. The terrorist leader, who went by the nom de guerre El Para, had little respect for his diminutive and frail young charge. "He is ugly and even shorter than [French president Nicolas] Sarkozy," said El Para in the early 2000s. "I think that he has an [inferiority] complex, and that he's even a little jealous of me." But Abou Zeid climbed through the hierarchy and was soon granted rare permission to live with a woman—a sign of his importance within the organization. In 2002, he issued his first fatwa, declaring all young Algerians who completed their compulsory military service to be legitimate targets of GSPC attacks. Abou Zeid would soon earn a reputation as one of the GSPC's most rabid idealogues—and perhaps its most merciless killer.

In 2003, the paratrooper-turned-jihadi El Para enlisted Abou Zeid in a scheme that would gain notoriety as one of the most audacious criminal operations in the history of the Sahara. Between late February and April, he and his Islamist militia kidnapped thirty-two Western tourists—French, German, Swiss, and Dutch—from a stretch of scenic desert road in southeast Algeria. The terrorists picked off four or five foreigners at a time as they rode motorcycles or four-wheel-drives down the highway—known as "the Graveyard Piste" because of the ancient Tuareg cemeteries that lie along the route—and disappeared with them into the wilderness.

At first El Para, Abou Zeid, and their gang did not announce their crime: a German military reconnaissance plane captured pictures of abandoned vehicles on the desert floor, and other imagery indicating that the tourists had been abducted, divided into two groups, and marched into the desert. One thousand two hundred Algerian soldiers and police joined German counterterrorism forces on a search by camel and helicopter through mountains and canyons. Not long afterward, a letter discovered by a scout under a tree revealed that the GSPC had been behind the abductions.

In May 2003, Algerian Special Forces raided a canyon, killed fifteen kidnappers, and carried seventeen hostages to safety. El Para, whom the French news media would come to call "the bin Laden of the Sahara," and Abou Zeid escaped the carnage and took the remaining fifteen hostages, fourteen Germans and one Dutchman, on a two-week-long trek south into Mali. The captors forced their female hostages to wear hijabs—Islamic veils—improvised out of handkerchiefs and towels and fed the captives little but porridge mixed in a pail with muddy water. One forty-six-year-old German woman died of heat stroke during the flight through the desert and was buried in the sand. The bedraggled group took refuge in Mali's Adrar des Ifoghas massif, a wilderness of eroded sandstone and granite hills, ancient riverbeds filled with sand, and boulder-strewn valleys that begins forty miles north of the provincial capital of Kidal. In an early example of what would become regular practice for the region's jihadis, El Para and his men, including Abou Zeid, sent word to the Malian and German governments that they would free their hostages in exchange for a multimillion-dollar ransom.

The man whom Mali's president designated as the government's representative in the hostage negotiations was Iyad Ag Ghali, a prominent Malian Tuareg from Kidal. Like all Tuaregs, Ghali came out of a culture of Sufism—the moderate, mystical form of Islam that had long dominated northern Mali. He was also a skilled fighter, a natural leader, a poet, a songwriter, a spiritual searcher, and a killer. As dangerous as these jihadis were, Ghali would emerge, ironically, as the biggest threat of all to the region's stability.

His first exposure to violence had come early. Born around 1957 in a nomadic encampment north of Kidal, Ghali was the son of a Tuareg soldier who had sided with the Malian government during a failed 1963 rebellion, when Tuareg secessionists rose up against newly independent Mali to try to establish their own state— Azawad, meaning "the land of pastures." When Iyad Ag Ghali was about six years old, a rebel commander shot his father in the head and killed him. Ten years later, after a devastating drought struck the north and killed nearly every camel, sheep, and cow in the region, the teenage Ghali fled the country, hitchhiked and walked across the desert for weeks, and ended up in Tripoli, the capital of Libya. He survived, like thousands of other Tuareg exiles, known as *ishumar* (from the French word *chômeur*, or unemployed), by doing odd jobs—gardening, carpentry, housepainting, and herding cattle, goats, and sheep.

After a couple of years of this hardscrabble existence, Ghali founded a small Tuareg rebel movement in Tripoli—it consisted of a one-room office, a fax machine, and about thirty members—and began laying plans for a new Tuareg insurgency. Though rebels had killed his own father, Ghali had witnessed the brutality of the Malian military government while growing up in Kidal—the governor carried out summary executions of suspected dissidents in the town square—and his associations with young Tuareg exiles in the cafés of Tamanrasset and Tripoli had heightened his sympathies for the rebel cause. In his early twenties, he underwent training at a military camp in the Libyan Sahara established in the early 1980s by Qaddafi, ostensibly to prepare the Tuareg exiles for another uprising, but primarily to train disposable young fighters for Libya's military adventures in Africa and the Middle East. Ghali fought in Qaddafi's Islamic Brigade alongside the Palestinian Liberation Organization in Lebanon during the Israeli invasion in 1982, hunkering down for weeks in bunkers near Sidon as Israeli warplanes bombarded PLO targets. He also joined in a 1987 infantry and tank assault in the Chadian desert against the forces of the dictator Hassan Habré, whom Qaddafi was seeking to depose. The Chadian army surrounded and killed thousands of Qaddafi's troops, forcing Ghali's Tuareg unit to flee across the border.

Ghali fell in with a group of Tuareg fighter-musicians in a barracks at Qaddafi's camp called the Artists' House. It turned out that he had a flair for poetry, and he soon began writing lyrics for them. The music, similar to that of the great guitarist Ali Farka Touré and also known as "the desert blues," often consisted of nothing more than two or three chords, call-and-response vocals, a melancholy tone, and a single repetitive, hypnotic phrase. Ghali's song "Bismillahi," or "In the Name of God," would become the unofficial anthem of Azawad, the independent state that many Tuaregs wanted to carve out of northern Mali, stretching from the Niger River north to the Taghaza salt mines, and northeast of Timbuktu to the modern-day border with Mauritania. "In the name of God, we rise up and begin/The revolution in the company of all our brothers," the first verse proclaimed. "Like true warriors we are going to trample on the enemy/Yes, in the name of God, we rise up and begin." In his ballad "Pendant Toute Une Nuit," or "All Night Long," Ghali declared his rapturous love for an unnamed woman: "My eyes are still lost in the stars/Crushed by a nostalgia that envelops me like a tent/I'm invaded by memories of your soft words/As if you were speaking now beside me."

In June 1990 Ghali led about one hundred men, armed with ten aging AK-47 rifles, across the Malian border. They attacked remote military camps, surprised the poorly trained Malian troops, achieved several quick victories, captured arms and vehicles, and drew hundreds, then thousands of Tuaregs to their cause. "Tuaregs didn't go to school, weren't in the army, and didn't have any positions in the government," one rebel commander who fought alongside Ghali explained to me. "We had to return to fight a war so we would be accepted as Malian citizens and have equal rights."

Experienced in close combat with light weaponry after years of fighting in Qaddafi's Islamic Brigade, the rebels picked off the government troops with lethal accuracy. They captured the imaginations of many in the West. The French historian Pierre Boilley described the "eternal Saharan mystique" of "a veiled nomad perched on his camel and brandishing his AK-47. . . . These men no longer carried the sword at their side like their fathers but instead waved the 'Kalach' . . . the arm of all resistance movements, of dissidence and revolt."

Each evening the rebels gathered around campfires and listened to warrior-musicians play guitar and sing martial songs written by

Ghali and other commanders. The rebel-musicians' bootleg cassettes were passed around the north, glorifying their combat and drawing more young men into the insurgency.

The rebellion ended with a temporary peace accord in January 1991, and Ghali arrived to a hero's welcome in Bamako. Mali's government conceded much of what Ghali and his rebels had asked for—millions of dollars in development money, integration of the fighters into the army and civil service. "He was Clint Eastwood, John Wayne, and Che Guevara rolled into one," said Mohammed "Manny" Ansar (the family name means "defenders"), a Tuareg law school graduate from the dunes north of Timbuktu, who first met Ghali in Bamako at the time of the signing ceremony and organized a dinner for him with Tuareg business and student leaders. As a reward for his persuading many Tuaregs to renounce violence, the regime made Ghali a presidential security adviser, and gave him a villa in Bamako and salary to keep the peace. But Ghali never renounced the goal of Tuareg independence, maintained close ties to the rebels, and kept his options open.

At this time Bamako was emerging as a world music capital, and Ghali's musical connoisseurship continued to develop. Every Sunday he and Manny Ansar—then a development official for a Norwegian charity and aspiring music producer—organized outdoor concerts at a picnic site in the shade of a mango tree by the Niger, just outside Bamako. The concerts featured a small group of Tuareg musicians with whom Ghali had fought in the battlefields of the north, led by a Carlos Santana lookalike named Ibrahim Ag Habib. Habib and his fellow ex-rebels transfixed their growing audiences with songs about heroic assaults on desert strongholds, the power of companionship in the Sahara, and their yearning for a homeland.

Ibrahim Ag Habib, who cited influences ranging from Egyptian pop to Elvis Presley and Jimi Hendrix, called his band "Kel

Tinariwen"—"People of the Desert"—which he soon shortened to Tinariwen. In January 2000 Ghali invited Habib and the other Tuareg musicians to perform at a Tuareg folklore festival in the desert north of Kidal. Two thousand nomads gathered in a valley of red sand between mountains and dunes for three days of camel races and indigenous music, much of it filmed for national television. No foreign tourists attended this nomadic gathering, but the event, Ansar would later say, would serve as his inspiration for the three-day concert series that he would call the Festival in the Desert. Ansar and a few fellow Tuareg promoters inaugurated the festival in 2001 with live music and camel racing in the dunes north of Kidal. Iyad Ag Ghali provided security for the event. Two years later, Ansar gained total control of the festival and moved it to Essakane, a traditional meeting place for members of his clan, near Timbuktu, where—thanks to his shrewd marketing and the appearances of famous Western musicians—it began attracting a significant number of visitors from around the world.

But even as he became an aficionado and a promoter of Malian music, Ghali was being drawn into Islamic fundamentalism. During the winter of 2002, four missionaries from the Tablighi Jama'at movement, based in Pakistan, arrived in Kidal and began preaching to the Tuaregs. Founded in the northern Indian state of Uttar Pradesh in the early twentieth century, Tablighi Jama'at is ostensibly a peaceful sect whose adherents emulate the austere lifestyle of the Prophet Mohammed—sleeping on rough mats on the floor, using twigs to brush their teeth—and spend forty days a year overseas on door-to-door prosletyzing missions. "The Pakistanis are up there converting all the former Tuareg rebels," Ansar was told by a friend living in northeast Mali. "They're all becoming devout." Even Ghali, Ansar learned to his surprise, had begun attending mosque on a regular basis and had expressed keen interest in what these strict Muslims had to say.

In 2002, Ghali studied at the main Tablighi Ja'maat mosque in France, located in the suburb of Saint-Denis, outside Paris. (This was the same suburb where French police would hunt down and kill the Islamic State terrorist Abdelhamid Abaaoud, the architect of the November 13, 2015, attacks.) Later that year he visited the movement's complex of mosques, madrassahs, and residential compounds near Lahore, in eastern Pakistan. Each November, four million people—the largest congregation of Muslims after the hajj—descend upon the complex for the three-day *itjema*, or gathering, sleeping on mats in a huge mosque, listening to a marathon of sermons, and praying in the streets. Life, he told Ansar upon returning home, "is like a waiting room in an airport when you are in transit," a brief interlude before the "real journey" begins. "You had better be prepared," he admonished Ansar, while reclining on pillows and thumbing through a copy of the Hadith.

By 2003, Ghali had begun to frequent a Salafi mosque in Bamako with ties to Tablighi Jama'at. One afternoon, Manny Ansar arrived there to find Ghali seated on a mattress in a small prayer room, a stubbly beard forming on his cheeks. Ansar looked at the cramped cubicles, the dirty mattresses, the bearded acolytes, and politely declined Ghali's invitation to stay there for a four-day weekend. At this point, Ghali had given up his rich diet of lamb and couscous, his bespoke suits and his embroidered boubous. He seemed to subsist on nothing but milk and dates, and dressed in a white djellaba, a long Middle Eastern robe, and short trousers that ended well above his ankles, the clothes favored by fundamentalist Muslims. He had removed all the photographs and paintings from his house, made his wife wear the hijab, and kept her confined to the home. And he began giving away his prized possessions, handing an expensive Rolex watch to another former Tuareg rebel. Ghali confided to Ansar that he was saying "twice as many prayers" as those required by Islam, because "of all the things I have done that I regret."

Ansar was mystified by his friend's devotion but tried to remain open to it.

"You must not lose yourself entirely in religion," Ansar told him. "You were the one who created these problems for the state and for the society, so you have to stay in charge, to maintain the peace."

Ghali waved him off.

"He began to lose his friends, his acquaintances, and he became solitary. He entered a different world," Abdallah Ag Alhousseyni, a Tuareg former rebel and a singer-guitarist in Tinariwen, told me many years later.

"You know the Festival in the Desert is not something constructive. It won't speak well for you before God after you are dead," Ghali lectured Ansar. "You have to leave it behind, and consecrate yourself to God." Ghali thrust into his hands a book written by a Salafi scholar about the proper way to pray. "Manny, you have to read this and respect it, and put into practice what you find," he said. "You have to give yourself over to God, because you are a Muslim."

"Leave me alone for five more years," Ansar said. "Then I'll stop everything and follow your advice."

"No, no, that's too late," Ghali warned. "You don't know if you're going to die today."

It was during this period of Iyad Ag Ghali's religious transformation that El Para retreated with his hostages to the low-lying Adrar des Ifoghas massif of northern Mali. These were the same strongholds where Ghali had grazed herds of goats and cattle as a boy, where he had encamped as a Tuareg rebel in 1990, and near where he had held his 2000 Tuareg music festival, the precursor to the

Festival in the Desert. "Iyad approached the German ambassador, and said, 'I have the ability to make contact with the jihadis,'" recalled a former comrade. One of Ghali's relatives, an Islamic scholar and imam in northeastern Mali, had become one of the first Tuaregs to join the Salafi Group for Preaching and Combat, and he might well have facilitated the contact between Ghali and the radicals— including the ringleader, El Para, the rickets-blighted Abou Zeid, and the one-eyed Belmokhtar, the last of whom did not participate in the kidnapping but, a consummate businessman, became involved in the ransom talks.

Mali's president, Amadou Toumani Touré, named Ghali the government's intermediary with the jihadis, and, the comrade recalls, "The Germans gave him the vehicle to carry out the mission. Iyad found the kidnappers in the mountains, and they had a long parley." Shortly after that encounter, German diplomats carried three suitcases filled with five million euros cash on a military plane to Bamako to deliver to the kidnappers. Ghali loaded the suitcases into a Land Cruiser and drove back to the kidnappers' Saharan sanctuary. There, El Para and his men counted the money on a blanket in the sand. Ghali earned a new Land Cruiser for brokering the deal—and the trust of three of the region's most fanatical jihadis. The hostages were released on August 17, 2003.

American officials were alarmed and outraged by the German government's capitulation to El Para's ransom demand. They believed that it had established a dangerous precedent. The Germans tried to keep the payment quiet, but, said Vicki Huddleston, the U.S. ambassador to Mali between 2002 and 2005, "everybody knew about it as soon as it happened." Reports circulated that the GSPC had spent the money on weapons in Mauritanian gun bazaars, and on recruiting fighters for jihad.

7

Nobody in Mali was sure how to counter the jihadi threat. Mali's president, Amadou Toumani Touré, was more concerned about the Tuareg rebels and shrugged off the growing presence of Islamic extremists in the Malian desert. A former army paratrooper who had brought down a military dictatorship in 1991, President Touré had quickly overseen a democratic transition and surrendered power to the civilian president, which earned him admiration around the world. As an elder statesman, he campaigned across Africa for the eradication of Guinea worm disease, a parasite that causes debilitating blisters all over the body. Since reentering political life and being elected the country's president in 2002, he had become a close ally of the West, but seemed to believe that Mali could remain insulated from post-9/11 realities.

French military intelligence had closely tracked Mokhtar Belmokhtar and was well aware of his pull and capacity for violence.

In 2002, according to *Le Monde*, the director of France's Territorial Surveillance Directorate noted that Al Qaeda was in direct communication with Belmokhtar. French intelligence feared that Belmokhtar was helping the terrorist group recruit jihadis of North African origin living in France. But the French were scaling down their military activities in the Sahel. Aside from running a small training program for Malian officers at the Special Military Academy of Saint-Cyr, in Brittany, they embedded just a handful of French officers with Malian soldiers in the field, and maintained a small number of soldiers, including Foreign Legionnaires, in base camps in the Sahel. The French ambassador to Mali did not believe that the Salafi Group for Preaching and Combat constituted much of a threat, according to Vicki Huddleston. He appeared far more worried, she said, about the U.S. government's increasingly aggressive attempts to project its military influence in the region.

General Chuck Wald, the hard-charging deputy commander of the U.S. European Command, was leading those efforts. In a series of meetings at the European Command headquarters in early 2003, Wald and his top aides assembled a "family tree" of suspected jihadis on the Algerian-Malian frontier. "We wove them all together," Wald recalled a decade later. "We had names, relationships, and how they contacted one another." Belmokhtar was considered the most dangerous figure on the list.

Wald and his deputies believed that they had an opportunity to destroy the jihadi threat in the Sahel before it metastasized into something much more pernicious. The Americans, including officials from the National Security Agency, the Drug Enforcement Agency, the Central Intelligence Agency, the Defense Intelligence Agency, and the Federal Bureau of Investigation, considered round-the-clock aerial surveillance of the fighters from manned aircraft, a Special Forces raid on their training camp, even bombing the group from a B-52. Wald liked the destruction wreaked by the big planes, which can carry up to seventy thousand tons of bombs. In Afghanistan ten B-52s had inflicted eighty percent of the damage to Taliban positions in the first three months of the war. But he was aware that the attack would likely be perceived as overkill. Wald ultimately settled on a strike using Tomahawk cruise missiles, which can hit a target with accuracy from six hundred miles.

First however, they would have to secure the approval of Vicki Huddleston, the recently arrived ambassador to Mali. Wald called Huddleston on a secure phone line, told her he was "concerned" about Islamic militants operating in northern Mali, and said he would send down two deputies to Bamako to brief her. Days later, the men, both high-ranking military officers, were ushered into a secure room at the U.S. embassy. Huddleston and her country team—the defense attaché, USAID director, head political officer, and deputy chief of mission—gathered around the satellite photographs that they had spread out on a table. Huddleston scrutinized the images—about ten rows of men, one hundred fighters in all, the rifles, the horses, a handful of SUVs around the perimeter, and the desert setting.

"What are they doing?" Huddleston asked.

"They're training," a deputy replied.

"What are they training for?"

"We don't know."

"Well, what's the plan?" Huddleston asked.

"We would like to remove them."

As Huddleston remembered the conversation, Wald's deputies specifically stated that they planned to launch a missile at the fighters, whom they labeled "really bad guys"; Wald insists that it was presented to the ambassador as one of several options. The deputies also said, Huddleston claims, that Wald was not willing to give the Malian government advance warning of the attack. Wald suspected that radical Islamist sympathizers had penetrated President Touré's circle, and that they would leak the information about the impending air strike.

Huddleston considered the European Command's request. A Colorado-born, former Peace Corps volunteer and a seasoned diplomat, Huddleston had run the U.S. interests section in Cuba and served as ambassador to Madagascar before arriving in Bamako in November 2002. She had also served as the deputy chief of mission at the U.S. embassy in Port-au-Prince at the time of a coup d'état by the Haitian military that overthrew the country's elected president, Jean-Paul Aristide, in 1994. As U.S. forces massed at Guantánamo Bay were preparing to remove the junta by force, Huddleston participated in negotiations between the Haitian coup leaders and a U.S. delegation, including former president Jimmy Carter and retired Joint Chiefs of Staff chairman Colin Powell, that led to the reinstatement of Aristide and averted an invasion. She was an advocate of restraint, dialogue, inclusion, and transparency, and she was troubled by Wald's advocacy of a covert missile strike inside Malian territory. Huddleston also worried about civilian casualties. Given the distance between the closest possible launch site and the training camp, she calculated that the missile would take between thirty and sixty minutes to reach the target—enough time for innocents to wander into the kill zone. Moreover, she still hadn't seen any evidence that the group was preparing a terrorist attack. Huddleston isn't sure that Wald's deputies ever confirmed the presence of Mokhtar Belmokhtar. But even if the deputies had identified the one-eyed jihadi as being among the fighters, Huddleston told me, she wouldn't have approved his killing. "He was not associated at the time with the Salafi Group for Preaching and Combat," she recalled a decade later. "We knew him only as a bad guy who smuggled cigarettes."

Huddleston pressed Wald's deputies for specifics. "Tell me exactly who's out there," she demanded.

The deputies admitted that they had no idea. "But give us your approval and we'll work on it."

She sent them back to Vaihingen with a message for Wald: "I don't want you bombing them," she said.

Wald was infuriated. Huddleston, he believed, had lost a golden opportunity to eliminate the radical Islamist threat in a single air strike. Her opposition confirmed his impression that U.S. ambassadors in Africa focused too much on "soft" issues—nutrition, education, and health—and were out of step in a world of globalized terror. "There was a resentment that we [military types] were even hanging out in Africa," Wald said. "The thinking was, 'what are you mucking about my area for? You're just going to mess it up.'" He also believed that the diplomatic corps was jealous of its military counterparts: four-star generals enjoyed easy access to many African leaders—"they love the U.S. military," he said—while ambassadors sometimes had trouble getting a foot in the door. Still, he resigned himself to Huddleston's decision overruling him. "We pushed it, but when the State Department says 'you're a bunch of assholes' what are you going to do?"

For her part, Huddleston believed that Wald was something of a cowboy who was willing to act without considering the region's complexities—or the possibility of blowback. "Wald doesn't think," she would say a decade later. "It is full speed ahead no matter what." She felt vindicated a few weeks later, when U.S. intelligence revealed that the military drills had nothing to do with jihad. Belmokhtar had been training fellow Arabs for a battle against a rival Arab clan—the culmination of a long-running Hatfield–McCoy rivalry over water rights, representation on village councils, and other issues. Tribal chiefs had hired Belmokhtar to prepare their kinsmen for battle.

Just after the intelligence report clarifying the nature of Belmokhtar's desert training came out, Wald left Germany on a scheduled visit to Bamako. He flew on his military plane from Stuttgart, first paying a courtesy call on Mali's popular president, Amadou Toumani Touré. In the evening, Wald pulled up to Huddleston's walled-off residence near the Niger River, a modern one-story villa surrounded by a garden filled with palm trees. Wald thought that Huddleston had gotten the "wrong impression" of him and wanted to ease the tension. "She didn't know us well at the time," he said. Fruit bats hung from the fronds of the palm trees in Huddleston's garden, swirling around at twilight, swooping low over the swimming pool. Unkempt thickets of bamboo grew behind the verandah. The household staff cooked their meals on small fires in the back garden. Huddleston had filled the airy rooms with Bambara crocodile masks and elaborate wooden doors carved by Mali's animist Dogon tribe—along with colorful folk art from Haiti that she had collected during her tour there.

"I guess you came to thank me," Huddleston told the general. In her view, she had probably saved his job by vetoing the missile strike. Wald laughed, and little more was said on the subject.

Huddleston and Wald traveled north to Timbuktu in Wald's plane the next morning, sitting across from each other on comfortable leather chairs in a private cabin. Wald was eager to see the Sahara, and assess the security situation there. The ambassador, slender, with brown hair cascading down below her shoulders, and the crew-cut general with a football player's physique made an odd couple, with starkly different views on projecting America's power in the world, but both agreed that northern Mali needed to be carefully monitored, and they found that they enjoyed each other's company.

The jet followed the course of the Niger River, a strand of silver that wound through a pancake-flat, desolate landscape. *A lot of places to hide out there*, Wald thought. After two hours they descended toward Timbuktu. The military pilot circled twice, at low altitude, over warrens of flat-roofed, dun-colored buildings a few miles south of the river. Then they touched down on Timbuktu's tarmac airstrip, to an official greeting from the mayor and many civil servants attired in turbans and flowing traditional Malian gowns.

Timbuktu was beginning a tourist boom, but Wald couldn't help noticing how backward the place was: unpaved streets, tumble-down mud-brick houses, and, it seemed, many unemployed young men. He toured the Ahmed Baba Institute, the government library funded by UNESCO that, thanks to Abdel Kader Haidara, now contained one of the world's largest collections of medieval Arabic manuscripts. Then Wald visited Timbuktu's Djingareyber Mosque, a mud-walled trapezoid with two limestone minarets, designed and built by one of the medieval world's great architects, Abu Es Haq Al Zaheli, in 1327 on a commission from Musa I, known as Mansa Musa, the emperor of Mali. In one of the three inner courts of the hulking fortress—influenced by the great pyramids of Egypt—the imam handed Wald an embossed business card on quality paper, with the holy man's website printed beside his email address.

"Imam, you've got your own website?" Wald asked, surprised. Later, he spotted a cybercafé and remembered a conversation that he had recently had with Algerian intelligence officials: Algerian extremists, they had told him, recruited potential jihadis via the web in Internet cafés just like this one. Wald was startled to see that modern technology had reached one of the most remote corners of the world. *Maybe we don't know this area as well as we thought we did*, Wald thought.

Though they disagreed over Belmokhtar, Huddleston and Wald collaborated successfully on a program to train soldiers in several Sahel countries to pursue El Para, the Algerian parachutist-turned-jihadi-kidnapper who had abducted the thirty-two Western hostages in the Sahara. As part of the Pan-Sahel Initiative, launched by the Office of Counterterrorism within the U.S. State Department in November 2002, the U.S. team gave the troops all-terrain vehicles and taught them how to track the kidnappers using such means as satellite telephone intercepts and on-the-ground intelligence. After collecting his ransom in August 2003, El Para had escaped from his mountain redoubt in northeastern Mali. Troops from Mali, Niger, and Chad, backed by U.S. on-the-ground intelligence and aerial reconnaissance, pursued the jihadi leader back and forth across the Sahara for months. Chadian rebels captured him in 2004 in the remote Tibesti Mountains in northern Chad and turned him over to Algeria, which convicted him of terrorism and locked him away for life for "creating an armed terrorist group and spreading terror among the population."

But his two deputies, Belmokhtar and Abou Zeid, both fellow members of his jihadi organization who had participated with him in the hostage-for-ransom operation in the Algerian and Malian Sahara, remained at large. And U.S. intelligence had come to regard Iyad Ag Ghali as a double threat—a former Tuareg rebel who was capable of restarting the rebellion in northern Mali, and a potential bridge between the secular Tuareg rebels and the radical Islamists, both of whom were occupying the desert and sometimes smuggling drugs and other contraband together. Although Ghali was still ostensibly a Malian government security adviser and was close to the Malian president, "We knew he had close contacts with the Salafis," said Huddleston. "We were concerned."

Huddleston took a road trip through the north of Mali in late 2003, trying to assess support for the radicals among Tuareg and Arab clans. She was alarmed by what she found. The embassy had been distributing money—about half a million dollars since she got there—on modest projects in the desert, building wells and other light infrastructure with the hope of winning over the local population. She traveled by four-wheel-drive with her security team through Belmokhtar's territory, north of Timbuktu, and arrived after a day's drive through the arid bush in an Arab village where he had taken a twelve-year-old bride. The mayor and other nota-bles put on a reception for Huddleston. Huddleston thought, "Bel-mokhtar is probably in the crowd watching me." The place, she felt, was "full of tension. It was a powder keg." Later Huddleston traveled three hundred miles across the Sahara to Kidal, the remote Tuareg outpost in the northeast corner of the country, in the shadow of the Adrar des Ifoghas massif, where she paid a call on Iyad Ag Ghali. She found the Tuareg leader in a government building in the center of Kidal, a dun-brown backwater of twenty thousand people, where herders drove packs of camels through the wide sand-swept streets, and a Malian flag fluttered from atop a turreted French-colonial-era fort perched on a pile of rocks. Ghali was serving as the president's security adviser as well as the unofficial leader of his Tuareg clan. He was "a good-looking guy with a turban, a nice beard, and pierc-ing eyes," she remembered. "He looked the part of a desert warrior." For half an hour they talked about U.S. assistance programs in the Kidal region, and about the importance of keeping a lid on restive Tuaregs.

"We don't need the resurgence of the rebellion," she told Ghali.

"Of course not," he agreed.

Ghali's deepening Islamic devotion also worried Huddleston. Although the Tablighi Jama'at sect presents itself as a peaceful group, it had sometimes served as a stepping-stone to jihad. Zacar-ias Moussaoui, the only person to be charged in the United States in the September 11 attacks, was a Tablighi Jama'at follower in France, as was Hervé Djamel Loiseau, who had died during the 2001 U.S. bombardment of Tora Bora in Afghanistan. John Walker Lindh, the "American Taliban" captured by U.S. forces after the Battle of Qala-i-Jangi, near Mazar-e-Sharif, had joined the Afghan radicals after a flirtation with Tablighi Jama'at. And at the very moment that Hud-dleston was meeting with Ghali, two young Tablighi Jama'at follow-ers from Great Britain were heading down a path toward terrible violence. The two men would soon attend a terrorist camp in Pakistan, then return to the United Kingdom to plan and execute the July 7, 2005 suicide attacks on the London Underground and on a double-decker bus, in which fifty-two people died and more than seven hundred were injured, many maimed for life.

"You'd better not be involved in terrorism," Huddleston cautioned Ghali.

"Oh, no, ma'am," he replied.

8

By 2007 the Salafi Group for Preaching and Combat, the Islamic extremist organization that had been formed a decade earlier from the remnants of Algerian rebel groups, and that had announced itself by kidnapping dozens of European tourists in the Sahara in 2003, was evolving into one of the best financed and most lethal terrorist organizations in the world. At the end of 2004, the GSPC had acquired an ambitious new emir, Abdelmalek Droukdel, a thirty-four-year-old Algerian from the agricultural town of Meftah, fifteen miles south of Algiers, who had established his jihadi credentials as a holy warrior in Afghanistan, and who sought alliances with the most violent figures in the international jihadi network. One to whom he reached out was Abu Musab Al Zarqawi, the Jordanian-born commander of Al Qaeda in Mesopotamia, then fighting a guerrilla war against the U.S. military in Iraq, and blowing up Iraqi Shi'ite Muslims with the objective of inciting a civil war. Droukdel tried to enlist the homicidal Al Zarqawi in a plot to kidnap French civilians and trade them for El Para, but the plan never got off the ground. When a U.S. drone killed Al Zarqawi, Droukdel vowed revenge on a jihadi website: "O infidels and apostates, your joy will be brief and you will cry for a long time . . . we are all Zarqawi."

On the fifth anniversary of the 9/11 atttacks, in 2006, bin Laden's deputy, Ayman Al Zawahiri, announced the formal merger of Al Qaeda and the GSPC. Exactly three months later, the GSPC bombed and fired on a convoy near Algiers carrying employees of Brown & Root-Condor, a joint venture of the U.S. Halliburton Group and Sonatrach, the Algerian state-owned oil company. The company was expanding military bases in southern Algeria. An Algerian driver was killed, and nine workers, including an American and four Britons, were wounded.

The Salafi Group for Preaching and Combat changed its name to Al Qaeda in the Islamic Maghreb in January 2007. AQIM declared that its primary goal was bringing down the Algerian regime and replacing it with an Islamic state, and Al Zawahiri proclaimed that the organization would also become "a bone in the throat of American and French crusaders." Almost immediately AQIM unleashed a series of devastating attacks in the Sahel. Terrorists blew up the front of the Algerian prime minister's house and a police headquarters in Algiers, killing twenty-three people and injuring more than 160, and car-bombed the offices of the United Nations, also in Algiers, killing sixty. Among the dead were U.N. staffers from Denmark, Senegal, and the Philippines.

The leaders of Al Qaeda in the Islamic Maghreb operated from villages hidden deep in the mountains of Kabylie, a hundred miles east of Algiers, largely beyond the reach of Algeria's security forces. Under Droukdel's command, the group developed a tightly hierarchical structure. Two leadership committees, the fifteen-member Council of Notables, led by Droukdel, and a fourteen-member

Shura Council, led by Abdu Oubeida Al Annabi, another veteran of the Afghan jihad, determined targets and priorities, established links with other terrorist groups around the world, and maintained a public presence through audio speeches, videos, and website communiqués. The great majority of these men were mujahideen who had earned their stripes with the GIA during the Algerian civil war and with the Salafi Group for Preaching and Combat, AQIM's predecessor, in the early 2000s. Some had received training with Al Qaeda in Pakistan or Afghanistan; nearly all were kidnappers, drug smugglers, and murderers. These two command structures presided over six committees—political, judicial, medical, military, finance, and foreign relations—and divided their territory of operations into two zones, the "Central Emirate," including northern Algeria and Tunisia; and the "Sahara Emirate," including northern Mali, southern Algeria, Niger, and Libya.

Droukdel and his fellow commanders in the Kabylie identified northern Mali—with its weak security forces, vast swath of desert, and growing presence of Western tourists and development workers—as both a vital source of revenue from drug trafficking and kidnappings, and a sanctuary for its fighters. The jihadi organization subdivided northern Mali into two zones, administered by rival emirs. Abdelhamid Abou Zeid controlled the territory around Kidal. The region belonging to Mokhtar Belmokhtar lay north of Timbuktu. Each led a *qatiba*, or brigade, of 150 to 200 fighters. Abou Zeid had named his unit the "Tarek Ibn Ziyad Brigade," after the Moorish general who conquered Spain in the eighth century. Belmokhtar called his brigade "Al Moulathamine," or "The Masked Ones."

Largely autonomous but expected to produce large sums of money for AQIM, the Al Qaeda militiamen moved through the desert in all-terrain vehicles, oriented themselves with GPS systems, and picked up food, ammunition, fuel, batteries, and even replacement vehicles from cachés buried in the sand. A home video made by a fighter of the Tarek Ibn Ziyad Brigade, captured in 2010 after a shootout with Algerian security forces, showed the men sleeping in caves, making their own clothes on manual sewing machines, repairing their own vehicles, and subsisting on water from the region's handful of streams and an unvarying diet of roots and lizards.

Abou Zeid was an austere figure, a brutal executioner, wholly committed to Islamist ideology. "There is a commercial aspect to what he does but it is mainly about jihad," one Western terrorism expert in Bamako told *Jane's Terrorism and Security Monitor*. Belmokhtar was "a businessman with radical tendencies" who operated according to his own code: he viewed soldiers, customs agents, and other government agents as fair game in his holy war, but he usually refrained from killing civilians. The two men competed bitterly for the attentions of their bosses in the Algerian mountains—but their rivalry was good for Al Qaeda's balance sheet. It fueled a wave of abductions of Westerners for ransom that would, over the next four years, contribute as much as $116 million to AQIM's coffers.

In April 2008 AQIM gunmen seized two Austrian tourists in Tunisia's southeastern Sahara, the first abduction of Westerners by jihadis in the desert since 2003. Al Qaeda released those hostages after 252 days of captivity when Austria reportedly paid a $6.4 million ransom. The wave of kidnappings accelerated. In December 2008, Mokhtar Belmokhtar's brigade intercepted a vehicle carrying two Canadian diplomats on a road outside Niamey, Niger, shoved them into a pickup truck, drove them hundreds of miles through the Sahara, and held them in a series of desolate jihadi camps. A month after that abduction, Abou Zeid's commandos ambushed three vehicles bringing tourists to Mali from a Tuareg music-and-culture festival in Niger. The gunmen grabbed four middle-aged and elderly European hostages and carried them off to another desert encampment. That June, in a change of tactics, two Al Qaeda gunmen shot dead Christopher Leggett, a thirty-nine-year-old American English teacher, in Nouakchott, the capital of Mauritania. Al Jazeera released a statement from AQIM's spokesperson saying that Leggett had been executed "for his Christianizing activities."

Soon it was back to kidnapping. In November 2009, Al Qaeda commandos attacked a convoy on the main highway through Mauritania, and seized three Spanish aid workers. Two weeks later kidnappers under Abou Zeid's command grabbed a French aid worker from his hotel room in Ménaka, a town in eastern Mali. And days later, in a familiar modus operandi, the Islamists seized a vacationing Italian couple from their vehicle on another desolate road in Mauritania. The kidnapping, an AQIM spokesman said, was in revenge for "the crimes [of the Silvio] Berlusconi government [of Italy against] the right of Islam and Muslims in Afghanistan and Iraq." Abou Zeid struck again in the spring of 2010, with the spectacular abductions of four French workers for Areva at a uranium plant in northern Niger, and the seizure of a seventy-eight-year-old retired French engineer, Michel Germaneau, also in northern Niger, where he was working for a charity organization.

Robert Fowler, one of the two kidnapped Canadians, who was serving as United Nations special envoy to Niger at the time of his abduction, was one of the few Westerners to get a sustained look at Mokhtar Belmokhtar. The AQIM emir appeared periodically at the desert camps where he and his colleague were being held. "He was relatively slight, with a heavily weathered and deeply lined face and curly black hair," wrote Fowler, who had suffered a compression fracture in a vertebra as a result of his multi-day journey through the desert immediately after his abduction. Fowler described Belmokhtar as a "revered leader" who exuded a sinister magnetism. "He had thin lips set in a straight line, and his mouth twisted from time to time into a ghost of a cold, almost wry smile. His most distinguishing feature was a deep almost vertical scar that began above the middle of his right eyebrow, crossed his right eyelid, and continued across his right cheek, disappearing into his moustache." Belmokhtar's crew was sustained by a fanaticism that impressed Fowler. "They would sit chanting in the full Sahara sun for hour after hour," he observed. "They seemed to have no trouble recruiting. The youngest among them was seven . . . and the voices of three of the others had yet to break. Parents, we were proudly informed, brought them their sons as 'gifts to God.'"

Fowler also described one interaction that set off in sharp relief the different personalities of Belmokhtar and his jihadi rival in northern Mali: Abou Zeid. On April 21, 2009, the Canadian government paid a mere 700,000 euros, then worth about $1 million, for Fowler's and his fellow Canadian diplomat's release—a deal negotiated by Belmokhtar himself, to the consternation of his superiors. Fowler was driven to a rendezvous point in the desert just as Abou Zeid's men arrived with two female Western hostages. Both had been seized after the music festival in Niger. After five months of fear, hunger, ovenlike heat, stultifying boredom, and brutal mistreatment by Abou Zeid and his men, both women suffered from dysentery, and the arm of one had swollen and turned necrotic from a scorpion bite. Their governments had sent them medicine during the negotiation process, but Abou Zeid had withheld it from them. "I recoiled with horror at the sight of those small, troubled white faces, twisted with pain," Fowler recalled. Belmokhtar inspected the women and, with a "thunderous look on his face," gave them dysentery pills from a medical kit. Abou Zeid's callous reputation solidified seven months later. The British government, following a long-standing policy, refused to meet his brigade's demands for the release of sixty-two-year-old plumbing contractor Edwin Dyer: a multimillion-dollar ransom and the release from a British prison of Abu Qatada, the radical Jordanian cleric whom Belmokhtar had known since the Afghanistan jihad of the 1980s. In June 2009, Abou Zeid beheaded the Briton. Prime Minister Gordon Brown condemned Dyer's "barbaric" murder, and avowed that "it strengthens our determination never to concede to the demands of terrorists, nor pay ransoms."

Other European governments did not display the same resolve. Understandably unwilling to see their citizens subjected to brutal treatment and possible execution, and disregarding U.S. and British government admonitions that the ransom payments were only fueling Al Qaeda in the Islamic Maghreb's recruitment efforts and arms purchases, they turned over tens of millions of dollars to the kidnappers and pressured the Malian government as well to make painful concessions. The jihadis released one Spanish aid worker in March 2010 and her two male compatriots five months later, in exchange for a total ransom paid by the Spanish government that has been estimated as high as $12.7 million; they also freed the Italian couple north of Gao after four months, in a trade for four radical Islamists held in Malian prisons.

Belmokhtar and Abou Zeid supplemented the ransoms they received from European governments with growing profits from international drug trafficking. They had started in that business in the early 2000s, employing Tuareg and Arab couriers to carry cocaine overland through Mali from Equatorial Guinea, a narco-state on the Atlantic Coast controlled by Colombian drug traffickers. By the latter part of the decade, the drug cartels, with Al Qaeda in the Islamic Maghreb intermediaries, were shipping huge quantities of cocaine by air through the Malian Sahara. In 2009 nomads discovered the charred carcass of a Boeing 727-200 in the Sahara north of Kidal. It had offloaded as many as ten tons of cocaine, according to a United Nations intelligence report, and, while attempting to take off, had become stuck in the sand. The crew had abandoned the plane and set it on fire to cover their tracks. Recovered flight logs revealed that the plane had made repeated flights between Colombia and Mali, suggesting that a vast and lucrative drug trafficking network existed between the two countries. With their coffers full of cash, their numbers growing, and their logistical capabilities improving, the terrorist group, U.S. officials believed, would soon become capable of attacking Western embassies in the region, and exporting their terror overseas.

In 2005 the Pentagon had launched the Trans-Saharan Counterterrorism Initiative, a six-year, $500-million program aimed at strengthening the armies of Mali, Mauritania, Niger, Chad, and a dozen other northern African nations. Special Forces commandos and Navy SEALs were rotated in to instruct hundreds of Malian soldiers and officers in basic military tactics, from assembling weapons to first aid, to patrolling the desert on foot and in vehicles. The Americans ran trainees through six-week courses conducted three or four times a year near bases in Mopti, Bamako, Gao, and Timbuktu. The army, the trainers recognized immediately, was in desperate shape. The soldiers' rifles, mostly AK-47s from the former Eastern bloc and China, had broken stocks, clips, and slings. Ammunition was decades old and stored in dampness or extreme heat. Troops showed up for weapons training without a single bullet in their clips. Flying in by helicopter to a Malian military base in the far north to observe the training in 2009, Marshall Mantiply, the U.S. defense attaché, noted the soldiers' mismatched uniforms, cracked boots, and headgear ranging from turbans to baseball caps. The men looked "unsoldierly," he thought. The recruitment of rank-and-file troops "was attracting the dregs of the society—all the problem children, failures in school, delinquents, and criminals," one Malian presidential adviser acknowledged to me several years later. Most of these Malian recruits had grown up in extreme poverty, and they lacked even the most basic skills for functioning on the battlefield. Mantiply observed one war zone simulation exercise that called for soldiers to replace a military truck driver who had been "shot and killed" in an ambush. The troops refused to participate; not a single one of them, it turned out, knew how to drive.

It was not the first time that the Malian army had proven itself an untrustworthy partner in the field. During their pursuit of the Algerian terrorist leader known as El Para through the desert near Mauritania back in 2004, a U.S.-trained Malian brigade had been closing in on his hideout when El Para and his men suddenly broke camp and escaped across the border into Niger. Somebody inside the brigade, the U.S. learned, had tipped off the jihadi commander that the soldiers were getting close. At the time, General Chuck Wald, the deputy commander of the European Command, had vowed angrily that he would "never" work with the Malian armed forces again. Colonel Didier Dacko, a U.S.-trained brigade commander who would become the commander in chief of the Malian military, would admit: "Esprit de corps did not exist."

Adding to the frustration and sense of drift, the U.S. government was locked into an acrimonious debate about how best to train the Malian troops. Vicki Huddleston was now working out of the Pentagon as the deputy assistant secretary of defense for Africa, overseeing the counterterrorism campaign against the jihadis in the Sahara. Initially opposing Wald when she had been ambassador, Huddleston had shifted her position radically as terrorism grew in the region. She now believed that the objective of the U.S. training mission should be nothing less than the "termination of Al Qaeda in the Islamic Maghreb." She urged the new ambassador to Mali, Gillian Milovanovic, who arrived in the country in the fall of 2008 and who had significant say over how the training program should be run, to create a quick reaction force of elite Malian troops to destroy nests of Al Qaeda militants.

Milovanovic thought that Huddleston's goal was "ludicrous," she would say half a decade later. It would take years to build Malian SWAT teams from scratch, she argued with Huddleston in meetings at the Pentagon. Even the army's most elite units, known as ETIAs, were in sorry shape. Milovanovic noted in a confidential cable that a U.S. Army captain had introduced her to "one, rather unimpressive soldier, an older, rail thin man with a scraggly beard and bloodshot eyes who had been lounging against a motorbike in a dirty T-shirt inside a warehouse. [The captain] explained that in spite of appearances, this was one of ETIA's best men, noting that he had been one of the survivors of a July 4 ambush of a Malian Army patrol by Al Qaeda in the Islamic Maghreb."

Milovanovic argued that the army should establish a presence only on well-traveled desert roads and limit itself to hunting down Al Qaeda's weapons and fuel caches. "We won't train the guys to look for Al Qaeda in little Toyota trucks and get ambushed," she said. Huddleston believed it was a tepid approach that was guaranteed to fail.

But in Milovanovic's view, the Pentagon brass was unwilling to put its money where its mouth was. Six months after arriving in Bamako, Milovanovic flew to Washington to attend her first meetings at the Pentagon, and was "stunned," she recounted, by the discrepancy between the amount of money the Defense Department claimed to be spending on Mali and what she had seen in the field. "It was a huge canard," she said. Tens of millions of dollars went to cover the transport and housing of U.S. trainers, but were misleadingly counted on the balance sheet as direct aid to the Malian military. Equipment was constantly promised but rarely delivered.

Huddleston shot down a proposal by Milovanovic and her defense attaché to provide the poorly equipped Malian air force with a pair of Cessna Caravans—durable turboprops that can be used to transport troops, bomb enemy positions, and conduct aerial surveillance. Huddleston believed that the Malian air force would allow the airplanes to fall apart or use them to attack Tuareg separatists—"their own people"—instead of their intended targets, the jihadis. That left the air force with a couple of Soviet-era MiG-21 fighter jets that hadn't been off the ground in years, two 1960s Navy Cessnas that barely stayed in the air on the cannibalized parts of a third plane, and four eight-seat Mi-24 helicopter gunships, or Hinds, that had been grounded after a Ukrainian pilot was shot dead in action against Tuareg rebels.

Between 2008 and 2010, a period of alarming growth for Al Qaeda in the Islamic Maghreb, the Malian armed forces received from the United States a single shipment of military hardware: thirty armored trucks. The trucks lacked communications gear, and months went by before the Pentagon bothered to send technicians to install the equipment. The radios rapidly drained the truck batteries, making them useless for long-range desert deployments. The trainers finally placed tags on the dashboards in Bambara, the main language of southern Mali, and French.

"Don't turn the radio on," they read.

By contrast, the French government, which had once shrugged off the jihadis' growing presence in the Sahel, had, by late 2009, became far more aggressive against them. AQIM had ambushed and murdered four French tourists, including three members of the same family, during a roadside picnic in Mauritania in December 2007—prompting the cancellation the next year of the annual Paris–Dakar motor rally. The group injured a Frenchwoman in a gun attack on the Israeli embassy in Nouakchott, in February 2008, and killed a French engineer, along with eleven Algerian civilians, in the explosion of two booby-trapped cars in Lakhdaria, Algeria, that June. In August 2009, Abdelmalek Droukdel, the Algeria-based leader of the group, denounced France as the "mother of all evils"; days later, an AQIM terrorist detonated a suicide bomb in front of the French embassy in Nouakchott, killing himself and injuring three passersby, including two embassy staffers. "The French realized AQIM was a growing danger," Vicki Huddleston told me.

"They considered it the biggest foreign terrorist threat that France faced."

Having lost all confidence in the abilities of the Malian army, France shifted its focus to conducting joint counterterrorism operations with the better-trained Mauritanian military. On July 22, 2010, French and Mauritanian Special Forces flew out of Nouakchott, crossed 1,100 miles of desert, and attacked an AQIM camp in Tigharghar, in Mali's Adrar des Ifoghas massif, north of Kidal, where, French intelligence indicated, the septugenarian aid worker Michel Germaneau was being held prisoner. The commandos killed six Al Qaeda militants but failed to rescue Germaneau, who may have been moved from the camp just a few hours before the raid. In retaliation, Abou Zeid ordered his beheading—and may have carried it out himself. "As a quick response to the despicable French act, we confirm that we have killed hostage Germaneau in revenge for our six brothers who were killed in the treacherous operation," Al Qaeda in the Islamic Maghreb's leader in Algeria said in a message broadcast on Al Jazeera television. "Sarkozy has [not only] failed to free his compatriot in this failed operation, but he opened the doors of hell for himself and his people." The Barack Obama administration, unhappy about a military coup that had unseated the elected Mauritanian government two years earlier, was lukewarm about the joint operation. "So by 2010 the United States and France had reversed their roles," recalled Huddleston. "The French were being far more proactive in their pursuit of Al Qaeda."

U.S. officials believed that Mali's president, Amadou Toumani Touré, remained oblivious to both the jihadis' growing strength and his own army's rot. After Malians voted him back to the presidency in 2002, corruption in the military ranks had deepened. Senior officers rose in rank because of connections rather than merit. Military commanders in the north were suspected of colluding with Al Qaeda in the drug trade. ATT, as he was known, often seemed to pretend that the radical Islamists didn't exist. The jihadis didn't pursue the Malian army—as long as they were left alone to smuggle cocaine and kidnap the occasional Westerner. "The [government's] attitude was, 'it was best not to poke the hornet's nest,'" Defense Attaché Marshall Mantiply told me. "Why send the troops out on suicide missions?"

Ambassador Gillian Milovanovic met Touré two times in June 2009 at the presidential palace, a sprawling whitewashed villa perched atop an extinct volcano. Her exasperation mounting, Milovanovic warned him that Al Qaeda in the Islamic Maghreb's use of northern Mali as a safe haven and the killing of the British hostage Edwin Dyer were "rapidly tarnishing" the country's image. "Do something," she urged him. Touré made Milovanovic a firm promise to go after Al Qaeda—as long as the United States delivered more military equipment and logistical support. Milovanovic left the meeting feeling that Touré had at last seemed to understand the danger facing his country, she cabled Washington, but others expressed their doubts. "The level of inaction at the presidency was akin to firefighters deciding to sleep through alarm bells at the firehouse," one high-ranking Malian official reported to the U.S. embassy.

As AQIM continued to gain strength in northern Mali, Iyad Ag Ghali was, as U.S. intelligence officials and diplomats had feared, making a turn toward jihad. After serving as a hostage negotiator, diplomat without portfolio, and presidential security adviser, Ghali had tilted back toward violence in 2006, when he had briefly joined forces with a perennial Tuareg troublemaker in Kidal, who was angry about being passed over for a military promotion. The pair had raised a rebel force, driven out government troops, and captured Kidal. Then Ghali crossed back to the government side and helped the president obtain the release of dozens of Malian soldiers held by the rebels.

Then, in late 2008 Ghali unexpectedly announced that he was

leaving Mali. He had had enough of politics and Tuareg rebellion, he told friends, rivals, and Western diplomats, and had decided to accept a low-level diplomatic posting in the Malian consulate in Jeddah, the largest port on the Red Sea, and the second largest city in Saudi Arabia after the capital, Riyadh. "I want to be near the Great Mosque of Mecca, where I can pray five times a day," he explained to the music impresario Manny Ansar, who worried that the assignment in Saudi Arabia might push Ghali over the edge.

Jeddah's King Abdulaziz University, the fundamentalists' nerve center, has been an incubator for some of the most virulent strains of Wahhabism. Osama bin Laden studied business administration there and received religious instruction from Mohammed Qatub, the brother of the Islamist revivalist Sayud Qatub, who established the ideological underpinnings of violent jihad against the West. Abdullah Yusuf Azzam, the Palestinian Sunni theologian whose sermons on cassette had enthralled the aspiring young jihadi Mokhtar Belmokhtar, was a lecturer there before he recruited committed young Islamists to fight a holy war in Afghanistan against the Soviets in the 1980s, and founded Al Qaeda with bin Laden. Ghali escaped the drudgery of his sweltering office on a back street in Jeddah to seek out Wahhabi radicals, possibly at the university and at some of the city's 1,300 mosques. Saudi intelligence kept a close eye on him. In August 2009, a Saudi militant with links to Al Qaeda blew himself up at a gathering at the Jeddah home of Prince Mohammed bin Naif, the deputy interior minister and a leading antiterrorism figure. After the failed assassination attempt, counterterrorism forces intensified a crackdown on those suspected of links to Al Qaeda. It was around this time that the Saudi government declared Ghali persona non grata and expelled him. "I don't think he was flipped there," one close associate told *The Atlantic Monthly* four years later. "I think he'd already begun to change. But the fact that he was pushed out . . . shows that his personal beliefs had begun to match up in a very tangible way with extremist ideology and behavior."

When Ghali returned to Bamako from Saudi Arabia in late 2009, he began frequenting Bamako's Green Mosque, a Salafi gathering place, where he preached the virtues of Shariah law to a large and enthusiastic following. On a Friday morning in 2009, he invited his friend Ansar to meet him there following afternoon prayers. In front of the mosque, as Wahhabis in long beards and robes walked past, Ghali again tried to coax him into the fundamentalist fold.

"Are you sure you're not heading down the road of violence?" Ansar asked him.

Ghali shook his head emphatically. "We are pacifists," he said.

Ansar saw Ghali a final time in February 2010. He was driving north from Bamako to the Festival on the Niger, an annual four-day concert, founded in 2005 as a southern Malian counterpart to the Festival in the Desert, and held on a barge moored off the riverbank in Ségou, 140 miles north of the capital. Ghali's distinctive, bright orange four-wheel-drive overtook his car on the two-lane road and disappeared around a curve. Minutes later, Ansar spotted the vehicle at a gas station and parked beside it. Although his relationship with Ghali had grown distant in recent years, Ansar felt a keen desire to see his old friend. In high spirits about the music festival, Ansar recalled fondly the intimate jam sessions that he and Ghali had attended with a few friends on his rooftop and by the Niger River in the mid-1990s, before Tinariwen had achieved international acclaim, and before Ghali had fallen in with the Salafis.

Ansar remembered vividly the chain-smoking, music-loving, club-hopping bon vivant that Ghali had been in those days; the poet and lyricist who had written romantic ballads as well as martial songs for his friend, the singer-guitarist Ibrahim Ag Habib;

and the hedonist who never prayed and hated being woken before noon. After parking his car, Ansar walked into the service station's adjoining restaurant. Ghali was seated at a table in the corner with his wife, with whom Ansar had once also been on friendly terms. Wearing a hijab, she kept her eyes fixed on the table, refusing to look at him. Ghali wore a white skullcap and a white boubou over black pants. He looked austere, yet still filled up the room with his presence. He greeted Ansar with a curt hello.

"You are going where?" he asked.

"I'm heading for the festival in Ségou," Ansar replied.

Ghali's face sagged. He looked at Ansar with what seemed to be a mixture of pity and contempt. "In his mind, I was an old friend whom he had once loved, and whom he hadn't been able to save from the grip of Satan," Ansar recalled. All common ground between them, it was instantly clear, had been lost. After an excruciating silence that seemed to drag out for minutes, Ansar mumbled goodbye and walked out of the restaurant.

9

In 2011 the Mamma Haidara Commemorative Library in Timbuktu was fast becoming one of the world's most innovative manuscript conservation centers and a symbol of Timbuktu's cultural renaissance. Abdel Kader Haidara had taken on twelve employees. A grant in 2007 from Dubai's Juma Al Majid Center for Culture and Heritage had allowed him to build a laboratory for the repair and digitization of his manuscripts, and to create an annex with four gleaming exhibition rooms and a conference center. Haidara showed off to a visiting European reporter his new lab and his state-of-the-art photographic equipment; he used a digital camera rather than scanner, he explained, because the ultraviolet scanning technology could ignite the linen-based paper and the ferrous inks and destroy the manuscripts.

In his workshop, Haidara had begun manufacturing acid-free paper for restoring the manuscripts to mint condition—previously imported at a high cost—and he talked with the reporter about establishing a side business selling it to tourists and exporting it. A digitization seminar was taking place on the top floor of the library, its heterogeneous participants—"Arabs with short beards, Tuaregs with turbans and reading glasses, African faces," the reporter observed—reflecting Timbuktu's historic role as a melting pot of ethnic groups. Haidara was making plans to release a CD containing translations of an Arabic text about conflict resolution—"The Westerners come over here and try and tell us they invented it all," he told his visitor—while awaiting the arrival of a team of South Africans from University of Cape Town for a manuscript conservation symposium.

Haidara was becoming an international man of letters. After the success of his first trip to the United States in 2003, for the inaugural American exhibition of African manuscripts, held at the Library of Congress, Haidara had been much sought after by libraries and museums around the world. He traveled frequently to New York, Washington, Atlanta, Chicago, Berlin, Paris, Brussels, Amsterdam, Geneva, and other capitals, receiving honors, serving on academic panels, and acting as the master of ceremonies at traveling exhibitions of the Mamma Haidara Library's manuscripts. He acquired a network of friends and colleagues abroad, became confident navigating his way through European and American cities—though he never mastered English—and found his world opening up in ways that he couldn't have dreamed a decade earlier. He developed a familiarity with Western customs—though when he traveled in the West, he always dressed, as he did at home, in the traditional Malian robe, the boubou—learned about American and European religion, literature, music, and cuisine, and more practically, exchanged knowledge with Western counterparts about manuscript valuations and conservation techniques. At the same time, he would recall years later, "I tried to remain as modest as I could, as I had always been in Timbuktu." He maintained the same friends in Timbuktu as he always had—boyhood playmates, associates from the world of manuscripts, along with the city's intellectuals and imams.

As Haidara's international and domestic profile rose, friends and elders pressed him to play a more active role in Timbuktu's society by running for local office, becoming a government functionary, even joining the High Council of Islam, an Islamic civil society organization that spanned ideologies from Sufism to Wahhabism and provided social services and charity across the country. But Haidara always refused. He believed that participation in public life invited trouble, and that the role would compromise his dedication to the city's libraries.

Like most of Timbuktu's population, Haidara visited the shrines to the city's Sufi saints occasionally, and he participated with enthusiasm every January in the Mawloud festival, a week-long celebration of the birthday of the Prophet that centered around the public reading of the city's most cherished manuscripts, including both Korans and secular volumes. From time to time he consulted books about Islamic jurisprudence, the *fikh*, in his own collection when confronted with thorny problems in his marriage and his work. But religion did not play a major role in his life. What drove him most was a belief in the power of the written word—the rich variety of human experience and ideas contained between the covers of a book.

Haidara was not a wealthy man, but the Ahmed Baba Institute had generously remunerated him for fifteen years—he had earned substantial bonuses during his forays through the Malian bush—and he had accumulated enough money to expand his passion for manuscript collecting far beyond the borders of Mali. On one trip to New York City, while browsing in an antiquarian bookshop in Manhattan, he came across an eighteenth-century volume of history from the Ottoman Empire, written in gilded Arabic letters and filled with maps and designs; the bookseller wanted $1,500 but Haidara, the expert negotiator, offered $800 and walked away with it for $1,000. The Ottoman history became one of the most valued volumes in his collection.

His life had changed in other ways. Haidara had a newborn son, who was born months prematurely and handicapped, unable to walk, sit up, or speak, a burden that would come to weigh heavily on Haidara's life. Following the tradition of many successful Sorhai men, Haidara around this time took a second wife—a high-ranking Malian diplomat. But Haidara's second marriage caused his first wife anguish, according to a close friend, and she berated him for his treatment of her. "The only time I ever saw him frazzled was after he married his second wife," the friend said several years later. "He came to me, crying, and he said, 'I had no idea that this would happen.'" The first wife grudgingly made her peace with the situation, tolerating his visits to Bamako to spend time with the second.

His turbulent personal life notwithstanding, Haidara had become a subject of glowing profiles in the international media. "Haidara is a man obsessed with the written word," wrote Peter Gwin in a lengthy piece, "The Telltale Scribes of Timbuktu," that appeared in *National Geographic* in early 2011. "Books, he said, are ingrained in his soul, and books, he is convinced, will save Timbuktu. Words form the sinew and muscle that hold societies upright. . . . Thousands upon thousands of words infused with the full spectrum of emotions fill in the nooks and corners of human life." Gwin visited Haidara at his home near the Sankoré Mosque and found him looking over a nineteenth-century missive from Timbuktu's elders to the sultan of Massina that supposedly showed evidence of a democratic awakening in Timbuktu. "He can spend hours sitting among the piles, dipping into one tome after another, each a miniature telescope allowing him to peer backward in time," wrote Gwin. The manuscript revival in Timbuktu, the author noted, was having a spillover effect, prompting the Aga Khan, the spiritual leader to fifteen million Shi'ite Ismaili Muslims and a multimillionaire philanthropist whose wealth—derived mostly from religious contributions—has been estimated at as high as $3 billion, to restore a medieval mosque in the city. Muammar Al Qaddafi had purchased the government-owned Sofitel resort in expectation of future academic congresses being held there.

In the *National Geographic* profile, Haidara downplayed the hostage taking, drug running, and other criminal activities being carried out by jihadis and Tuareg rebels in the desert around Timbuktu. "Criminals, or whoever else it may be, are the least of my worries. Termites are my biggest enemies," he told Gwin. "In my worst dreams," he said, "I see a rare text that I haven't read being slowly eaten."

In January 2011, the month that the *National Geographic* profiled Haidara, events were set in motion that would shatter Haidara's complacency. A popular revolt drove out Tunisia's dictator, Zine El Abidine Ben Ali, and President Hosni Mubarak in Egypt fell a month later. Protests erupted against Qaddafi in Benghazi, in eastern Libya, and security forces killed more than one hundred demonstrators. Rebellion spread across the country. By the end of a month, Qaddafi's government had lost control of much of Libya. Qaddafi claimed that Osama bin Laden had put "hallucinogenic drugs" in Libyans' Nescafé to turn them into rebels, and vowed not to step down until he had cleaned Libya house by house of the "rats" and "cockroaches." At other times he vowed to die like a "martyr." NATO forces, acting on a United Nations Security Council resolution, enforced a no-fly zone in Libyan airspace and attacked Qaddafi's army. NATO bombs pulverized barracks, TV stations, communications towers, and Qaddafi's residential compound in Tripoli.

Haidara was astonished by the reversal of Qaddafi's fortunes.

Five years earlier the Libyan leader had made a state visit to Timbuktu—a three-day affair at the height of Qaddafi's regional influence that had served as a showcase of his most erratic and megalomaniacal tendencies. In honor of the Prophet Mohammed's birthday, the "King of African Kings," as he called himself, had traveled by road the 606 miles to Timbuktu from Bamako, losing his escort, President Amadou Toumani Touré, en route, and taken up residence in a Moorish-style villa—La Maison Qaddafi—that he had built on the edge of the city. Timbuktu had been papered over with Libyan flags, banners of welcome, and life-sized posters of the Libyan leader. On his second evening he presided over a bizarre ceremony at Timbuktu's soccer stadium, flooded with so many lights that it blew out the city's electrical grid. Qaddafi called upon all nations to embrace Islam, denounced the Nobel Peace Prize–winning French aid group, Doctors Without Borders, as Western spies, declared George W. Bush and French president Jacques Chirac to be as "impure as beads of sweat," and advocated the creation of a unified Sahara "in which imperialism will perish." Then he flew back on his presidential jet to Tripoli without bidding Touré goodbye, leaving the Malian leader sitting in the airport terminal confused and humiliated, "with his head in his hands," according to the Algerian ambassador to Mali. Now Qaddafi's own regime was about to perish, and Haidara was incredulous at how fast the unraveling had happened. He didn't yet imagine that the violence in Libya could reach across the Sahara to Timbuktu.

That spring, several hundred Tuaregs in Mali answered Qaddafi's desperate plea for assistance. They departed for Libya in small convoys of SUVs, drove through the desert at night to avoid detection, gathered at mercenary camps, and joined Tuareg veterans who had left Mali for Libya years before and had served as mercenaries in Qaddafi's army. One company of young Tuaregs rushed north through the Sahara to the coastal city of Misrata, where Qaddafi's forces had surrounded the rebels and were starving them into submission. But as they approached the city, pausing for a night in a date palm plantation at the edge of the Sahara, NATO planes pounded government positions and broke the siege. "We knew that we had no chance," recalled one young mercenary from Timbuktu, who had come to Qaddafi's rescue in gratitude for his solidarity with the Tuareg separatists. "Qaddafi was going to die." At that point, he recalled, his Tuareg commander said, "It's time to go back to Mali."

Tripoli, the Libyan capital, fell in late August. Days later, looters ripped off the unguarded double gates of a compound marked "Schoolbook Printing and Storage Warehouse" on the outskirts of the city. Inside the three-building complex, a poorly disguised arsenal, they pulled out antiaircraft missiles and thousands of other pieces of military ordnance. The scene was repeated across Libya. In the beds of their pickup trucks the fleeing Tuaregs placed a stockpile of antiaircraft guns, 12.7-millimeter machine guns, rockets, mortar tubes, artillery shells, BM-21 and BTR-60 ground-to-ground and ground-to-air missile launchers, and huge amounts of ammunition. Then they headed home.

It's an age favorable to war, sang the band Terakaft, a desert-blues contemporary of Tinariwen. *The years to come will be full of fury.*

Convoys filled with Tuareg fighters and heavy weaponry traveled back to Mali through Niger. Eventually they arrived in an ancient riverbed of white sand called Zakak, tucked in the far northeast corner of Mali, near the Algerian border. By fall hundreds of fighters had gathered there, heavily armed and primed for rebellion. They called themselves the National Movement for the Liberation of Azawad, or the MNLA, the latest iteration of a dozen groups and movements that had formed over five decades to advance the pipe dream of Tuareg independence. Another four hundred men, equally well armed, camped in the desert a hundred miles away.

Al Qaeda in the Islamic Maghreb was also plundering Qaddafi's abandoned armories, Belmokhtar told a Mauritanian newspaper in November 2011. Convoys of trucks dispatched by the jihadi group had rumbled across the Libyan desert in the immediate aftermath of Qaddafi's fall, loading up with shoulder-fired surface-to-air missiles, known as MANPADS, antitank RPGs, Kalashnikovs, heavy machine guns, explosives, and ammunition. A United Nations report stated that a convoy intercepted in the Niger desert that fall carried "645 kilograms of Semtex plastic explosives and 445 detonators—meant for Al Qa'ida in the Islamic Maghreb camps in northern Mali."

In late October, desperate to prevent another Tuareg uprising, President Touré dispatched Iyad Ag Ghali to northern Mali with cash, food, and an offer to integrate the secular Tuareg rebels into the Malian army. Following Ghali's expulsion from Saudi Arabia for associating with known jihadis, and his return in disgrace to Mali, Touré had relegated him to a small office with little to do. But no other figure in the government, Touré believed, could persuade the rebels to disarm. Looking out over a sea of fighters wearing turbans neatly folded atop their heads and mismatched camouflage uniforms, Ghali, a burly, black-bearded, and still imposing figure at fifty-five, instead urged them to elect him their commander. He had crossed over to the other side once more, perhaps calculating that he had worn out his welcome with Touré's government and had more to gain by taking up the insurgents' cause.

The rebels responded with insults. Uncomfortable with Ghali's Islamic fervor, and suspicious of his links to the Malian government, they overwhelmingly rejected him. "He was a good friend of Amadou Toumani Touré," one young rebel would explain. "How could we trust him?"

By now Ghali had set himself on a course of rebellion from which there would be no turning back. Humiliated, the Tuareg leader climbed back into his vehicle, and, in a cloud of sand and dust, retreated across the desert to his stronghold, Kidal. He had money—at least 400,000 euros provided by Abou Zeid's Tarek Ibn Ziyad Brigade of AQIM—and influence as the leader of the 1990 Tuareg rebellion, and his Islamic fervor struck a chord with several hundred members of his clan. In the following weeks Ghali created a new militia, including disaffected Tuareg members of the Malian military, restless former freedom fighters who had never adjusted to peace, and unemployed young men in Kidal. This force would be marching under the black banner of jihad. Ghali named his army "Ansar Dine," or Defenders of the Faith, and he called for the implementation of Shariah law in the territory that it controlled.

In November 2011, Ghali and the two commanders of Al Qaeda in the Islamic Maghreb in Mali, Mokhtar Belmokhtar and Abdelhamid Abou Zeid, sat down to parley in the Zakak riverbed. It was familiar territory for all of them: not far away rose the Adrar des Ifoghas, the mountain redoubt where Ghali had first met them years earlier during the negotiations to free the European hostages. There, the Malian Tuareg and the Algerian Arabs officially sealed their jihadi alliance.

At nine o'clock one evening, two years later, I headed out of my Timbuktu hotel in the darkness for a clandestine meeting with a Tuareg secular rebel who had, I had been told, witnessed the jihadis' fateful meeting in the desert. I rode on the back of a Tuareg guide's motorcycle, bouncing over sandy alleys in the darkness. A bright yellow moon cast a weirdly elongated shadow of the motorbike on the rippled sand, and smudges of light here and there illuminated the doorways of groceries, cafés, hair salons, and other shops still open at this late hour. We passed the mud-brick ramparts of the Sidi Yahya Mosque, and the festering heaps of garbage at the edge of the city's main bazaar, and then the alleys widened into broad, sandy tracks, marking the start of Abaradjou, a newer neighborhood of villas and half-built houses hidden behind high walls, where many of the city's Tuaregs lived.

We found Yusuf—a tall twenty-six-year-old with an aquiline nose, his head wrapped in a pale blue turban—sitting on a bed in a spartan back room at his mother's house. He had been living in a refugee camp in Mauritania, and had snuck back into Timbuktu for a few days to visit relatives in secret; animosity toward the Tuareg insurgents remained high in Timbuktu two years after the uprising, and he was terrified that his presence here would be discovered by some of his neighbors. Hence, he had insisted on a late night rendezvous, when the streets were empty and people were hunkered down inside their homes. Speaking quietly, clearly nervous, he told me that Ghali and the Al Qaeda jihadis "talked for hours" on a carpet laid out in the sand, not far from where he and his secular Tuaregs were encamped. "It happened at night, under the light of the moon," Yusuf recalled.

After securing an alliance with his fellow jihadis, Ghali proposed to the Al Qaeda commanders that the Islamists join forces with the secular Tuareg rebels. The two groups had little in common: the Tuaregs wanted to create a secular independent state called Azawad that they had been fighting for for half a century. The jihadis sought to create a caliphate in northern Mali in which they would impose Shariah law, train terrorists, and steadily expand their Islamist state across northern Africa. The group had already made an alliance with Boko Haram, in northern Nigeria, the brutal Islamist terrorist group that has murdered as many as ten thousand Nigerians since its founding in the northern town of Maiduguri in 2002. The deal between the Tuareg rebels and Al Qaeda would be a marriage of convenience that would allow them to pool their fighters and the heavy weapons they had stolen out of Qaddafi's armories, overwhelm the weak Malian army, and carve an independent state out of a region as large as France. As American intelligence officials and diplomats had feared, Iyad Ag Ghali was now serving as the midwife to a pact between Malian Tuareg independence fighters and Algerian Arab Islamists—the two prime destabilizing forces in the Malian Sahara.

The secular Tuaregs were divided. Many considered the "The Bearded Ones" dangerous people and feared being associated with them.

"I knew Al Qaeda. I knew their reputation, their criminality," said Yusuf, brewing me a cup of tea. He had always considered himself to be "relaxed" about religion, he insisted. "These were people who were being hunted by the international community. How could we be joining forces with them?"

The majority, however, believed that they had no choice. The route to independence, they said, required making unsavory compromises. Alone the Tuaregs would certainly fail. An alliance with Al Qaeda in the Islamic Maghreb would guarantee their victory.

10

At one o'clock in the afternoon on Friday, November 25, 2011, a beige pickup truck carrying four armed men approached the walled compound of a backpacker's guesthouse on the northern edge of Timbuktu. Most of the city's population was in mosque for Friday afternoon prayers, and the streets were nearly deserted. "The vehicle made a single tour around the block, to see if there were people in the streets," a young eyewitness told me a year later, as we drank black tea with milk at dusk in his auto repair stall across the alley from the hotel. "They looked this way and that way, up and down the street. Two sat in the cabin, and two in the back. All of them wore turbans, and robes. Then they stopped in front of the gate."

Inside the stone-walled compound, three travelers—a Dutchman, a Swede, and a Briton—were eating lunch on an outdoor terrace beneath a cloudless blue sky, while the Dutchman's wife dozed in a tent pitched on the roof of their Land Cruiser. "I heard the dog barking, and I came outside. There was somebody in the courtyard, with an AK-47, and he said, 'Go back inside,'" said the reception-ist, as we stood on the rooftop of the hotel in faint pink light, a full moon hanging low over a landscape of mud-walled huts, and the dunes of the Sahara beyond. "He shouted at the tourists, *'Allez, allez, allez,'* and that's all I heard." The gunmen prodded the three Europeans into the street—taking no notice of the Dutch woman who lay, frozen in fear, inside the tent—and pushed them into the bed of the vehicle.

At that moment, an unlucky German tourist returning to the hotel from an errand walked into the kidnapping. Resisting an order to get into the vehicle, he was shot in the head at point-blank range and killed instantly. The two gunmen climbed into the rear of the vehicle with their hostages, fired three times in the air, and drove "at a leisurely pace," the young eyewitness said, past the crumbling and ne-glected Monument of Peace, past a handful of Tuareg tents, and into the desert. They left the German's corpse lying facedown in the street, the blood from his head wound trickling into the sand. It was the first time that Al Qaeda in the Islamic Maghreb had succeeded in carry-ing out an attack inside Timbuktu. The abduction came just thirty-six hours after seven AQIM gunmen entered a small hilltop hotel in the town of Hombori, one hundred miles south of Timbuktu, roused two French geologists from their sleep, dragged the dazed, terrified men into a vehicle, and disappeared with them into the desert.

The murdered German whose body had been left lying in the road had been part of a tour group that had arrived in Timbuktu the day before on a boat cruise downriver from Mopti, organized by Sleeping Camel Safaris in Bamako. The young Australian owner had assumed that Timbuktu was well protected by the Malian army and had not hesitated to send his clients there. The three kidnapped Europeans had been traveling on their own, by motorbike and four-wheel-drive, across West Africa, and had also discounted reports about instability around Timbuktu. That afternoon, the Malian army moved eighty frightened Westerners into the Hotel Bouctou, placed them under heavy guard, and evacuated them on the presidential jet the following morning.

In Bamako, the Tuareg music impresario Manny Ansar was organizing the thirteenth edition of the Festival in the Desert, the three-day concert featuring indigenous and foreign bands. After being inspired to cocreate the event by Iyad Ag Ghali, Ansar had introduced the festival to Essakane, a traditional Tuareg meeting place of rippled white sand dunes forty miles west of Timbuktu, in January 2003. It had become a global phenomenon and, for a while anyway, a symbol of hope in Africa. Robert Plant, the cofounder of Led Zeppelin, had played on the stage in 2003 with Tinariwen and in a "campfire jam session" with Ali Farka Touré, generating a flurry of attention in the Western press. "It was a journey of revelation—one of the most illuminating and humbling experiences of my life," Plant would tell *Rolling Stone.*

The French Basque guitarist-vocalist Manu Chao, and Damon Albarn, the front man of the British pop group Blur, had performed there in the following years, and prominent guests had included the Ethiopian model Liya Kebede, on a fashion shoot for *Vogue,* and Princess Caroline of Monaco, who had handed out prizes at the camel races in 2006. "Swords turn to guitars, democracy blooms, and music helps bring a sense of national unity," wrote Tom Freston, the founder of MTV, in *Vanity Fair,* of his 2007 trip to Essakane with Jimmy Buffett and Island Records founder Chris Blackwell. "The festival has been vital in bringing foreigners [to northern Mali], with its irresistible invitation to three days of Saharan magic, world music, and cross-cultural community—the only place in the world where Robert Plant can share a bill with West African griots [traveling poets, singers, and storytellers] and Tuareg bluesmen," noted James Truman in a lengthy piece on Malian music in *Condé Nast Traveler* in 2008.

Yet both *Condé Nast* writers were so swept up in the romance of this "African Woodstock" that they had missed signs of growing danger. Tuareg clan intermediaries had warned Ansar that Al Qaeda in the Islamic Maghreb militants regarded the festival as an abomination, a "Sodom and Gomorrah" that would have to be expunged. "You invite nonbelievers to your festival, who drink alcohol and commit sins in our dunes," they told him through clan elders, forcing Ansar to increase security at the event and watch his own back. Freston's piece in *Vanity Fair* contained just one cautionary note, which barely registered at the time. "Manny [Ansar] congratulates us on our bravery for defying the recent U.S. State Department travel advisory warning U.S. citizens to stay away from the festival," he wrote. "Needless to say, we know nothing about this." Freston made light of reports of "banditry, factional rivalry, and carjackings" in this "lawless area." It sounded, he joked, exactly like Los Angeles.

In 2010, the wave of kidnappings carried out in the Sahara by AQIM had obliged Ansar to relocate the Festival in the Desert to Timbuktu, where, he believed, Malian security forces could better protect it. The kidnappings-murder of the four Westerners inside Timbuktu now exposed the total inadequacy of their measures. Nevertheless, the musical stars were lining up again. For the sixth time in a decade, the featured performers would be Tinariwen, the Tuareg practitioners of the desert blues, who had gained an impassioned following around the world and the imprimatur of some of the West's most influential music critics. Other stars who had committed were Vieux Farka Touré, the thirty-one-year-old son of the late Ali Farka Touré, who had died of cancer in 2006; and Oumou Sangaré, described by Freston in *Vanity Fair* as "Mali's most popular female singer and its greatest advocate for women's rights—a true diva." And Ansar was holding discussions with one of the world's most recognizable musicians and celebrities: Bono. The lead singer of U2 and peripatetic human rights activist was considering making a twenty-four-hour visit to the festival after inspecting a Millennium Village antipoverty project near the river town of Ségou with Columbia University professor Jeffrey Sachs. Bono was the latest in a long line of Western rock stars who had become entranced by the music of Mali, in particular the desert blues of Tinariwen.

Still clinging to the hope that he could reverse Mali's sagging fortunes as a tourist destination, President Touré promised Ansar that he would send in tanks and hundreds of troops, including members of his Presidential Guard, to secure the festival. "The entire *état-major* of the Malian military will be in Timbuktu, the minister of defense, all the top military chiefs," he assured the promoter. He begged Ansar not to cancel. "There will be more security in Timbuktu than in Bamako."

On Thursday, January 12, 2012, Al Qaeda in the Islamic Maghreb threatened via the Internet to kill the two French geologists it had seized in Hombori in November, and the three European tourists it had grabbed in Timbuktu the next day. The group announced that it was preparing for "military operations" against the Malian state and warned the hostages' home countries—France, the United Kingdom, the Netherlands, and Sweden—not to intervene or else invite the deaths of its captured citizens. Bono's private jet landed at Timbuktu airport at eight o'clock Friday evening. Ansar, both dreading and thrilled by Bono's visit, found the musician relaxing on a sofa in an onboard salon with his wife and friends, including Renzo Rosso, the founder and owner of Diesel, the designer jeans line. A music video was playing, and the group was in a convivial mood. Dressed in black, eyes shielded behind his blue-tinted glasses, Bono asked Ansar whether he thought that Timbuktu was safe. Ansar, disconcerted by the contrast between the dust, poverty, and violence of Timbuktu and the cocoon of privilege, wealth, and celebrity that he had just entered, stammered that he believed it was.

President Touré deployed armored vehicles and troops on the

perimeter of the concert. Three thousand people, including two hundred foreigners, and Malians from across the country—men, women, and children, Tuaregs in traditional dress, Bamako and Mopti professionals in Western clothing—gathered in fifty-degree Fahrenheit temperatures, bundled in jackets and vests. Bono was escorted to a VIP box for the evening's concert. The star and his entourage, guarded by a dozen troops, spent the night at the Hôtel La Maison, a French-owned villa in Timbuktu's Sankoré quarter. The next day he took a hike alone past the military perimeter and into the dunes, while Ansar—his escort for the twenty-four-hour visit—waited in high anxiety.

On the festival's last evening, Saturday, January 14, Bono climbed onto the stage to perform with Tinariwen. "The concert had been going on for an hour when projectors lit up the crowd and a clamor erupted. Bono, the leader of U2 and guest star, had arrived," reported an article in *Jeune Afrique*. "Dressed in black, jerking to his left, then to his right, the Irishman raised his hand and shouted, 'We are all brothers here!' This unleashed a wave of hysteria from young girls who tried to climb onto the stage, without success. His four body-guards watched over him, as did military security."

Bono improvised with the Tuareg band, trying out a few French phrases, dancing with the Tinariwen singers and guitarists. "Music is stronger than war," he declared, before boarding his jet and flying back to Bamako.

Four days later, Iyad Ag Ghali led a coalition of heavily armed fighters on a bloody sweep across the north. At dawn on January 18, they attacked a remote army camp at Aguelhok and besieged the troops until the government forces ran out of ammunition. Ghali and his men overran the compound, took ninety soldiers prisoner, manacled them, lined them up in two rows, and executed them by cutting their throats or shooting a single bullet into each man's head at point-blank range. "It was us or them," he told a Bamako journalist in a satellite phone conversation from an undisclosed location in the desert. The French accused Ghali's men of committing an "Al Qaeda–style" atrocity. Days later they encircled an American-built military base called Tessalit, a few dozen miles south, and prevented convoys from reaching those inside. Food and water ran short. At the Malian government's request, U.S. planes dropped emergency rations to the beleaguered Malian troops and their families, but the camp fell in the middle of March after a six-week siege. Witnesses described a panicked flight, and the abandoning of mortars, rocket launchers, and tanks.

Enraged by the massacre at Aguelhok and the humiliating retreat from the base at Tessalit, soldiers rioted on March 21, 2012, at an old military compound outside Bamako. They stole weapons from the armory and marched toward the hilltop presidential palace, which was lightly protected at the time, because most of the elite presidential guard had been dispatched to the north to fight the rebel army. Amadou Toumani Touré and his wife slipped out of the marble-walled villa in the darkness, walked down a steep trail through the brush to a waiting vehicle, and disappeared into the night. Mutinous soldiers rampaged through the palace, stealing TVs, bed linens, wall hangings, and electrical fixtures, then looted shops in Bamako. The new ruling military council was led by a U.S.-trained captain, Amadou Sanagou, remembered by former U.S. Defense Attaché Marshall Mantiply as an unprepossessing figure who had often joined fellow officers at Mantiply's home in Bamako on weekends, watching soccer matches on his television. The military body dissolved Mali's constitution and democratic institutions, imposed a curfew, and closed the borders. The army was "putting an end to the incompetent regime of Amadou Toumani Touré," a spokesman declared. Touré took refuge at the embassy of Senegal, and flew to asylum in Dakar.

To some extent the collapse had been beyond Touré's control:

he could not have foreseen the Arab Spring and the NATO bombing that led to the toppling of Qaddafi, nor the looting of Libya's arms depots that would give the Tuareg rebels and their radical Islamist allies the wherewithal to defeat the Malian army. But he had ignored pleadings by Western ambassadors and his own generals to supply and strengthen his army and move decisively against the jihadis, and he had scurried away like a hunted animal into the night.

The jihadis, meanwhile, seemed unstoppable. Eight months earlier Al Qaeda in the Arabian Peninsula, which answered, like its counterpart in the Maghreb, to Osama bin Laden and Ayman Al Zawahiri, had captured Zinjibar, the capital of Yemen's Abyan Province, and declared it the twenty-first century's first caliphate. It was the initial step in Al Qaeda's goal of sweeping away Muslim and Arab secular regimes and replacing them with a pan-Islamic fundamentalist state. Further emboldened by their victories in Mali, the radicals would pursue this goal with increasing aggressiveness. The triumph in Mali would inspire, at least in part, the seizure of much of Syria and Iraq by the Islamic State between 2013 and 2015.

The endgame in Mali had begun. Demoralized troops abandoned their bases. Iyad Ag Ghali and his jihadis captured Kidal on March 26. They overran Gao, the north's largest city and onetime capital of the medieval Songhai Empire, two hundred miles downriver from Timbuktu, on March 30. At the same time that the jihadis were marching on Gao, secular Tuareg fighters advanced through the desert, and made camp forty-two miles north of Timbuktu. The director of Timbuktu's most popular radio station, Radio Communal Bouctou, a sixty-seven-year-old elder who was a respected member of Timbuktu's majority Sorhai tribe, took the initiative to form a committee comprised of spokespeople for the city's main ethnic groups. They charged themselves with making face-to-face contact with these Tuareg rebels to plead with them not to take the city by force.

The Sorhai elder, joined by a representative of the Bellas—lower-caste black speakers of Tamasheq who had served as slaves to the higher Tuareg castes during precolonial times—and a spokesperson for the Peuls, traditionally pastoralists along the Niger River, left the city at sunset on Friday, March 30. Darkness fell quickly, and soon they were enveloped by the black desert night broken only by the phosphorescent glare of their headlights. They drove for an hour, making nervous conversation. Three miles from the rebel position, they called their contact on his satellite phone. "Turn off your headlights," he ordered. The delegation groped their way forward on a track illuminated only by the stars, and found a gathering of rebels and four SUVs parked around a wool blanket in the sand.

The three spokesmen shook hands with the rebel group, and at the commander's grunted invitation sat down on the tattered blanket. The night was so dark that the Timbuktu representatives could not see "five feet" beyond this intimate gathering, the radio director recalled; there might have been an entire army lurking behind them. The rebels' cigarettes formed tiny pinpricks of orange light, and cast a glow upon the men's features—haggard after months of camping in the desert. They stared at one another in silence. The station director asked the commander to spare Timbuktu.

"I cannot," he answered. "We are ready to take Timbuktu tonight."

"Just give us the time to prepare the population for your arrival."

"How much time do you want?" he asked.

"Two weeks."

"We will give you until Thursday."

The committee members shook hands with the commander and his men, climbed into their vehicle, and drove back through the night. The next morning, the radio man announced on air that Timbuktu's residents had been given another six days. But the rebels were already on the move.

11

Abdel Kader Haidara had watched the advance of the Tuareg secular rebels and their jihadi partners with relative calm. He believed that the latest uprising would be concentrated in the northeast of Mali, several hundred miles from Timbuktu, like the other full-scale rebellions and minor insurrections he had lived through in the previous twenty years. He wasn't especially worried, and he barely discussed with friends and colleagues the attacks on government army bases that were taking place in remote corners of the desert; the rebellion seemed far away. In March 2012, he traveled with a small group of fellow librarians and conservationists to a provincial town in neighboring Burkina Faso to assist a government library with a manuscript digitization project. On the drive home, they learned that Mali's military had declared a coup d'état and sealed the country's borders. Haidara and his team spent another week stuck in Burkina Faso. At last, during the last week in March, the frontier opened, and they drove to Bamako.

Arriving in the capital, Haidara grasped for the first time the gravity of what was happening—the collapse of the government army, the speed of the rebel advance. He spent one night in Bamako, and then decided that he had to go home. "Abdel Kader, you mustn't go now. It's dangerous," friends and colleagues advised him. Haidara shrugged off the warnings. Heading north with a driver in his SUV, he spent the first night out of Bamako with friends in Sévaré, a town on the Niger River, halfway between Bamako and Timbuktu, and the site of the region's only airport.

"Don't go to Timbuktu," his hosts begged him.

"I've got to go," he said. "I have things to do there, and if I'm not there, I won't be at ease. Even if there's a war going on, I need to be there with my family."

Haidara departed at dawn with his driver. Four hours into the trip, they encountered heavy traffic coming from the north. People were on the run. A long caravan of vans, trucks, small cars, all-terrain vehicles, minibuses, coaches, motorcycles, and jeeps snaked along the rutted highway, with many people traveling on foot, all enveloped in a cacophony of honking horns, revving engines, and screeching brakes. Soldiers, teachers, clerks, librarians, traders, housewives, market women, children, most of the population of Timbuktu, it seemed, hung from the windows of overheated cars and buses, clung to the backs of motorcycles, balanced on the bus roofs with bundles of clothing, bulging suitcases, mattresses, duffel bags, footlockers, cardboard boxes. It was a seemingly endless flight of humanity enveloped in a cloud of dust, diesel exhaust, and desperation, all anxious to escape the rebel takeover.

For the first time, the horror of what was happening in his hometown struck Haidara. Yet he had already come this far, and it felt too late to turn back. As he continued traveling north, the flow of panicked people continued. Refugees on the roadside advised him to turn around. The paved road soon surrendered to a red-earth track that wound past geological oddities—saw-toothed mesas, fingerlike pillars of red sandstone rising sharply between sloping buttes. Then the track disintegrated further into two shallow grooves through the sand. Haidara rode on for a hundred miles past a sea of thorn trees, shallow depressions, and dried riverbeds, until he crossed a wide, barren slope and arrived at last at the Niger River.

Tuareg secular rebels had taken Timbuktu that morning, driving into town in eighty vehicles flying the separatist tricolor—green, red, and black, with a yellow triangle at the hoist—and the ferries had stopped running. Haidara searched the barren mud bank until he found a pirogue for hire to cross the wide waterway, and said farewell to his driver. They motored at a steady pace for about twenty minutes on a wide diagonal course across the Niger. The yellow-sand north bank, with its rolling dunes and clumps of low bushes, grew ever closer, until clusters of mud huts and palm trees appeared, and they moored the boat in the small port of Korioumé, eleven miles southwest of Timbuktu. A friend picked him up in a battered Mercedes. On the stretch of highway to Timbuktu, which ran past rice fields irrigated by the Niger, Tuaregs in fatigues, armed with Kalashnikovs, seemed to be waiting behind every tree. The insurgents searched the car, ripped open bags, and interrogated them a dozen times.

"Where are you coming from?"

"Bamako."

"Where is your own vehicle?"

"I left it on the other side."

A hot gust of wind blew sand across the asphalt road as Haidara and his companion passed through the southern entrance gate to Timbuktu—two eight-foot-high square pillars constructed of small blocks of limestone. Gunfire rang out, some of it unnervingly close. They advanced cautiously into town. The flag of Azawad, the independent homeland that the Tuaregs had dreamed of, now hung from the City Hall, the governor's headquarters, and the district courthouse. In the vacuum left behind by the fleeing police and army, looters, including some Tuareg rebels, were rampaging across the city, breaking into houses, shops, and government offices, and grabbing everything they could. Haidara was stopped and frisked, and the car was searched at more Tuareg rebel checkpoints. Haidara's friend dropped him off at his home in the Bella Farandja neighborhood, on the eastern edge of the city, bordered by the desert. They wished each other good luck.

Behind the twelve-foot-high walls of his compound, in the stone courtyard, he was reunited with his wife and their five children. Several nieces and nephews and three household employees were also lodging at the Haidara home. The shooting continued through the night and into the next day, making it all but impossible to sleep. At last the gunfire died down, and he ventured into the main marketplace and Timbuktu's government district. He walked past looted shops, the gutted City Hall, and other administration buildings that had been trashed—their doors removed, documents scattered, windows smashed in.

One thought ran through Haidara's mind.

They're going to break into our libraries, and steal everything inside, and destroy the manuscripts. What do we have to do to save them?

While Haidara took refuge inside his family compound on the chaotic afternoon that he first came back to town, the "Bearded Ones" also arrived in the city. The radical triumvirate, one Malian Tuareg and two Algerian Arabs—Iyad Ag Ghali, Mokhtar

Belmokhtar, and Abdelhamid Abou Zeid—sitting side by side in a Toyota Land Cruiser, led a convoy of one hundred vehicles flying black jihadi flags. They took up positions across Timbuktu, put a stop to the looting, hoisted black banners in place of the Tuareg tricolors, and demanded that their secular Tuareg allies withdraw outside Timbuktu's municipal boundaries. Outgunned and intimidated by their supposed partners, the secular Tuaregs grudgingly pulled out of Timbuktu, establishing bases at the port of Kabara five miles south of Timbuktu, and at the airport three miles outside town. Then, having quickly gained the upper hand, the jihadis announced themselves to Timbuktu's apprehensive civilians.

On the morning after the jihadis rolled into Timbuktu, a clerk at the Hotel Bouctou, a two-story establishment of limestone blocks with a wide rear terrace that faced the Sahara, urgently summoned the owner, Boubacar Touré, from his home. Once the Hotel Bouctou had been Timbuktu's most popular drinking spot—a magnet for Western tourists, local guides, and trainers from the U.S. Special Forces. It was here, during a two-hour stopover in Timbuktu as a *Newsweek* correspondent in 1995, that I had first encountered Boubacar Touré, and here, eleven years later, that I had listened to the recorded music of Ali Farka Touré while noting the four U.S. Special Forces trainers discreetly drinking beer on the terrace. But by the spring of 2012, the hotel, like every other enterprise connected with Timbuktu tourism, had fallen on difficult times.

Boubacar Touré, a gregarious man in his fifties, rushed over to the hotel, a five-minute drive from his home, and observed three Toyota Land Cruisers, black flags fluttering from their radio antennas, parked before the entrance. "Twelve bearded terrorists from all over the world—Pakistan, Somalia, Saudi Arabia—stood beside them," Touré recalled a year later as we sat in plastic chairs in a sand plaza in front of the hotel, beside a thick grove of acacia trees, joined by members of his staff and friends. Behind the establishment, sand blew across a stark landscape of dunes, scrawny acacia trees, hobbled camels and domed cardboard-and-plastic tents, inhabited by resettled Tuareg nomads who were too poor to rent housing in the town.

As Boubacar Touré stepped out of his vehicle on that first day of the occupation, he noticed a hunched figure carrying a black-and-gray Kalashnikov and protected by the scrum of bodyguards. The jihadi was under five feet tall, with a hawklike face and a black turban whose loose ends framed an unkempt graying beard. The weapon in his hands seemed comically large for a man of his childlike stature. In a voice barely louder than a whisper, he introduced himself as Abdelhamid Abou Zeid, the emir of Timbuktu. He was looking, he said, for a place to stay for him and his men.

"Who are your clients?" Abou Zeid asked, cocking his head in a peculiar way.

"We've worked with tourists, businessmen, government officials, whoever can pay," Touré replied.

"You mean you work with the whites?" Abou Zeid asked. "You work with the infidels?"

Touré struggled to contain his resentment. Touré's business had been near collapse for several years because of the drug running and kidnappings carried out by Al Qaeda in the Islamic Maghreb. And since Al Qaeda militants had shot dead the German tourist in November 2011, and abducted three other Europeans, the hotel hadn't had a single guest. "Mr. Abou Zeid, tourism has been ruined," he said. "My employees and their families are hurting. You are kidnapping tourists, and you are killing them. What are you going to do about it?"

"We're going to see," Abou Zeid muttered.

Boubacar Touré knew that he should probably be more cautious. Abou Zeid was a murderer who had not only executed two Western hostages, but probably also killed many Muslim civilians in his native Algeria. But Touré refused to be intimidated by the terrorist leader and his gang of thuggish bodyguards. He had always been one to speak his mind, and he made the calculation that the Al Qaeda emir had no desire to alienate his new subjects immediately by murdering them. He also saw this face-to-face encounter as perhaps his only opportunity to extract what he could for years of hardship.

"No, no, that's not acceptable," he told Abou Zeid, surprising himself with his temerity as he pressed the terrorist chief. He felt almost as if he were speeding down a road and couldn't get off, gaining speed, exhilarated and heedless of the consequences. "Either you give me money to help the families of the people working here," he said, voice rising, "or you find another solution."

Abou Zeid "stared and stared," Touré recalled. Then, abruptly, he turned around, stepped back into the Land Cruiser, and stormed off with his entourage.

The self-appointed emir of Timbuktu returned to the hotel the following day. On this visit he brought his partner, Iyad Ag Ghali, with him. They made a curious pair, Touré thought—the hunched and crippled Arab and the robust Tuareg, who towered over his Algerian counterpart. The new rulers surveyed the grounds, toured the corridors, and strolled through the restaurant, staring at its bottles of gin, vodka, and whiskey prominently displayed on shelves behind the bar. They had decided to make the Hotel Bouctou their headquarters, they announced. But first, some changes would be made.

"You take out all the bottles of beer and other alcohol, all the photos, from both of your buildings and then we will see if we can work here," Ghali told him. Touré smiled ruefully. He had won Al Qaeda in the Islamic Maghreb's business, he realized, but it would end up costing him dearly. He called together his staff.

"Get rid of everything, every bottle we have, and every photo we have," he said.

The Hotel Bouctou staff dutifully took down images of traditional Timbuktu life—camel herders, Niger River fishermen, weavers, and musicians—from the halls and public areas, and stripped the guest rooms as well. Then they dug a trench behind the hotel and dumped in hundreds of bottles of beer, wine, and hard liquor. They smashed the bottles with hammers. Great foaming puddles of beer mixed with amber rivulets of scotch and bourbon, blood-red pools of burgundies, and clear streams of vodka, sinking into the sand amid explosions and cascades of shattering glass. Touré forlornly watched thousands of dollars' worth of liquor dribble away, as Ghali and Abou Zeid looked on approvingly.

Abou Zeid and Ghali held their first meeting with city elders in the Hotel Bouctou dining room the following afternoon. Abdel Kader Haidara remained at home, intent on avoiding drawing attention to himself. Fifty people, including the mayor of Timbuktu, sat in hard-backed white chairs around two white rectangular tables in a shabby space dominated by the now empty blue-painted bar. Sunlight filtered through windows covered with pink blinds. Dozens of armed Islamist militants, and three or four secular Tuareg commanders, sat on benches on the room's perimeter. Iyad Ag Ghali addressed the crowd in French.

"Peuple de Tombouctou, nous sommes vos nouveaus maîtres," he began. People of Timbuktu, we are your new masters. "From this moment on, we plan to develop Islam in the city of Timbuktu."

The imam of Sidi Yahya Mosque, one of Timbuktu's oldest and most venerated houses of worship—finished in 1440 after forty years under construction, famed for a pair of Moroccan-style wooden doors that, according to a local legend, were meant to remain closed until the End of Days—interrupted him. "We don't want to listen to this," he shouted. "Get out of our city. Give us back our peace. We don't want your kind of Islam here."

Elders reacted in alarm. "Don't talk like that. These people are barbarians," one whispered. "They will kill you."

The imam waved him off. "How dare you say you're going to 'teach us Islam'? We were born with Islam. We have had Islam in this city for one thousand years."

Ghali turned to Abou Zeid.

"We're going to have to replace the imams in this town," he said.

The meeting dissolved in acrimony.

A week later, Iyad Ag Ghali and his men took over Radio Communal Bouctou, the only one of the city's seven radio stations that had stayed on the air after the occupation. The station's eclectic programming had reflected the city's mix of ethnic groups and cultures: news in Arabic, Songhoy, Tamasheq, and Hausa; call-in talk shows in which residents in this city of about 54,000 discussed their problems, marital or political; news broadcasts from Radio France International; and many genres of music. The jihadis presented the program director with a USB stick, containing the Koran in MP3 format, and ordered him to play verses in sequence throughout the day and night.

Fiery sermons delivered live by Ghali, threatening whippings and amputations, marked the only deviations from the program. "We used to go into forty-seven villages around the Niger River and record their traditional music," the station's director, a grizzled sixty-seven-year-old with sunken cheeks, told me as we sat on the porch outside the studio at City Hall many months later. "But when the jihadis took over, there was nothing but the Koran." The Islamist militant who had been placed in charge of the station seized twenty years' worth of cassettes—folkloric music, interviews, benedictions—stuffed the confiscated tapes into four rice bags and carted them off to be burned.

As Ghali ranted on the airwaves about Shariah law, the jihadi leaders made a few tenuous attempts to ingratiate themselves with Timbuktu's populace. They coordinated shipments of food aid with the Red Crescent Society, expropriated looted ambulances from the unruly Tuareg rebels and returned them to the city's hospital, and agreed to meet twice a week with a committee established by the city's religious figures, doctors, teachers, and neighborhood representatives. Though asked to participate in the committee, Abdel Kader Haidara kept his distance. He had other work to do.

At the end of April, Abou Zeid, Ghali, and their secular Tuareg counterparts even invited this group of Timbuktu notables, who called themselves the "Crisis Committee," to celebrate the declaration of Azawad's independence. Ibrahim Khalil Touré, a sixty-seven-year-old book collector, private museum owner, and leader of the Djingareyber quarter, reluctantly accepted the jihadis' invitation, and persuaded many of his colleagues on the committee to join him. "I went to this celebration—and they told us 'we have occupied Azawad, and we have an obligation to find a way to live together,'" said Touré, a leonine figure whose copper skin contrasted sharply with his lily-white turban and emerald boubou. We were sitting on carpets in a second-floor receiving room in Touré's home on an alley in Djingareyber, a medieval quarter dominated by the fourteenth-century mosque of the same name. The salon was decorated with Tuareg swords and dusty family photographs, and a gas-operated "cooling machine" stirred up the stultifying air, rattling as we talked.

Abou Zeid and Ghali, joined by Mokhtar Belmokhtar, now the commander of Gao, had been convivial hosts, Touré said, welcoming the elders to a villa near the port, and leading them to a banquet table covered with bottles of Fanta, Sprite, and Coke. Jihadi butchers slaughtered a sheep and roasted it on a spit on their behalf. The jihadi commanders struck a reasonable tone. "Shariah is going to come little by little, and if you want it faster, we'll bring it faster,"

Abou Zeid assured the committee members, while Ghali grunted and said nothing.

"Abou Zeid had a preternatural calm about him," Touré recalled many months later. "Perhaps he had a rock-hard heart beneath, but he smiled, he seemed calm, and he was in total control. He never shouted, never raised his voice. And when you were listening to his soothing voice, you were obliged to become calm yourself." For five hours the delegates and the jihadis prayed, feasted, and talked. They exchanged mobile phone numbers, shook hands, and said goodbye. "We will work together, there won't be any problems," the jihadi leaders assured them.

The era of good feelings did not last. Black flags soon covered every municipal building in Timbuktu. Billboards for Orange cell phones, Air Mali, Coca-Cola, and other products were ripped down, and armed fighters from Al Qaeda in the Islamic Maghreb and their Ansar Dine partners swaggered through the streets, intimidating anyone who crossed their path. Estimates on their numbers varied, but most citizens put the figure at between five hundred and one thousand militants in Timbuktu, making them all but unavoidable in every neighborhood of the city. Almost immediately after declaring Azawad's independence, in late April, the jihadi commanders deployed squads of enforcers, bearded men wearing black turbans and blue vests with the words "Islamic Police" written in French and Arabic—as well as a handful of teenagers who were still too young to grow beards—who fanned out across Timbuktu in pickup trucks flying black jihadi flags. "Everything happened little by little," Ibrahim Khalil Touré recalled. "They destroyed the beverage warehouses and the bars. They appointed a judge who was responsible for morals, and he enjoyed his work. He began personally arresting women and menacing them because they weren't properly dressed—with veils that covered the whole face, robes that covered everything but the hands."

The Islamic Police screeched around corners and swooped down on unsuspecting people in a cloud of dust, snatching cigarettes out of the mouths of pedestrians and arresting women and girls who went about unveiled, or who wore perfume, bracelets, or rings. They brought many of these women at gunpoint to the Commercial Bank of Mali, a three-story, sand-colored building that had been looted immediately after the occupation. Its warrens of offices had been converted into cells and interrogation centers, and an ATM booth in front—a sweltering cubicle sealed by an iron gate—became a punishment chamber where the offending girls and women were forced to stand for hours, deprived of food and water. The black-turbaned, AK-47-toting enforcers stormed through Timbuktu's market, flogging women for failing to cover themselves. "I saw three members of the Islamic police beat a fish seller because she wasn't properly covered," one trader recounted to Human Rights Watch. "They told a middle-aged woman selling mangos to cover up but she refused. They started hitting her; she tried to protect her face, all the while saying defiantly, 'No, forget it. You people took the village and drove away all our business, it's you who must submit to Shariah.' They beat her five, ten, twenty times but still she refused."

Islamist authorities banned musical cell phone ringers, insisting that only Koranic verses were acceptable. When one boy's ringer played a tune as he walked past Islamic Police headquarters, "he frantically tried to hit the answer button in his pocket," a witness recalled. "They told him to come but the youth talked back; two Islamists whipped him with a switch until he bled, saying, 'If we were the Malian army you wouldn't be speaking to us like that!'" The jihadis forbade baptisms, marriages, and circumcisions, the joyful rituals of Timbuktu life. Wedding processions, noisy festivals of ululating women and banging tindé drums, vanished. Shops closed early and people stayed off the streets, fearful of running into

Islamic Police patrols. One former tour operator was sitting with friends at a sidewalk café, drinking tea and listening to music from the Côte d'Ivoire on his boom box, when a pickup filled with police pulled up in front of them; the jihadis told the gathering that the music is "condemned by God," and threatened them with pistols. "They removed the memory card from the boom box and three days later they returned it," the tour operator said. "They'd erased the music and put on Koranic verses."

The police broke up a gathering of boys and men watching the European Association's Champions League soccer match on TV, telling them that it was forbidden to watch television in public. A café owner was ordered to carry two foosball tables from outside into his establishment because "they are a bad influence for children. The boys should be praying, not playing in the street." Four Islamist gunmen randomly stopped a twenty-nine-year-old woman in the street, searched her, and discovered pictures of Western pop stars, including Celine Dion, on her mobile phone. They lashed her on the spot with a camel-skin whip. "I did not count how many times they hit me," she said. Islamist officers beat a group of boys and girls for swimming together in the river.

A seamstress who fled the north told Human Rights Watch, "The north feels dead. As a woman I can't dress up, wear perfume, go for a stroll with my friends. . . . They've even outlawed chatting in groups. They say instead of talking we should go home and read the Koran." By May perhaps one third of the population of fifty-four thousand had fled Timbuktu for Bamako or refugee camps in Mauritania and Burkina Faso, and the city fell into silence and stagnation. One Timbuktu resident lamented, "They've taken all the joie de vivre from our lives."

The Al Qaeda imams issued fatwas, which they announced on their radio station, decreeing prison terms or public whippings for unmarried couples, consumers of alcohol, people discovered listening to music, smokers, and men without beards or with trousers that extended to their ankles—all considered haram, or forbidden, according to certain Hadith cited by the extremists.

"The Prophet (peace and blessings of Allah be upon him) said: *Isbaal* (wearing one's garment below the ankles), may apply to the *izaar* (lower garment), the shirt or the turban. Whoever allows any part of these to trail on the ground out of arrogance, Allah will not look at him on the Day of Judgment," a Hadith declared.

"We were ordered to wear our beards like the Prophet," Ibrahim Khalil Touré remembered. "They would stop you on the street and hold your face and check. You could shave your head, your mustache, but you could not touch the beard."

In May, the Hôtel La Maison, a century-old limestone villa built around a tiled courtyard, where Bono and his entourage had spent a night in January 2012, was declared the city's Shariah Court. Overnight it became the most dreaded destination in Timbuktu. When I visited the hotel a year later, after the jihadi occupation had collapsed, the Tuareg caretaker escorted me upstairs to an arched verandah overlooking a mosaic fountain in the courtyard. (The French owner had fled to Europe in March 2012, days before the rebels seized the city.) Here, in two adjoining former guest rooms with log-beamed ceilings and thick stone walls, Islamic judges had presided over hearings and pronounced judgments. "They sentenced people to be flogged," the caretaker told me. In a plaza beside the market—nicknamed "Tahrir Square" because it became the center of tumultous changes and violence under jihadi rule—or in the Sankoré Square, in front of the mosque that once contained the finest university in Timbuktu, convicted criminals were stripped, and lashed with a camel-hair switch, a tree branch, or an electrical cord. The whippings often left open sores and welts.

Two hundred miles downriver, the largest city in the region was also experiencing the jihadis' onerous rule. In Gao, a city of mud-brick huts and the gaudy mansions of Arab drug traffickers, sprawling along the southern bank of the Niger River, the Islamists went on a rampage their first night in town. They turned their machine guns on a dozen bars and nightclubs that had constituted the city's only entertainment. Le Relais, Le Hero, Le Camping Bango, Le Petit Dogon, L'Auberge Askia, and other popular establishments were riddled with hundreds of rounds and reduced to smoldering ruins. The Al Qaeda spinoff group that ruled the city, comprised mostly of black Mauritanian and Malian Islamists, under the leadership of Mokhtar Belmokhtar, converted City Hall into the palace of justice, and implemented Shariah punishments. "When someone is arrested, the person is brought to the commissariat [Islamic Police] and interrogated [and held until trial]," said a witness. As many as ten suspects at a time were crammed, sometimes for two weeks, into a filthy, eight-foot-by-eight-foot concrete room with graffiti scrawled on the bare walls. "Trials are heard every Monday and Thursday, and the detained are transferred to the justice palace to be judged," the witness went on. "There are five judges, some of whom are foreigners, but no lawyers in this process, so the right to defense is not respected. The population can attend the trials which take place in a big room."

As in Timbuktu, the Islamic police also meted out punishments on the spot, beating and whipping dozens of people, some of them elderly, for drinking and smoking cigarettes. A bricklayer accused of drinking alcohol was handcuffed, held overnight at the police station, and given forty lashes with a switch made of camel skin and camel hair. "He hit me forty times, counting in Arabic and moving from the legs up my body," the victim recounted. "It was terribly painful, I had many welts." A man in his late sixties defied the Islamic police when they demanded he put out his cigarette, telling them: "I like smoking. I will smoke today, I will smoke tomorrow . . . in fact, I will smoke every day until the day I die. Is this the work of God, beating people for smoking?" They savagely beat him and threw him in jail overnight. A sickly septuagenarian smoker, beaten by a teenaged member of the Islamic Police, a witness said, "urinated on himself after about five strokes—the punishment for smoking is ten—it was too much for him."

Boys and adolescents became the jihadis' eyes and ears in the north, employed to lurk in alleys and spy on their neighbors. The militants also recruited boys for the Islamic Police, training them to shoot weapons in a makeshift firing range behind Timbuktu's main military camp, in a field that had belonged to the gendarmerie, the military police. "I saw them running, sometimes with their guns, sometimes not, and firing in the air. . . . There were about twenty-five to thirty people all mixed, about twelve or so were children. The trainer was a Senegalese, who's an officer in the Islamic Police," recounted one observer of the weapons course. A Timbuktu resident told Human Rights Watch that he saw boys as young as eleven riding about the city in vehicles driven by Ansar Dine militants, and joining the Islamic Police on foot patrols.

On Thursdays and Sundays, Ibrahim Khalil Touré and his colleagues on the Crisis Committee made their way through the alleys of Timbuktu. Touré gazed with contempt on the jeep-loads of turban-wearing Islamic Police that bounced through the streets. Billboards with Koranic quotations had replaced advertisements for consumer goods, and black banners flew from every municipal building. They walked through the doors of Timbuktu's City Hall—its windows broken in the spasm of looting—and took seats in a lightless, airless room with sporadic electricity. Across the conference table sat Abou Zeid and his cohorts. Abou Zeid, as usual, clutched his Kalashnikov. The contrast between the bulky semiautomatic and the diminutive, limping Al Qaeda leader had inspired a cutting remark among the denizens of Timbuktu: "How does he have the strength to fire it?" They shook hands across the table. Abou Zeid and his jihadis spoke Arabic; the men of the Crisis Committee spoke French, and a Timbuktu imam served as the interpreter. The two sides discussed medical treatment, electricity, food distribution, and education. All social services had degraded under the occupation, because of the exodus of government engineers and other experts, and the shortage of capable replacements.

The conversations were cordial. "We had no choice but to keep talking to them, because we had to safeguard lives," Ibrahim Khalil Touré told me. When the jihadis decreed that boys and girls must learn separately, the committee members dutifully put together a plan to divide up the schools. When Malian government officials in the south refused out of fear to cross into jihadi territory to administer national examinations, the committee arranged for hundreds of buses to bring students down to Mopti, the nearest town of any size in government-controlled territory. But beneath the measured dialogue, the members of the Crisis Committee seethed. "We are a city that has had Islam for one thousand years," Ibrahim Khalil Touré told me months later. "We had the greatest teachers and universities. And now these Bedouins, these illiterates, these ignoramuses, tell us how to wear our pants, and how to say our prayers, and how our wives should dress, as if they were the ones who invented the way."

After years of spartan conditions in desert camps and caves, the new rulers of the north settled into their lives of urban comfort. Five times a day, at prayer time, Abou Zeid and his entourage made their way to one of Timbuktu's three Wahhabi mosques, including the butterscotch fortress perched on a dune at the edge of the Sahara, a stone's throw away from Abdel Kader Haidara's house. "They would pray with their rifles in the mosque, with their shoes on the prayer carpets," Ibrahim Khalil Touré remembered with disdain— the mark of "primitives," he said, who had spent much of their lives praying in the desert sands. At sunset, Abou Zeid retreated to the terrace of the Hotel Bouctou, the same spot where U.S. Special Forces troops had sipped beers between training sessions with Malian recruits, to relax with his fellow commander, Iyad Ag Ghali. At night the Algerian either slept in his suite on the ground floor of the Hotel Bouctou or camped in the dunes.

Then, abruptly, after one week, Abou Zeid checked out of the hotel. The jihadi commander settled the bill with crisp hundred-euro notes that a minion peeled from bundles of cash stored in the back of a Land Cruiser. *Ransom and drug money*, owner Boubacar Touré thought. Abou Zeid moved with a handful of cohorts into the Moorish-style villa that Qaddafi had had built in 2006, isolated in the dunes and surrounded by a grove of palm and pine trees. Abou Zeid, according to Touré and other witnesses, was often seen in the company of a boy about ten years old, who was believed to be his son; nobody had any idea where he kept his wives.

Timbuktu residents observed clandestine deliveries of food during the night, and heard reports that the two French geologists kidnapped in Hombori and the three European travelers taken in Timbuktu were imprisoned inside the villa. There were other sightings of the hostages at an Arab militant's home on the northern edge of Timbuktu—a cleaning woman spied the stricken faces of white men peering from the barred upstairs windows. One man swore he had seen the prisoners being led from a car, blindfolded, and marched into the Hôtel La Maison.

In Gao, a somnolent town of wide streets of reddish sand lined with mud-brick compounds, and sturdier concrete villas behind metal gates, Mokhtar Belmokhtar occupied a peach-stucco ranch house behind high walls in the prosperous Château quarter. He was joined by a ten-year-old son, named Osama, in honor of his spiritual mentor, Osama bin Laden, and one of his Arab wives, who often visited from Algeria. Down the street, fifty Hausa-speaking jihadis from the northeastern Nigerian terrorist group Boko Haram—including suicide bombers, assassins, and, it is believed, the movement's fanatical leader, Abubakar Shekau, who would two years later organize the kidnapping of 276 girls from a secondary school in Chibok—occupied the former headquarters of a welfare agency, and trained in a former government military camp outside the city. Belmokhtar moved around Gao in a four-vehicle convoy, and, when he appeared in public, a retinue of armed men surrounded him. He had his hair cut by a favorite barber, bought lamb in the downtown market, and on one occasion visited the government hospital to be treated as an outpatient for malaria. "Please take care of the Prince," his entourage told the nervous staff physicians, who did their best to remain calm in the presence of the jihadi commander.

Like Abou Zeid, the Prince preferred to leave the city in the evenings. In a canopied pinasse, escorted by three boats filled with armed men, Belmokhtar and an Al Qaeda lieutenant he had fought beside in Afghanistan often motored from Gao's harbor to the Pink Dune, an eighty-foot-high mountain of sand on the far bank of the Niger. From the knife-edge summit of the giant dune, its surface intricately scalloped by the constant wind, Belmokhtar could gaze upon a landscape that had not changed much since Al Hajj Askia Mohammed Touré, the greatest ruler of the Songhai Empire, surveyed the scene from the same vantage point five centuries earlier. The river curved and divided into channels as it flowed past dozens of cookie-cutter islets. In the other direction lay the Sahara, a flat ocher sea speckled with yellow grass. At sunset the bodyguards slaughtered a sheep and grilled it atop the dune, which turned from orange to pink in the fading light. Belmokhtar camped beneath the stars.

12

At his home in the Bella Farandja neighborhood, Abdel Kader Haidara paced the courtyard for long periods of reflection, pondering how to respond to the rebels' seizure of Timbuktu. Largely thanks to Haidara's initiatives, the city now had forty-five libraries, ranging from small private archives to ten-thousand-volume collections with exhibition spaces and conservation and digitization facilities that rivaled those in Europe and the United States. Most prominent were Haidara's Mamma Haidara Commemorative Library in the Sankoré neighborhood and the Ahmed Baba Institute, housed since 2009 in an $8 million complex built by the South African government. The forty-five libraries served as repositories for a total of 377,000 manuscripts, ranging from four-hundred-page, leather-encased volumes to single folios, including some of the greatest works of medieval literature in the world.

The immediate threat to the manuscripts from the looting in

Timbuktu had passed, but Haidara was gradually realizing that they faced a greater danger. He knew that many of the works epitomized the reasoned discourse and intellectual inquiry that the militants, with their rigid views of Islam, their intolerance, and their hatred of modernity and rationality, wanted to destroy. It was inevitable, he was coming to believe, that the manuscripts would become a target.

To be sure, jihadi spokesmen had appeared on radio and on television twice soon after their capture of Timbuktu, to reassure people that "we won't harm the manuscripts." But Haidara and most of his friends and colleagues dismissed the promise as a public relations ploy. "They went on television and assured us, 'we know the value of the manuscripts, and we vow to protect them.' And that's the moment that people got afraid. We knew that they were lying," said Sane Chirfi Alpha, Timbuktu's director of tourism and a close friend of Haidara.

Timbuktu's population, Chirfi explained, was savvy enough to understand that the mere act of acknowledging the manuscripts' existence implied that the jihadis had them in their sights—and would turn against them when the time was right. "We could read between the lines," Chirfi went on. "They told us that we had deviated from Islam, that we were practicing a religion full of innovations, not based on the original texts." Deborah Stolk, the director of the Prince Claus Fund in the Netherlands, a major funder of manuscript conservation in Timbuktu, initially downplayed the peril, though it became clear to her later that the texts were endangered. "These manuscripts show a community in which science and religion coexisted and influenced each other," she said. "That community is not in line with the one envisioned by Al Qaeda."

Emily Brady had anticipated trouble in Timbuktu from the moment the coup d'état occurred in March. An American attorney, scholar, illustrator, translator (of an 1839 French *grimoire*, or book of the occult, entitled *Treasure of the Old Man of the Pyramids*), and poverty-eradication specialist in her fifties from Seattle, Washington, Brady (who requested that her real name not be used in this book) had first visited Mali in the 1990s. During that visit, she met Abdel Kader Haidara, and instantly became captivated by the manuscripts.

The texts, she told *The New Republic* in 2013, "do something for me nothing else ever has." While keeping her base, an ocean-side house just south of Seattle, Brady began spending more time in Mali: she apprenticed with master bookbinders in Bamako; studied Bambara, the language spoken by Mali's dominant ethnic group; married a young Malian, and purchased a house near the Niger River in Bamako, where she spent a good portion of every year. "I'm a book artist and book and paper conservator with one side of my brain and an attorney and governance specialist with the other," she described herself in an online Reddit chat about the manuscripts.

During her first encounters with Haidara in Timbuktu in the 1990s, Brady had been struck by the multifaceted and liberal society revealed by the works, by evidence of an artistic and scientific culture that had flourished alongside devout Islamic traditions in Timbuktu. She relished the manuscripts about musicology—"wonderful books about playing the lute," she said—and the epic poetry that often communicated powerful and illicit emotions through the clever use of imagery. "A poet would describe a relationship with tea when he was actually talking about a woman's sexuality," observed Brady. Both subjects, she knew, were anathema to the Al Qaeda zealots. From her home in the Malian capital, in consultation with Haidara, she had preemptively sent out letters to every contact in her database in late March 2012, a total of two thousand individuals and organizations, alerting them to the danger posed by the advancing jihadi army. She received no responses.

When the rebels seized control of Timbuktu, she recalled two years later, "Abdel Kader called me and he said, 'If we don't do something, the manuscripts are going to be affected. They're caught in a combat zone. They could become something of value to the jihadis politically.' We pleaded with donors [for money], and still nobody would help."

A few days after the occupation began, Haidara met with his colleagues at the office of Savama-DCI, the Timbuktu library association that he had formed fifteen years earlier.

"What do we have to do?" Haidara asked them.

"What do you think we have to do?" a colleague replied.

"I think we need to take out the manuscripts from the big buildings and disperse them around the city to family houses. We don't want them finding the collections of manuscripts and stealing them or destroying them."

"But we have no money, and we have no secure way to move them."

"Don't worry. I will find a solution for that," Haidara said.

Months earlier, the Ford Foundation office in Lagos, Nigeria, had given Haidara a $12,000 grant to study English at Oxford University in the fall and winter of 2012–2013. The money had been wired to a savings account in Bamako. He emailed the foundation and asked for an authorization to reallocate the funds to protect the manuscripts from the hands of Timbuktu's occupiers. The money was released in three days.

Haidara recruited his nephew Mohammed Touré, his sister's son, who had worked with Haidara at the library since he was twelve. Touré idolized his uncle and envisioned spending his life in manuscript preservation; Abdel Kader had tapped him as the family's next scholar, just as his own father, Mamma Haidara, had tapped him when he was in his teens. "I ran the library, I welcomed the delegations, the researchers, the journalists, anyone who came by," Touré told me when we met months later in the courtyard of

Villa Soudan, a French-run guesthouse on the east bank of the Niger in a neighborhood of embassies and walled-off villas in the Malian capital. He was twenty-five years old, a wiry man with a high-pitched voice, a fidgety, distracted manner, and a pair of cell phones that went off at regular intervals, one for work and one for personal affairs, prompting impassioned bursts of conversation in Arabic; French; Tamasheq, the language of the Tuaregs; and Songhoy, Touré's first language, spoken by the dominant ethnic group along the northern bend of the Niger.

Touré and his uncle reached out to people they trusted—archivists, secretaries, Timbuktu tour guides, and half a dozen of Haidara's nephews and cousins. In a coordinated effort, the volunteers went from shop to shop in Timbuktu's commercial district, buying, as discreetly as possible, metal trunks at a rate of between fifty and eighty a day. They reasoned that if everybody in the group limited his purchases to just two or three chests daily, the activity wouldn't attract suspicion. "It looks like ordinary baggage. And commercial activities were going on as usual during the jihadis' time," Touré explained. When the metal lockers were sold out, they bought lesser-quality ones of wood. When they had purchased every trunk in Timbuktu, they swept through markets in the riverside town of Mopti, a large commercial center in unoccupied territory about 240 miles to the south. When they had bought up every one in Mopti, they purchased oil barrels in Timbuktu and shipped them down by boat to Mopti workshops. In that bustling riverfront city, metalworkers broke apart the barrels and refashioned them into chests—there was nobody in Timbuktu who could do the work—and sent them back downriver to Timbuktu. In one month, they accumulated 2,500 trunks and moved them into storage rooms inside the city's libraries to prepare for the evacuation.

Haidara searched for safe houses to store the manuscripts. Unsure what kind of reaction he would elicit, he first broached the subject with a female cousin who lived in a house near his in Bella Farandja. "Listen," he told her. "I want to bring some trunks filled with manuscripts to your house, and I want you hide them there. It could be dangerous. Are you okay with it?"

"Of course. Why wouldn't I be? I'll open everything for you," she said. She led him to a storage room deep inside the house, filled with sacks of grain. "You are free to use this whenever you want." He reached out to dozens of other relatives and friends. Not a single one, Haidara said, turned him down.

At seven o'clock one evening in late April, Haidara, Moham-med Touré, and several other volunteers met in front of the Mamma Haidara Library and began the dangerous task of packing and mov-ing the manuscripts. They had waited until an hour after dark—when they could work inside the library without attracting the scrutiny of the Islamic Police, who were always on the lookout for suspicious activities. That would give them exactly two hours before AQIM imposed its nightly nine p.m. curfew. Being caught on the streets after that hour, all of them knew, would earn them an interrogation by the Islamic Police and a whipping or imprisonment. Carrying two trunks, the men moved silently across the courtyard, entered the main building, and locked the doors behind them. The rebels had cut the electricity in Timbuktu at night, obliging them to use flashlights—only one or two to avoid drawing attention. Whispering among themselves in the darkness, and guided by the night watch-man, they opened the cases in the main exhibition hall and delicately removed the volumes displayed inside. The flashlight beams cut through the darkness, reflecting off the exhibition glass, enveloping the men's faces and the yellowing manuscripts in an eerie glow. Fear-ful of discovery but excited by the work, they passed the manuscripts down the line and laid them gently inside the footlockers.

Into the trunks went some of the most valuable works in Abdel Kader's collection. One prize was a tiny, irregularly shaped manuscript that glittered with illuminated blue Arabic letters and droplets of gold—a twelfth-century Koran written on the parchment of a fish, and a centerpiece of the Mamma Haidara collection for generations. There was a 254-page medical volume on surgery and elixirs derived from birds, lizards, and plants titled *Remedies of Internal and External Maladies Affecting the Body*, written in Timbuktu in 1684, shortly after the Moroccans ended their occupation and a second intellectual flowering began in the city. A 342-page, eighteenth-century manuscript with sparkling red-inked calligraphy and a fist-sized hole gouged out of it by termites had been selected for display by Haidara to show the extraordinary destructive power of these minute and sharp-jawed creatures. A Koran written in looping Maghrebi script with diagonal and vertical marginalia lay beside a book of Sufic philosophy opened to a cryptic black-and-white diagram. It consisted of eight concentric circles that compared the goodness and brilliance of the original Islamic thinkers to that of subsequent generations. Another prize of the Haidara collection, reflecting Haidara's belief that Islam in its purist form was a religion of peace, was a manuscript on conflict resolution between the kingdoms of Borno and Sokoto in what is now Nigeria, the work of a Sufi holy warrior and intellectual who had briefly ruled Timbuktu in the mid-nineteenth century. He had been a jihadi, Haidara argued, in the original and best sense of the word: one who struggles against evil ideas, desire, and anger in himself and subjugates them to reason and obedience to God's commands.

After emptying the exhibition cases, they groped their way in the darkness down hallways, concerned that their flashlight beams would be seen by patrolling Islamic Police, and worked methodically in the conservation labs and library shelves where the bulk of the manuscripts were held. They kept close track of the time, limiting themselves to two hours, packing in as much as they could, often in silence, listening for every suspicious sound. The manuscripts ranged from miniature volumes the size of a contemporary mass-market paperback to large, encyclopedia-sized works, and required artfully arranging, in near-total darkness, to maximize the use of space, like assembling the pieces of a jigsaw puzzle. Because of the speed with which the volunteers were forced to work and the shortage of funding, they used no cushioning, no cardboard boxes, and no humidity traps to protect them from potential damage caused by squeezing and jostling. "The manuscripts are jam-packed in metal footlockers. This means that they are being subjected to risks of damage for lack of padding or protection from one another," Emily Brady would explain in a Reddit-based plea for funding one year later. "Every time a footlocker is moved, the manuscripts rub against each other causing damage."

When they had finished the packing, they sealed the chests with padlocks, locked the door of the library behind them, and hurried home down shadowy alleys, keeping a sharp eye out for Islamic Police patrols. The following evening, they returned to the library, picked up the lockers, which now required two men to lift each one, wrapped them in blankets, and loaded them onto mule carts. The packing and transport continued across Timbuktu every evening over the following weeks, employing a total of twenty volunteers. Haidara told nobody outside his fellow librarians what he was doing—not even his immediate family. His wife and children noticed that he was going out every evening and returning late, but he shrugged off their queries. He didn't want to give them additional reason to worry.

One night a year after the evacuation, a guide led me through the rubbish-filled alleys around Timbuktu's outdoor market to a rendezvous with a mule-cart driver who had participated in the operation. The skinny young man stood nervously in the street in the twilight and mumbled in broken French that he had picked up dozens of trunks from the Mamma Haidara and other libraries. "We moved them by night, always at night," he told me, but declined to shed more details or even to give me his name; the occupation of Timbuktu by the jihadis was over, but Al Qaeda was still lurking in the desert just outside town, and nobody yet had the confidence to admit his role in Haidara's secret smuggling operation. "I can't say anything more," he said, and slipped away in the darkness.

In the busy hours between seven and nine at night, before curfew, when the streets were still full of pedestrians and traffic, and their transport would fit in with the bustle of ordinary Timbuktu life, this young man and many others led their donkeys through the sand, cart wheels creaking, and knocked on the doors of designated safe houses belonging to dozens of families connected to the Savama-DCI network. Everything had been prearranged: the mule-cart drivers, couriers, and hosts carried the footlockers by candlelight or flashlight down hallways and stacked them inside storage closets. "They were owners of libraries and their families—sisters, cousins, brothers, nephews. We used dozens of them," Mohammed Touré said.

At the end of May 2012, while the clandestine rescue was gathering momentum, Haidara traveled to Bamako for an emergency meeting with UNESCO. A dozen UNESCO officials, Mali's minister of culture, and twenty reporters assembled in a conference room at the Ministry of Culture. With cameras and digital recorders on, Haidara was asked to discuss the peril facing Timbuktu's manuscripts.

Haidara refused to comment. "If I talk about the situation in front of you here, I could worsen the problem," Haidara told the reporters. Drawing attention to the manuscripts, he argued, would remind the jihadis of their value. The radicals might hold them as bargaining chips or destroy them out of spite. When the meeting ended, the UNESCO delegates asked Haidara how they should proceed.

"Stay silent," Haidara advised. "Do nothing. Leave it in our hands."

Haidara decided, after days of reflection, to remain in Bamako. He insisted that it had nothing to do with his personal safety: in the entire month since the rebel takeover, he had not had a single encounter with Abou Zeid, Iyad Ag Ghali, or any other jihadi in the city. He had deliberately kept a low profile, and none of them had sought him out, or appeared to have noticed him. But he was finding it increasingly difficult to stay in touch with his donors around the world, to keep them updated on the dangers in Timbuktu and to prepare them to donate money should the situation require it. Haidara had a second home in Bamako where he lived with his second wife, the Malian diplomat, whenever he came to the capital, but before the troubles started she had taken up an embassy position in Paris; he told her nothing about the rescue operation, determined to shield her from worry.

Haidara designated Mohammed Touré his proxy in Timbuktu and settled into a drab rented apartment a few blocks from the Niger River, which soon became a refuge for relatives who had fled the north. (He felt it inappropriate to move into his second wife's home with members of his first wife's family.) Haidara brought down his three oldest children so that they could continue their education. Amid the insecurity and violence that had enveloped Timbuktu, many of the city's teachers had fled, forcing their secondary schools to shut down. The children now shared space with their grandmother—the mother of Haidara's first wife—and numerous aunts, uncles, and cousins. And the relatives kept coming. With the exception of two short visits to Timbuktu over the following six months, during which he quietly met with his nephew Mohammed Touré and others participating in the rescue, and gave them encouragement, Haidara would remain in Bamako until the end of the occupation.

13

On a windswept morning during the summer rainy season, Sane Chirfi Alpha, Timbuktu's director of tourism and a member of the city's Crisis Committee during the now-ended occupation, guided me in a four-wheel-drive over rolling dunes to the football-field-sized graveyard at the edge of the city, surrounded by a low orange wall perforated with ornamental, Moorish-style apertures. Clad in a white skullcap and white robe, Chirfi, a sad-faced and taciturn man in his forties, stepped out of our car, opened the padlocked gate with an iron key, and led me on foot across a field of mottled sand, barren except for a scattering of thorn trees. We threaded our way past overturned clay cisterns, pottery shards, stones, chunks of concrete with names and birth and death dates scratched into them, and other crude markers for the dead.

Abruptly we arrived at a ten-foot-high pile of bricks, stones, and earth. There was nothing to suggest that it had been, until the previous year, the mausoleum of one of Timbuktu's most revered saints, among 333 Islamic scholars—including several members of the Timbuktu resistance who were executed by the Moroccan invaders in front of the Djingareyber Mosque in 1591—viewed by the city's residents as divine.

On the 1st of July 2012, a Friday, Chirfi told me, dozens of Ansar Dine militants under the command of Iyad Ag Ghali blocked the entrances to this cemetery and a second one in Timbuktu with their vehicles. Ghali's men approached the shrines, wielding pick-axes, hammers, and chisels, and, with cries of *"Allahu Akbar,"* or "God is the Greatest," smashed them into rubble. The attack came a day after Ghali's men had broken into the courtyard of the Djingareyber Mosque and knocked down three small mausoleums while the imam looked on in horror. Jihadi imams appeared on television and in Timbuktu's mosques the day after the cemetery attacks and explained their actions to a shocked, demoralized population. "They said that saints are not acceptable in Islam," Chirfi said, as the wind howled over this desolate sight. They made it clear that they would continue until all the shrines in Timbuktu were destroyed.

The worship of saints and the construction of shrines had spread through much of the Islamic world following the death of the Prophet Mohammed, including Persia, Iraq, the Hejaz region of the Arabian Peninsula, and the Maghreb region of Africa. But it was not until the eighteenth century, when Muhammad Abd Al Wahhab, the spiritual mentor of Timbuktu's jihadis, began his campaign of religious purification, that such rites and practices began to be seen as heretical. As part of his fanatical quest to drag Islam back to its seventh-century roots, Al Wahhab raged against prayers to the dead, worship at tombs and shrines, the veneration of saints, the erection of tombstones, even the celebration of the Prophet's birthday. Those who indulged in such practices, Al Wahhab preached, were guilty of idolatrous superstition, polytheism, and blasphemy, and deserved to be killed, their daughters and wives raped, and all of their possessions confiscated.

Al Wahhab's preachings drove his followers to carry out rampages that would inspire the jihadis centuries later in Timbuktu. In 1801, the Wahhabi forces of Abdul Aziz Ibn Muhammed Ibn Saud seized control of Najaf and Karbala, the two holiest cities in Shi'ite Islam, and destroyed the tomb of Hussein Ibn Ali, the grandson of Mohammed, and that of his father, Imam Ali, the son-in-law of the Prophet. Two years later, when the Saudis captured Mecca from the Arabian Hashemite clan, they destroyed a shrine above the tomb of the Prophet's daughter Fatimah as well as the tomb of his first wife, Khadijah. "Beware of those who preceded you and used to take the graves of their prophets and righteous men as places of worship," the Wahhabis declared, citing a Hadith, "but you must not take graves as mosques; I forbid you to do that."

For centuries the Sufis of Timbuktu had carried out their rites unmolested. Even under the yoke of the nineteenth-century jihadis, they had continued to enter these *zawiya*—simple mud huts bearing little ornamentation, except, perhaps, a carved wooden door and a bed of white linen draped over a bier—to commune with their local spirits, reciting certain prayers over and over, in a mystical ceremony called the *dhikr*. "We pray to them for everything we look for in life," a seamstress would explain to an investigator from Human Rights Watch months after the 2012 attacks. "The barren pray to have children; the pregnant pray for a safe birth; mothers pray for their children to be healthy, safe, and marry a good man or woman. If you, or a family member, are to travel, we pray to deliver us safely home."

Weeks after demolishing the tombs of Sufi saints in emulation of Ibn Saud's fanatical army, the jihadis consolidated their control over northern Mali. The Islamic militants had already outmaneuvered their secular Tuareg partners—implementing Shariah law against their wishes, pushing the Tuaregs to the outskirts of Timbuktu. But in Gao, the Tuareg rebels still clung to a modicum of power, occupying most major municipal buildings, including City Hall and the governor's mansion overlooking the Niger River. Those days ended abruptly at the end of July.

The spark occurred early one afternoon. A Tuareg rebel tried to steal a popular schoolteacher's motorcycle on a street in Gao and, when the teacher resisted, shot him dead. Residents of Gao were already angered by an epidemic of looting carried out in late March and early April by the Tuareg occupiers. "Over the period of several days, the town of Gao was thoroughly, systematically, and comprehensively pillaged—the government offices, banks, schools, hospitals, and churches, the warehouses and offices of international humanitarian organizations, the houses of government officials," a Gao resident told Human Rights Watch. "Everything that the state and residents of Gao had worked to construct for the benefit of the population was stripped away in a matter of days." Now enraged crowds gathered at the gates of the governor's mansion, demanding that the Tuareg commanders turn over the murderer. Panicky Tuareg snipers fired from the villa's windows on the protesters, killing several. The Islamists seized on popular outrage and launched an attack against the Tuaregs, killing twenty-eight and driving them out of their strongholds in Gao after a day of fierce street fighting. The Tuareg rebels fled into the desert.

At their bases at Timbuktu's airport and harbor, the Tuaregs watched in terror. "We knew we would be next," said Yusuf, the young fighter I met at his mother's house on the outskirts of the city. Yusuf and hundreds of his comrades slipped from the city in a disorganized retreat, grimly aware that they had been humiliated and rendered powerless by their jihadi partners.

The vision of an independent Tuareg homeland that had inspired three generations of rebels, and that these men had realized for a brief and euphoric moment, in northern Mali in April, lay in ruins. "We lost our dream of Azawad," said Yusuf, who fled by motorbike to a refugee camp in Mauritania, where he joined tens of thousands of northern civilians who had escaped from the very depredations that Yusuf and his fellow rebels had inflicted. Until this point the Tuaregs, who had little tolerance for Salafism, had kept the radicals' most extreme impulses in check. With the Tuaregs gone, Al Qaeda in the Islamic Maghreb and Ansar Dine now felt free to turn the clocks back fourteen hundred years.

In a violent repudiation of his former life, Ghali declared war on the north's musicians. "We do not want Satan's music," a spokesman for Ansar Dine declared in August 2012. "In its place there will be Koranic verses. Shariah demands this. We must do what God commands." Ghali's jihadis destroyed instruments and sound equipment, and burned down rudimentary recording studios. In Niafounké, a Niger River town forty miles upstream from Timbuktu, and the home of the late desert-blues master Ali Farka Touré, jihadis threatened to chop off the fingers of Touré's protegés if they were caught so much as lifting a guitar. Ahmed Ag Kaedi, a Tuareg camel herder who doubled as the lead guitarist of Amanar, a Tinariwen-inspired group from Kidal, returned from visiting his camels in the bush in August 2012 to find his house vandalized and his musical equipment destroyed. Ansar Dine militants "saw my sound system and my instruments and they poured fuel on them and set them on fire," he recounted. "They talked to my sister and said, 'When Ahmed comes back tell him [that if] he plays music in Kidal again, we will come back and cut off his fingers.'"

The jihadis' Shariah punishments became more draconian. In August the Islamic Police in Timbuktu summoned Muhamen Bebao, twenty-three, a slim man with a wispy beard, to the court at the Hôtel La Maison and sentenced him to a month in jail and a $750 fine for purchasing a stolen mattress for $22. Bebao admitted purchasing the mattress from a friend—but claimed that he didn't know that the friend had seized it from a shop during the looting spree in Timbuktu in April. On the day before Bebao's scheduled liberation, he was given a new sentence: the amputation of his right hand. "When I heard the sentence I got weak," Bebao told me, as we sat in the office of a Bamako agency that provided some charity to maimed victims of Islamist justice. The police bound him to a chair with bicycle inner tubes. They dispatched a volunteer to the market to purchase a kitchen knife. Bebao received an injection of an anesthetic. He has only a foggy memory of being carried in the chair to the sandy depression behind the Libya Hotel, all that remained of a five-mile canal that Qaddafi had dredged, at a cost of millions of dollars, from the Niger River to his resort—and no memory of his hand being sawed off. "People think it's done with a single stroke, but it's with a knife, slowly cut, as if you're an animal," one witness to the amputation told me. Bebao woke up in pain in a Timbuktu clinic, he told me, as he displayed for me his empty sleeve. A local physician nursed him back to health, and he fled Timbuktu.

In late July, in a village outside Gao, Islamic Police arrested a man named Almahmoud and accused him of stealing livestock, saying that they had followed motorcycle tracks from the theft site to his house. After two weeks in a jail cell, "At around three p.m. they took me to the public square, which was full of people," he told a Human Rights Watch investigator. "They tied my hands, feet, and chest firmly to a chair; my right hand was tied with a rubber cord. The boss, himself, cut my hand as if he were killing a sheep. As he cut it, which took about two minutes, he shouted 'Allahu Akbar.' . . . I stayed in the cell for a week without seeing a doctor. . . . Later [the militants] gave me money to repair my motorcycle, and to buy tea and clothes and brought me back home. I am innocent: I didn't steal those animals."

Weeks later, in a village near Timbuktu, a local Tuareg shot dead a Sorhai fisherman during an altercation. He was swiftly sentenced to death. That Friday morning, pickup trucks equipped with loudspeakers circulated through the alleys of Timbuktu, ordering the population to Qaddafi's grand canal to witness the execution following the afternoon prayer. The jihadis ordered the director of Radio Communal Bouctou, renamed Radio Azawad, to announce the impending event. Five hundred spectators gathered along the barren depression that once was Qaddafi's grand canal, behind the Libya Hotel, now designated as the amputation and execution ground. The condemned man, riding in the back of a pickup, alit on the sand, dropped to his knees, and prayed. Abou Zeid and the Al Qaeda henchmen stood to one side, near the victim's mother, while a two-man masked firing squad fixed Kalashnikovs on the kneeling prisoner. Abou Zeid and his men cried, *"Allahu Akbar."* Then the executioners fired from fifteen feet away.

In the town of Aguelhok, near Kidal, Ansar Dine militants loyal to Iyad Ag Ghali dragged to the village square a young couple from a nearby rural area that had had a child out of wedlock. At five o'clock in the morning, before two hundred people who watched in silence, the Islamists dug two holes four feet deep, buried the couple up to their necks, and stoned them to death. "It was horrible," an eyewitness recounted, noting that the woman had moaned and cried out and that her partner had shouted something indistinct just before he died. "It was inhuman. They killed them like they were animals." An Ansar Dine spokesman defended the punishment. "They both died right away and even asked for this application," he said. "We don't have to answer to anyone over the application of Shariah."

Around the same time, a panel of five judges convicted four young men in Shariah court in Gao of robbing a bus at gunpoint— a crime that called for the amputation of the right hand and left foot. Hours later the men received their punishment. Four had their limbs hacked off in a military camp, the fifth was taken in a Land Cruiser to the Place de l'Indépendance, the main market square in Gao. Bodyguards of the police commissioner, a man named Aliou, bound the convicted robber to a chair with a rope and gave him an injection. "Aliou took two butcher knives, laid them on a piece of black rubber and said, 'Allahu Akbar' which the other Islamists repeated," a witness to the mutilation said. "Then he put one knife down, and with the other, cut off the young man's hand—it took but ten seconds to chop it off. He held it up for all to see. Another Islamist with a beard took the second knife, said 'Allahu Akbar,' and cut off the foot. The [jihadis] started to pray and said that they were doing what God asked them to do. Aliou ordered the man to be untied, and at the same time asked for a bag in his car. It was the bag with the four feet and hands amputated from the other thieves. He then placed the new foot and hand inside and they said, 'Allahu Akbar.'"

The jihadis' brutality drew the disapproval of even Abdelmalek Droukdel, the Algerian-based supreme emir of Al Qaeda in the Islamic Maghreb. For months Droukdel had looked askance at his underlings' provocative actions in Mali—the declaration of an independent state, the beatings and whippings of ordinary citizens in Timbuktu and Gao. While he sanctioned the bombings of government targets, terrorist attacks on embassies, and abductions for ransom of Westerners, Droukdel was coming to regard Ghali, Abou Zeid, and Belmokhtar as impetuous fanatics who were likely to alienate the very people they were trying to win over. Now, the accelerating wave of amputations, stonings, and executions confirmed his sense that they had gone too far.

But the three jihadi commanders, who had gotten used to acting with near-complete autonomy, ignored Droukdel's admonitions—and they even bragged about their brutality. In the new jihadi state, the Islamists created a parallel universe that combined medieval theology with twenty-first-century communication. They flaunted their absolute power and their Shariah punishments in YouTube videos, Twitter feeds, and website communiqués.

Some people defied the jihadis. In Gao, Mokhtar Belmokhtar's henchmen announced that a public amputation would take place at the Place de l'Indépendance at eight o'clock one morning. Thousands filled the streets leading into the plaza and blocked the way. "You will not do this in Gao," they proclaimed. The jihadis called off the amputation, then carried it out stealthily in the plaza before dawn a week later.

One hot summer night, Mohammed Touré, Haidara's nephew and chief assistant, left the headquarters of Haidara's library owners association, Savama-DCI, with a metal chest full of manuscripts. He had been working alone that evening, and as he locked the front gate behind him and stepped into the alley, one of Al Qaeda's most fanatical and unpredictable leaders, Oumar Ould Hamaha, fifty, known as "Red Beard," walked past the building with bodyguards. "He lived in the house right next to Savama-DCI, and I didn't even know that," Touré said. A pinched-looking man with large lips, a distinctive henna-dyed goatee, and an ever-present black turban, Hamaha had risen through the ranks of Al Qaeda to serve as the top lieutenant of Mokhtar Belmokhtar, and recently the two jihadis had become in-laws: Belmokhtar had taken one of Red Beard's teenaged daughters as his latest wife. Red Beard had become a notorious figure in Timbuktu—and much of the world—because of his televised threats against the West, delivered in flawless French, which this camel driver's son from Kidal had learned as a boy in a Timbuktu *lycée*, or high school. He shone a flashlight in Touré's face.

"What are you doing here?" he demanded.

"I'm sorry," Touré stammered, momentarily blinded by the

beam of light, "but soon we're going to be moving, and I'm transferring these manuscripts to a place where they'll be better secured."

"No," said Red Beard. "You're stealing them."

"Certainly not."

"You're moving them in the middle of the night, and who gave you the authorization to do so?"

"I . . . I didn't think I needed permission to move my own stuff."

Red Beard summoned the Islamic Police. Three pickup trucks filled with black-turbaned enforcers pulled up to the building. They too demanded to see Touré's authorization. When he failed to produce it, they arrested him.

"You are a thief," he was told.

Touré knew that the Islamists put little time between issuing Shariah judgments and meting out punishments. Grounded in Islamic scholarship, he cited Hadith and Koranic verses stating that proof of a misdeed was required before punishment was meted out.

"The proof is there. You were robbing this library," Red Beard said.

"It belongs to me," Touré insisted, "and I was moving the books to a more secure location."

"Prove it to me," Red Beard demanded.

"Fine," said Touré, improvising. "I will call the imams, and the chiefs of the quarter, and at nine o'clock tomorrow morning they will come and they will give testimony about who owns the library."

He bought himself time, but his fate was unclear. In Bamako, while Touré was being kept in custody, Haidara frantically made phone calls, contacting imams, neighborhood leaders, and librarians. The men worked through the night, assembling documents and affidavits attesting to Touré's affiliation with the Mamma Haidara Library and the librarians association, and his role as a custodian of the manuscripts. The witnesses gathered at the governor's office at nine a.m., with the Islamic Police, judges, Red Beard,

Abou Zeid, and other jihadi leaders. The judges interrogated the witnesses. Touré, unlike many of those judged by the north's Shariah courts, had been privileged enough to marshal the support of the city's most influential religious, business, and cultural figures. Twenty-four hours after his arrest, the judges told Touré that the evidence had been overwhelming in his favor and that he was free to go. That night he resumed packing. "There was only one objective: to save the knowledge of Mali, and I didn't consider my life worth anything compared to that," Touré said.

Not every librarian had gotten onboard at first. The curators of Timbuktu's Ahmed Baba Institute, the Kuwaiti- and Saudi-financed government library where Haidara had been employed collecting manuscripts in the hinterlands for fifteen years, hesitated. Soon after the rebels seized Timbuktu, twenty Al Qaeda fighters had occupied the institute's new $8 million headquarters, which contained about fourteen thousand manuscripts, and turned it into a weapons depot and dormitory. There they prayed, studied the Koran, ate, and slept in close proximity to the greatest treasures of Timbuktu's Golden Age, and trained with their Kalashnikovs and other weapons in the courtyards. But 24,000 manuscripts remained inside the original building—unknown to the occupiers and under the control of the Ahmed Baba staff. "These manuscripts are at risk," Haidara had told a gathering of Ahmed Baba employees in April. "They are our patrimony. There's no administration here, so it's our responsibility to get them out."

"We don't have the means to do this," he was told.

"I've got the means," Haidara assured the curators and staff. "You need to leave everything to me. It's my responsibility."

Some employees believed the occupation wasn't going to last, or trusted the jihadis' pledges to leave the manuscripts alone. Others were reluctant to cede control to an outsider, even one who had devoted half his life to building up the collection. "After the crisis, if the manuscripts are all missing, the director could say that we stole them," one curator told him. Dismayed by their passivity, Haidara had walked away. But he was tormented by thoughts of the manuscripts he had tracked down for fifteen years falling into the hands of Abou Zeid and his men, and, weeks later, he begged the director, who had fled to Bamako hours after the jihadis arrived in town, to act. "You designate two agents, they will meet with my agents, and we will get the manuscripts into our custody." Arrangements were made, and in Timbuktu, Mohammed Touré delivered chests to Ahmed Baba Institute volunteers. Supervised by Touré and other members of Haidara's team, the institute's agents worked through the night, for two consecutive weeks, safely evacuating all 24,000 manuscripts to designated safe houses. These books were among the last to be removed from the libraries of Timbuktu and placed in private family homes, according to Haidara's plan. By the end of that month, Touré and his team had transported ninety-five percent of the 377,000 manuscripts from Timbuktu's libraries to more than thirty safe houses around the city. The only significant collection that was still exposed was the thousands of manuscripts at the new Ahmed Baba Institute in Sankoré, occupied and declared a barracks by the jihadis.

Shortly after Touré's narrow escape from Shariah justice, Timbuktu's Crisis Committee requested a meeting with Abou Zeid to discuss the Islamic Police–led crackdown in the city. At the office he had commandeered in the governor's headquarters, he served the men soft drinks, greeted them by name, and inquired after their health and that of their families.

"Why are you whipping women, and putting them in prison

in that bank?" Ibrahim Khalil Touré demanded. "These people are Muslims, they are not animists. They are not unbelievers. They believe in God. How could you put these women in a cell like this, and not let them out to pray?"

Abou Zeid professed surprise. "Is that true?" he asked. "We'll have to have a consultation about this."

The encounter, committee member Ibrahim Khalil Touré said later, typified Abou Zeid. The Al Qaeda commander disliked confrontations and distanced himself from the crimes being committed under his authority. Abou Zeid conducted himself like "a gentleman," Touré said. "He always respected us." But they never forgot that Abou Zeid had final word in the city, and they considered him as brutal as the men who worked for him. "Abou Zeid was a cold man, but calm," said Touré. "He killed with a smile on his face."

In Timbuktu, after harassments and beatings by the Islamic Police for refusing to wear burqas—the veils that fully cover the face—the city's market women staged a protest. Dozens marched through the Sankoré neighborhood, waving the hated veils and shouting, "Down with Shariah law." Islamic police fired over their heads, and placed them in custody. They brought six ringleaders to the governor's headquarters, where Abou Zeid was waiting for them.

The Al Qaeda leader was seated on a sofa, flanked by the police commissar and the minister of moral enforcement. Abou Zeid stroked his ragged beard and refused to make eye contact with the women.

"What are the reasons that you women go to the market to do this work, and that the men stay at home, doing nothing?" he inquired in a soft voice.

"The men don't have any work," the leader, a fishmonger, shot back, "and if they steal to survive, you cut off their hands."

In the face of the most powerful jihadi in Timbuktu, a man responsible for the murders of two Western hostages, and the mutilations and whippings of many of her fellow citizens, she felt no fear, she remembered. She had little left to lose. She refused to put on her veil and kept her eyes fixed on Abou Zeid, as if daring him to look at her.

Abou Zeid stared at the floor.

"Our husbands don't have jobs," she went on, "and you want us to spend money on these veils? We don't have the money to buy such clothes. And when we buy them, you jihadis say they are not good enough, and send us back to buy more."

Abou Zeid spoke so quietly that she had to lean forward to hear him. "In our religion, women do not march," he said. "Women do not hold demonstrations."

His expression hardened. "We are the authorities here," he said, "and if you attempt to march or demonstrate again, anything that happens will be your own fault." Then the women were escorted from the room. From that point until the end of the occupation, the market women refrained from further protests, but they refused to wear the despised niqabs. For their act of passive resistance, they were made to feel the extremists' wrath. "Mostly the jihadis were targeting young women and men who were seen together in the streets," the fishmonger recalled, "but every Friday, they would come by the market after mosque to beat us."

14

Emily Brady, the manuscript conservator from Washington state, had been urging Haidara to evacuate the manuscripts to government territory from the first days of the jihadi takeover. Haidara had always given her the same answer: "It's still not time." He couldn't bear the thought of again scattering the treasures that he had consolidated in Timbuktu. They were meant to be in the desert, he insisted, the place where they had been created, traded, and stored for centuries. But Haidara was coming to realize that at some point he would have to remove them.

"You must get them out," Western embassy officials and several of his benefactors in Europe and the Middle East advised him. "These are terrible people. They will destroy everything before they leave."

In the summer of 2012, a confluence of events prodded Haidara toward the drastic step that he had been delaying for months. The jihadis of Timbuktu went on their rampage in July, destroying a dozen Sufi shrines. In August, Libyan Wahhabis, known as Najdis, outdid their Timbuktu counterparts. They desecrated dozens of graves in a Sufi cemetery in Tripoli's Old City, knocked down a mausoleum in Misrata and three in Tripoli, bulldozed and blew up the shrine of a fifteenth-century Sufi scholar in the Mediterranean coastal town of Zlitan, and fired mortar rounds at the mosque and library of Al Asmari University in the same city. The shells ignited a fire inside the library that burned thousands of manuscripts to ashes. "This is clear: what people are now doing in terms of digging up old graves and demolishing mosques is contrary to the Sunnah and the sayings of scholars," Abdelrahman Al Gharyani, the grand mufti of Libya, the spiritual leader of the country's Sunni Muslim community, declared, in a futile attempt to curb the Salafis' rampage. The wave of destruction served as a frightening premonition of what could lie in store for Timbuktu.

Haidara recalled, "I knew we didn't have much time."

Compounding the pressure on Haidara was the north's economic collapse and the consequent breakdown of law and order in Timbuktu. Livestock trading and butchering were staples of the region's economy, but Tuareg and Arab herders, fearful of being accused of collaboration with the occupiers, fled the Timbuktu area and took all of their animals with them. (Together, the Arabs and Tuaregs comprised about forty percent of Timbuktu's total population.) Arab shopkeepers boarded up their stores, many of which had been ransacked during the early wave of looting in Timbuktu. The tourist industry had long ago withered and died, and local government services ground to a halt. With the banks looted, it became impossible to take out money. Most residents of Timbuktu became dependent on their relatives in Bamako, Mopti, and other cities in the south, who brought them periodic infusions of cash. The growing unemployment and deepening poverty set off a wave of burglaries and robberies. Gangs burst into private residences and snatched anything they could lay their hands on. "We began to panic," Emily Brady remembered. "We said, 'Okay, pretty soon there will be nothing to be seized but the manuscripts. We've got to get them out.'"

Brady perceived an opportunity: at the end of July the secular Tuareg rebels had fled from Timbuktu. Faced with a shortage of fighters, the jihadis had been obliged to dismantle all but two checkpoints between Timbuktu and government territory. Controls on the roads going south had all but disappeared.

"It's time," Brady told Haidara.

"It's time," he agreed.

Sitting across from each other in Brady's sunlit dining room in Bamako, where she was still spending much of the year, Haidara and Brady discussed the logistical challenges that lay ahead of them. Transporting hundreds of thousands of priceless and fragile artifacts over 606 miles of unpredictable terrain would, they understood, be dangerous and hugely expensive. They would need to hire couriers and drivers and rent hundreds of trucks, four-wheel-drive vehicles, and taxis. They would require cash for bribes, spare parts, repairs, and gasoline. Brady calculated a budget of $700,000, and she and Haidara reached out to their contacts around the world. After hesitating in the initial stage of the rescue, donors had seen what the jihadis were capable of doing and many rushed to contribute. Haidara secured $100,000 from one of his most generous benefactors: Dubai's Juma Al Majid Center. The rescuers appealed to other longtime supporters, including the Prince Claus Fund in the Netherlands. "We're desperate," Brady said. A grant of $135,000 came through. A Kickstarter campaign raised another $60,000. The Dutch National Lottery, one of the richest cultural foundations in the Netherlands, wired $255,000 to Bamako.

Brady turned next to the director of a Dutch government

development agency in Bamako. European missions in Mali had plenty of unspent money in their coffers, because of a European Union embargo on bilateral aid to the Mali government since the military coup; the Dutch came up with another $100,000. Key Bank, an American regional institution headquartered in Cleveland, Ohio, arranged for those dollar contributions to be sent by wire transfer to Malian banks. The money was deposited into the Bamako accounts of trusted merchants in Timbuktu. The merchants then turned over cash, as needed, to Haidara's team.

In Timbuktu, Mohammed Touré cast about for sturdy four-wheel-drive vehicles—few were in good shape in the city—and recruited drivers and couriers. Emily Brady and Haidara were reluctant to use the same teams over and over—fearful they would be recognized and arrested—so they advised Mohammed Touré to hire as many couriers as he could. They ended up with hundreds. The majority were teenagers, the sons and nephews of Timbuktu's librarians—people whose loyalty would remain unquestioned.

At dawn one morning in late August, Mohammed Touré parked a Land Cruiser in front of a safe house in Timbuktu and loaded it with five chests filled with 1,500 manuscripts from the Mamma Haidara Library. Each chest was four feet long by two feet wide and two feet deep, and could snugly fit up to eight stacks of manuscripts—which ranged from single sheets, or folios, to thick volumes encased in leather covers. He draped a blanket over the footlockers, and climbed in the Land Cruiser beside the driver. Touré would be the test case, whose success or failure would determine the future of the operation.

A chill desert wind blew as they pulled away from the safe house and, beneath a brightening sky, drove south, past the Islamic Police headquarters in the former Commercial Bank of Mali, past a handful of once popular, now deserted guesthouses that lined the main street heading out of town, through the southern gate. The turbaned fighters who manned the first checkpoint on the southern outskirts of Timbuktu waved him through. They passed the municipal airport and there the tarmac ended. They crossed the Niger by car ferry and then for several hours drove unmolested on the sand track south, through an undulating landscape of dried-out riverbeds and faint patches of grass, scattered acacias, and scrub. In a market town called Douentza, they hit the second jihadi roadblock. Touré waved innocently, and they drove through without stopping.

They reached Konna, beside the Niger, a town of mud huts, labyrinthine alleyways, and a small mosque modeled after the Great Mud Mosque of Djenné. Konna marked the start of Malian government territory. Touré called Haidara on his cell phone and informed him with relief that he was now in the zone of safety. Then, just south of the line of control, his illusions of being safe dissolved. Malian troops—edgy, demoralized, and suspicious of anyone coming from the occupied north—stopped him at Sévaré, thirty-four miles south of the border.

The soldiers peered into the back. "What are you carrying?" they demanded. They pointed rifles at his chest and ordered him out. "Remove the trunks." One by one Touré and his driver pulled the manuscript-filled chests out of the rear compartment.

"What are you hiding here? Are you smuggling weapons?"

"No sir," Touré stammered, fearful that he would be thrown in prison or, this being wartime, even shot on the spot.

"Are you a spy? A jihadi?"

"No sir."

The soldiers smashed the locks on the chests with their gun butts, pulled out the volumes, and flipped roughly through the fragile pages. Touré kept silent as he watched them manhandle the precious volumes.

For two days and nights they kept him and his driver under guard in their spartan camp beside the roadblock, keeping him fed but refusing to explain why they were detaining him. He was frustrated, infuriated, but he kept his emotions under control. At last, they told him he could go. In Sévaré he paid off the driver and hired a new vehicle; the grueling drive over sand tracks and dirt roads from Timbuktu had damaged the suspension, steering box, and shock absorbers. Moreover, he was afraid that his captors had given the plate number to their comrades further south and they would stop him again.

This time, they stayed off the main road to Bamako, fearful of encountering more military roadblocks. They followed red-earth tracks through a landscape of skeletal thorn trees and dark sandstone outcroppings, occasionally passing herders with their goats, but few other signs of life. But the driver repeatedly lost his way. He was confused by the crisscrossing trails, and the four-wheel-drive vehicle, riding low because of the extra weight, broke down twice in the middle of flat, featureless brush. In the riverside town of Ségou—a pleasantly dilapidated town of rutted streets, motor scooters, donkey carts, and a few faded colonial-era villas 140 miles north of Bamako—Touré hit another military checkpoint marked by four-foot-high metal oil drums strewn across the road. "What's this? What are you doing? What are you smuggling?" they demanded. As Touré watched helplessly, the soldiers broke the locks with their gun butts for the second time, and rifled through the manuscripts one by one. He repacked, hired yet another vehicle, and got back on the road. By now he had had enough. Touré decided that the only way he could avoid further harrassment was to hire a military escort.

At a military post on the outskirts of Ségou he announced himself, explained his problem, and chatted with the local commander. "I need two vehicles filled with soldiers to get through the roadblocks. And I can pay you generously," he said. The commander assembled vehicles and troops. With military vehicles behind him and in front, Touré traveled the last 140 miles to Bamako without incident. At one o'clock in the morning, he paid the troops, shook hands with the men, and they turned around and returned to Ségou. Then, just down the road at the Porte d'Entrée, a mud-brown, double-arched gateway adorned with brown spires that resembled those of the Great Mud Mosque of Djenné, where the military searched every vehicle entering the capital, Touré found himself detained again. Exhausted and hungry, he was taken to a camp, thrown into a filthy cell, given nothing to eat or drink, and interrogated. Touré was permitted one phone call, to Haidara, who arrived at dawn with tea and bread, ate with him in his cell, and freed him with a "gift" to his jailers.

It had been a terrible ordeal that had lasted a week, yet no sooner had Touré delivered his cargo to Haidara than he returned to Timbuktu and prepared for the next journey. Touré would make more than thirty round-trips between Timbuktu and Bamako during the course of the rescue mission, personally saving tens of thousands of manuscripts. With each trip the going got easier: soldiers and police soon came to recognize him, and readily accepted his bribes in exchange for safe passage.

Every day, sometimes five times a day, Haidara traveled to the Porte d'Entrée, on Bamako's northern outskirts. Lengthy negotiations—and the invariable payment of gifts—allowed his couriers to slip through unmolested. Some returned to Bamako so shaken that they dropped out after a single mission, but most remained committed to the end. Haidara's supporters in Bamako stored rescued manuscripts temporarily in their houses, until a more lasting solution could be found. During the first ninety days, Haidara's couriers evacuated about 270,000 of the 377,000 manuscripts in Timbuktu, nearly three quarters of the books that had been held in the city's safe houses. Miraculously, despite being roughly treated by soldiers at roadblocks, all came through intact.

In July, when the jihadis took absolute control of the city of Timbuktu and instituted Shariah law, Haidara sent for his wife and their three younger children. Arriving in Bamako two days later, they settled with difficulty into their new home. Displaced relatives crowded the five rooms. The streets outside were noisy and squalid, a jumble of shabby concrete-block buildings and exhaust-spewing motorbikes. Haidara's wife, who had spent her life in Timbuktu, with the exception of her university years, fell into melancholy and barely ventured outdoors. Yet Haidara found it difficult to focus on his family's needs. The rescue effort, the responsibilities he felt toward Timbuktu's library owners and to his couriers, and the attachment he felt toward his own archive, overwhelmed all other concerns. "I had so many worries," he recalled months later. "They had entrusted everything to me. And if anything happened to their manuscripts, it would all be on my head."

"I saw him with the manuscripts, and I realized that this man has a direct relationship with them," said Emily Brady. "He feels as close to them as he does to his children."

And every day, it seemed, there was a new crisis, another risk of exposure. Early one morning, at the height of the smuggling operation, luck seemed to have run out for Haidara's nephew Mohammed Touré as he was exiting Timbuktu. Al Qaeda guards stopped his vehicle, searched the rear compartment, found metal chests filled with manuscripts beneath blankets, and ordered his driver at gunpoint to turn around. Islamic Police handed the cache—and Mohammed Touré—over to Abou Zeid. Once again, the twenty-five-year-old called upon every contact he had to bail him out of trouble.

Ibrahim Khalil Touré, the head of the Djingareyber neighborhood, influential member of the Crisis Committee, and close friend of Abdel Kader Haidara, paid another visit to Abou Zeid at the governor's headquarters, with the committee chairman. Both men vouched again for Mohammed Touré and "guaranteed" that the manuscripts were simply being taken out of Timbuktu for repairs. "That is the only reason, and then they will be brought back," Khalil Touré promised the jihadi leader. Perhaps Abou Zeid had other matters on his mind, or was feeling favorably disposed to Khalil Touré. "He had confidence in us, and we were his only liaison to the population of Timbuktu," Khalil Touré recalled. Whatever the case, Abou Zeid was willing to take Khalil Touré at his word. After forty-eight hours, to the surprise and relief of the Crisis Committee members, the emir of Timbuktu allowed Haidara's nephew to get back on the road with his cargo.

Touré had taken to sleeping at night in one of the empty exhibition rooms at the Mamma Haidara Library, to protect it from vandalism. Early one morning he heard a knock at the front door. When he opened it, Touré confronted three men carrying a video camera and a sound boom. They introduced themselves as a television documentary team from an international news channel, which had received permission from Ansar Dine and Al Qaeda in the Islamic Maghreb to document the conditions in occupied Timbuktu.

"You cannot come in," Touré told them, and double locked the door. Half an hour later, the film crew returned. This time they brought an escort of militants. The jihadis pushed their way inside and, as Touré stood by helplessly, led the crew through the library. Glass cases stood empty. The workshops where manuscripts were digitized, repaired with the strong Japanese Kitakata paper, and stored in moisture-proof boxes, were bare. "Where are the manuscripts?" the militants demanded.

"I . . . I have no idea," Touré said. "The proprietors must have taken them all. I don't know what happened."

The film crew and their jihadi escorts left, and Touré never heard another word about the incident.

15

During the fall of 2012 tensions in northern Mali were rising. After Iyad Ag Ghali's zealots demolished the tombs of Sufi Islamic saints in Timbuktu that summer, and began carrying out stonings and amputations under Shariah law, President François Hollande of France declared that the presence of a radical Islamic state five hours by air from Paris constituted an existential threat that had to be confronted. U.S. Secretary of State Hillary Clinton told the United Nations in September 2012 that "the chaos and violence in Mali [threatens] to undermine the stability of the entire region." In October, the United Nations Security Council affirmed Resolution 2071, calling for military intervention in Mali. By late fall, plans had been drawn up for 3,300 troops under the banner of the African Union and the Economic Community of West African States to invade the north, supported logistically by the United States and Europe. "As each day goes by, Al Qaeda and other organizations are strengthening their hold on northern Mali," warned General Carter Ham, the top U.S. military commander in Africa in early December, claiming that Al Qaeda was running terrorist camps and providing arms and explosives to the brutal Islamist group Boko Haram. Mali was emerging as a test case for international intervention: a barely functional state that had lost control over nearly two thirds of its territory to an army of jihadis.

Al Qaeda in the Islamic Maghreb responded with threats. "We warn all the countries that are planning aggression against us, [we will mete out] merciless punishment," vowed the rebel spokesman known as Red Beard, the father-in-law of the one-eyed jihadi leader, Mokhtar Belmokhtar, and the fanatic who had surprised Haidara's nephew in the act of secretly transporting manuscripts to a safe house. "We will bring this war to the center of their capitals. And we warn them, we have hundreds of holy warriors ready for martyrdom." Suicide bombers, he claimed, "are already in the capitals with their explosives." In late December, Ghali, Belmokhtar, Abou Zeid, and eight hundred fighters gathered near Essakane, the former site of the Festival in the Desert, for a war council. The music impresario Manny Ansar had no doubt as to why the location had been chosen. By assembling in the same corner of the Sahara where musicians and Western aficionados had once performed and partied through the night, AQIM was sending a message to all who had dreamed that a secular, liberal society could take root around Timbuktu. "It was no longer a place for sin, no longer for debauchery, no longer for the international hippies of the world," Ansar would say. "It was a place for jihad."

For ten days, according to a Timbuktu butcher who was hired to prepare food for the assemblage, the three jihadi commanders and their fighters trained, prayed, and feasted inside a near-impregnable natural fortress in the desert, a field of sand and acacia groves surrounded by serrated walls of sandstone, with a single narrow entry that could be easily guarded to keep out intruders. The jihadis had kidnapped a moderate imam from Timbuktu in revenge for his denunciations during Friday prayers, and forced him at gunpoint to lead the men in their devotions in an outdoor mosque in a clearing among the thorn trees. They ran for miles each morning, carried out simulated ground assaults, fired their Kalashnikovs at the cliffs, and wheeled out their mortars, rocket launchers, and howitzers, pulverizing boulders and gouging chunks out of solid walls of rock. At night they stoked their zeal by slaughtering cows and turning them over to the butcher, who divided the meat into hundreds of pieces. Or they ate *méchoui*—an entire sheep or lamb roasted on a spit—while sitting around campfires, telling tales about the Prophet. After ten days the entire convoy returned to Timbuktu. At the entrance to the city the jihadis posed for a film crew, brandishing their rifles in unison with the war cry, *"Allahu Akbar."*

One morning in early January, Mohammed Touré and other members of Haidara's rescue team watched more than one hundred pickup trucks carrying eight hundred men, with heavy weaponry mounted on the beds, rumble through the streets of Timbuktu. In clouds of dust the vehicles disappeared through the southern gate of the city and headed for the Niger River port of Kabara. Each vehicle carried as many as ten fighters brandishing Kalashnikovs and rocket-propelled grenade launchers. "They are off to war," thought Ibrahim Khalil Touré, who was apprehensive but also hopeful of a rout, and relieved that the confrontation was not taking place in Timbuktu. Five miles south of Timbuktu, the radicals inched past market stalls and assembled along the sandy bank of the river. There, they commandeered three ferries and shuttled their vehicles across the Niger. The operation lasted the entire day.

Their objective was Konna, the Niger River town of 35,000 people that marked the northern limit of Malian government territory. Five hundred Malian troops and a handful of trucks and armored personnel carriers formed a flimsy front line in the bush north of the town. Citizens along the two-hundred-mile route from Timbuktu had informed the army of the jihadis' approach, and the soldiers were given an extra advantage when the attackers became bogged down in the mud for twenty-four hours after detouring from the main highway to follow a hidden track toward Konna. The short winter rains had turned the back roads of the north into nearly impassable quagmires.

On the night of Wednesday, January 9, 2013, having extracted themselves from the mud, but having also lost any element of surprise, the jihadis launched their assault. Konna residents cowered in their houses, listening to the explosions of heavy weaponry and the crackle of Kalashnikov fire, and watching muzzle flashes light up the night. The five-hundred-man government force pushed back the Al Qaeda attackers after six hours. "The military returned to their camp to eat around dawn, after having repulsed the first jihadi attack. They thought they had achieved a victory," a schoolteacher in Konna told me a year later as we strolled past mud-walled compounds brightened with purple splashes of bougainvillea. A small mud mosque modeled after the Great Mud Mosque of Djenné—multiple spires, scaffolding made of bundles of palm sticks—rose over pools of mud, lagoons, and patches of marsh grass left from the winter rains.

"They ate, they were exultant," the teacher remembered. There were fist pumps and high-fives with Konna's denizens—expressions of satisfaction by men who had surprised themselves and staved off a disaster. "They were very pleased with themselves," the teacher went on. "All was calm—and then the jihadis returned at nine o'clock in the morning."

They had reinforcements this time. One hundred fifty pickup trucks filled with fighters attacked Konna from the north and the east. Another fifty vehicles from Gao circled around to the south.

"They flanked them, they entered Konna, they were everywhere," he told me. The jihadis fired heavy machine guns and rocket-propelled grenades. Soldiers fled in panic through the dirt streets, some stripping off their camouflage uniforms and begging locals for civilian clothes. Fifty soldiers were killed and hundreds wounded.

That Thursday afternoon, the Islamists occupied Konna and summoned people to the mud mosque. "Your town was long terrorized by the Malian government, and now we have taken it," a radical imam declared. "There is no mayor, no police, and no army. There is only us." Shariah law would take effect immediately, he said, ordering women to cover themselves or face a whipping in the town square. That evening, townspeople watched nine more vehicles roll into town from the direction of Timbuktu. At the head of the procession, clad in a white turban and pale blue boubou, savoring the jihadis' latest victory, was Iyad Ag Ghali. The capture of Konna had brought the jihadis one step closer to their goal: seizing control of the entire country and making a foreign intervention difficult, if not impossible. Ghali's apparent plan was to wait for the arrival in the south of Abou Zeid's militiamen, who were following a different road from Timbuktu. Then the two jihadi leaders would join forces on the highway, and lead their troops and vehicles all the way to Bamako.

16

Abdel Kader Haidara spent Thursday, January 10, the day that the jihadi forces of Iyad Ag Ghali captured Konna and prepared to advance further south, ensconced at the spacious, sunlit home of the American expatriate Emily Brady near the Niger River in Bamako. They had been raising money from European donors, running a crowdsourcing campaign, and sending cash to couriers in the north. Haidara was also dashing back and forth between Brady's home and the double-arched Porte d'Entrée marking the north entrance to the capital, receiving his couriers and guiding them and their precious cargo to twenty-five storage places around the city.

But the dramatic events on the ground had thrown the rescue operation into disarray. Hundreds of jihadi vehicles had just seized Konna, stranding the team's couriers and the manuscripts. Now they were threatening to take over all of Mali. The Malian army had fallen back to Sévaré, the site of the regional airport. But the

demoralized troops were in no condition to resist the jihadi onslaught, and their commander was talking openly about shedding
his uniform, slipping into the bush, and creating a guerrilla force to
combat the rebels.

Diplomats and Malian government officials in Bamako expected that the new front line would quickly collapse; from Sévaré,
the Islamist army would have an easy, seven-hour journey straight
down the highway to Bamako. Nothing would then prevent them
from turning Mali into "Sahelistan"—an armed terrorist state in
the heart of Africa. They would likely seize Western hostages for
ransom and institute Shariah law in the capital. An exodus of diplomatic families and other expatriates from Bamako had begun;
the U.S. embassy had initiated a test of its emergency notification
service to prepare for the evacuation of two thousand American
citizens. Neither Haidara nor the hundreds of thousands of manuscripts he had by now secreted in the homes of his partners would
be safe. There would be nowhere left to hide.

As the day wore on, Haidara kept a cell phone on each ear, and
a cell phone in each hand, receiving reports from his couriers every
few minutes: the sweat acted as an adhesive, gluing the devices to
his ears. "Bring me more tea," he said, signaling Brady's house-
keeper. He drank dozens of cups of heavily sweetened tea every day.
The sugar rush kept him going. But the constant stress had caused
his weight to balloon, raised his blood pressure, and given him a
gastric ulcer.

"You shouldn't drink so much because of your stomach," Brady
said. He waved her off and drank another cup.

While Haidara and Brady were confronting the growing danger
in the north, momentous decisions were being made a continent
away. At the Élysée Palace in Paris, the French president, François

Hollande, held an emergency meeting with his cabinet, took urgent calls from his ambassador in Bamako and from the interim Malian president, Dioncounda Traoré—the former leader of Mali's National Assembly, who had replaced the head of the military junta in a deal brokered by regional governments—and conferred with Barack Obama at the White House.

Since well before the jihadi takeover of northern Mali, the French had been intensifying their on-the-ground operations in the desert spaces that had been all but abandoned by the Malian military. In January 2011, following the abduction of two twenty-five-year-old French friends, Vincent Delory and Antoine de Léocour, from a restaurant in Niamey, Niger, a French surveillance plane had pursued Al Qaeda in the Islamic Maghreb through the desert into eastern Mali; there, French Special Forces ambushed the kidnappers, and the hostages were killed in the exchange of fire. Ten months later, a dozen French Special Forces commandos in Sévaré, near Mopti, were deployed to hunt for the abducted French geologists in Hombori. The French had lost patience with the Malian military—fed up with their complicity with drug traffickers and reports of their selling of weapons and ammunition to the radicals in the desert, convinced that they couldn't be induced to fight. "The French were disgusted [by the Malian army]," recalled Vicki Huddleston, then serving as the deputy assistant secretary of defense for Africa in Washington.

France's historic and linguistic ties to its former colony, the prospect of a jihadi-controlled state in Francophone West Africa, and the presence of eight thousand French expatriates in Bamako led Hollande quickly to a decision: France would take military action to rescue the country from Al Qaeda in the Islamic Maghreb. Hollande, the leader of a European power that had frequently intervened in French-speaking Africa in recent years, from Rwanda to the Côte d'Ivoire to the Central African Republic, with varying motives and varying degrees of support, this time enjoyed a strong popular mandate. In a poll, seventy-five percent of the French public said that they backed a rapid strike against the radicals. "The French people are ready to support a military operation as long as the objectives are clear and seem legitimate," one French defense analyst told *The New York Times*.

Hours after Iyad Ag Ghali marched triumphantly through the muddy alleys of Konna, people who lived near the Sévaré airport, thirty-six miles south, saw a helicopter land under cover of darkness and discharge fifteen white soldiers onto the tarmac. On Friday afternoon, January 11, a five-seat Aérospatiale Gazelle helicopter swept in low over Konna, and fired rockets at the militants' positions. "At first we thought it belonged to the Malian army," one trucker, who was burying the corpses of soldiers in a trench when the chopper arrived, told me a few days later, when I met him at a friend's house in Sévaré. He returned to Konna and climbed onto his rooftop, "but all I could see was dust." Militants fired back, striking the pilot in the groin, severing his femoral artery, and causing France's first fatality in the conflict.

A second Gazelle engaged the jihadis later that afternoon. After dark, four Mirage 2000D jets carried out precise strikes on twelve jihadi vehicles and the military camp on a rise overlooking the Niger River in Konna. Ghali and his militants piled their dead and wounded into the beds of pickup trucks and began their long retreat north. Dozens of bodies littered the streets.

The Konna schoolteacher whom I had been talking to about the battle a year after it happened escorted me to the abandoned military camp on a rise above the Niger, briefly seized by the jihadis, and then attacked by French aircraft. A twelve-foot-deep crater filled with twisted metal and concrete was all that remained of two barracks in which the jihadis had encamped overnight. Back at his kindergarten and day-care center, the teacher unfolded a crudely made jihadi flag—fashioned from a piece of white linen, with a black field in the center and a pair of black-and-brown Kalashnikov rifles drawn in the white margins—and laid it out in front of me. He had ripped it off the radio antenna of a destroyed jihadi vehicle as the Al Qaeda soldiers fled from Konna. "This flag lived only for nineteen hours—from Thursday the 10th of January at 3:45 p.m. to Friday the 11th, at 10 a.m," he had scrawled across the bottom margin.

Operation Serval, named after a small cat indigenous to the Sahara, gained momentum in the following days. French C-160 and An-124 transports airlifted ground troops, vehicles, and equipment into Bamako, and more French forces arrived by road from the Côte d'Ivoire. By January 15 France had eight hundred troops on the ground. The French government announced that it would triple the force to 2,500 soldiers by the end of January. Days later, the French bombed AQIM positions in the town of Diabily, near Djenné, captured by Abou Zeid and hundreds of his men on January 14. Hunkered down in the packed-dirt home of a Diabily farmer while his men camped under mango trees, the jihadi commander had planned to use Diabily as a base from which to continue his advance to Bamako. But French warplanes bombed them with precision, destroying dozens of vehicles. On January 17, the Islamists fled north under a withering French ground and air assault, camouflaging their remaining vehicles with so much foliage that they appeared to the population of Diabily like moving bushes.

The United States bore some responsibility for the Malian military debacle, having frittered away tens of millions of dollars on inadequate training of Malian soldiers. Now the Pentagon stepped into the fight: the United States airlifted hundreds of French troops and weapons aboard Air Force C-17 transport planes, refueled French warplanes with a KC-135 tanker aircraft, and provided drone surveillance. Vicki Huddleston, who had recently left the Department of Defense, called for vigorous U.S. "intelligence, equipment, financing, and training of a West African intervention force," in *The New York Times*.

While Malians were quick to applaud the American assistance, some Malian intellectuals attacked the French intervention as a neocolonialist enterprise, and lashed out at former president Nicolas Sarkozy for his central role in the NATO attacks that had unseated Qaddafi and destabilized the region. But most Malians, including Abdel Kader Haidara, seemed ready to forgive the French missteps in Libya, and welcomed them with tricolors and the gratitude of the liberated.

17

Abdel Kader Haidara's couriers were grounded, and war had broken out across the north. The French intervention had stopped the jihadis from capturing Bamako and declaring all of Mali a caliphate. But as hundreds of French troops advanced toward Timbuktu, the militants were enraged and threatening to take revenge. The manuscripts were at risk from both Al Qaeda, who seemed likely to lash out at anything that the West considered valuable, and from the French military, which had turned the entire north into a zone of gunfire and destruction. Missiles had slammed into jihadi barracks and military bases, command-and-control centers, villas appropriated by extremist commanders, and hundreds of vehicles. Mirage jets, Super Pumas, Tigers, Harfang drones, Alpha Jets, C-130s, and Mi-35s streaked across the skies of northern Mali. French helicopters pursued the radicals' convoys into the roadless desert. Ground forces moved north to Timbuktu and Gao and sealed the roads to

civilian traffic. A total of 791 footlockers containing 100,000 manuscripts remained hidden in safe houses in Timbuktu. They faced a
growing threat of being found and destroyed; Haidara could not
afford to wait. He was obliged to consider the only viable alternative
to the road: the Niger River.

Emily Brady had pressed him from the early days of the evacuation to bring at least some of the manuscripts to government territory via the river, but Haidara had refused. He was worried, he said,
about fast-moving currents and unpredictable winds, horrified by
the possibility that a pinasse could capsize and send his manuscripts
to the bottom of the Niger. But now that he had reluctantly changed
his mind, the mule carts that had carried the chests from libraries to
safe houses during the summer were called into action again. Down
rough tracks through rice paddies and vegetable fields, too narrow
for cars, the carts pulled stacks of trunks toward the river. Village
chiefs, whom Haidara had come to know in his travels throughout
the region, opened their mud-walled homes for temporary storage.
In Toya, a village of Sorhai fishermen, consisting of a few dozen
flat-roofed mud huts lining bare sandbanks about seven miles from
Timbuktu, the hereditary chief, Mohannan Sidi Maiga, played a
critical and clandestine role.

I visited Toya one sweltering August afternoon long after the
boatlift was over, chartering a pinasse at Timbuktu's main port of
Kabara—a thirty-foot-long craft with five pink-cushioned benches,
and a hull brightly painted in blue, yellow, and green arabesques.
The pilot motored the pinasse slowly down the center of the olive
green Niger. A canvas roof tethered to curving wooden supports
shielded me from the sun. The river widened, and a steady wind
blew across the bow, rocking the creaky wooden vessel alarmingly.
The landscape on either side of the river was brown and barren,
rising gently, speckled with grass and lone acacia trees. "The Niger,
with its vast and misty horizons, is more like an inland ocean than a

river," wrote Félix Dubois in *Timbuctoo the Mysterious*, which I had brought along with me on this journey. "Its waters break upon its banks in the monotonously cadenced waves of the Mediterranean shores; and when winds, grown violent in the desert, swell its waves into a great race, seasickness will convince the most rebellious that the river Niger is of kin to oceans."

After a turbulent, thirty-minute journey that made me understand Haidara's hesitancy about transporting the manuscripts by river, we arrived in Toya, clambered past women scrubbing their laundry with bars of thick brown soap in the shallows, and walked through sandy warrens to the home of Maiga, a lanky man in a red T-shirt and gray slacks, whose skinny arms hung to his knees. "When the jihadis arrived [in April 2012] we sensed the danger, and people from Savama-DCI visited us here to tell us that they might need our help," he told me, as we sat in plastic chairs beneath a burlap tarp, suspended by bamboo poles, in an outdoor meeting area next to his house.

One moonlit night in the middle of January, as the French ground forces rolled toward Timbuktu, the footlockers arrived in donkey carts. Maiga distributed them among the villagers. "Toya is off the track, it's a little more hidden than the main port, so we figured they would be safe here," he told me. Even so, Maiga knew that the Islamic Police could raid the village at any time. "The jihadis had passed through here many times during the occupation, to make sure that women were covered and that people were applying their version of Islam," he said. "They arrested nonmarried men and women, boys and girls, who were together. They tied their hands behind their backs and took them to Timbuktu."

While he and other village chiefs were preparing the manuscripts for transport by water, Haidara's team in Timbuktu traveled to Kabara, five miles south of Timbuktu. In the once bustling, now dead quiet port, where pinasses from Bamako and Mopti had, before the jihadi occupation, brought a steady flow of electronics, sacks of grain, and other goods—as well as Western tourists—to Timbuktu, the team struck up discreet conversations with boatmen. Most were idle, desperate for work, simmering with hostility toward the Islamists, and eager to pitch in to save the country's patrimony.

Haidara's team recruited dozens, and laid out the rules: Each pinasse would have two couriers and two captains, so that they could keep moving on the river twenty-four hours a day. No vessel could carry more than fifteen footlockers, to minimize losses should any boat be seized or sunk. The boats would load at beachfront villages such as Toya to avoid attracting the jihadis' attention. Their destination would be Djenné, located on the floodplain between the Niger and the Bani Rivers, 223 miles and two days south of Timbuktu. Once the footlockers had been unloaded safely in government territory, trucks, taxis, and other vehicles would receive the cargo and continue the journey to Bamako, 332 miles further south.

While Haidara and his team prepared to launch the boatlift, the jihadi army was in retreat. Two convoys of blood-streaked pickup trucks, led by Iyad Ag Ghali and Abou Zeid and filled with corpses and the groaning and bloodied injured, made their way back toward Timbuktu, while another convoy veered off toward Gao. Choking clouds of sand and dust rose above Abou Zeid and Ghali's caravans as they rolled for hours along the rough track beneath a sweltering sun. The militant leaders had planned to converge triumphantly with their forces in Bamako and declare Mali a jihadi state. But they had not anticipated the rapid intervention of the French army, and their miscalculation had brought about a debacle. Upon reaching Timbuktu, the militant leaders dropped the injured at the government hospital, buried the dead, and demanded that the director of Radio Azawad, formerly Radio Communal Bouctou, announce that the jihadis had defeated the Malian army.

"We killed and injured hundreds of them," Ghali declared.

"How many did you lose?" the director asked.

"That isn't your concern," the jihadi leader replied.

Soon the French army made its first aerial forays over the city. Drones and French warplanes buzzed in the skies, a portent of the coming attack.

The imam of Timbuktu's most venerated mosque, Djingareyber, approached the jihadi authorities, who had turned increasingly agitated and hostile, regarding a matter of great importance for the city's Sufis. Mawloud, the weeklong celebration of the Prophet Mohammed's birthday, and the most joyful occasion on Timbuktu's calendar, fell on the 21st of January, only days away. Originating as a Shi'ite festival in Persia in the twelfth century, Mawloud had arrived in Timbuktu around 1600, and it had been celebrated with gusto ever since. A period of feasting, singing, and dancing, Mawloud combined the rituals of Sufi Islam with a celebration of Timbuktu's rich literary traditions. It culminated with an evening gathering of thousands of people in the large sandy square in front of the Sankoré Mosque and a public reading of some of the city's most treasured manuscripts. For a city that had been starved of a reason to celebrate for nearly a year, the imam of Djingareyber saw Mawloud as a critical morale booster, a reed of hope for a despondent population.

The imam asked Abou Zeid for permission to plan the festivities. "Normally our *marabouts* read from our manuscripts for this festival," the imam explained.

"I don't have a problem with this, imam," Abou Zeid said, surprising the religious leader with his apparent receptivity. But Abou Zeid added that he was a fighter, not an intellectual, and would have to defer to his "religious experts."

Al Qaeda's minister of moral enforcement in Timbuktu listened impassively as the imam, joined by members of Timbuktu's Crisis Committee, made an emotional plea for the festival.

"That holiday does not exist," he announced when they had finished. It constituted a "reprehensible innovation." He cited a Hadith in which the Prophet had declared, "I urge you to follow my Sunnah and the way of the rightly guided caliphs after me; adhere to it and cling to it firmly. Beware of newly invented things, for every newly invented thing is an innovation (bid'ah) and every innovation is a going-astray."

"But it is sanctioned by other Hadith," the imam argued.

"Bring me proof," the bearded, turbaned morality minister replied.

The Sufi imams of Timbuktu, marabouts, and members of the crisis group created a "Committee of Proof" to assemble all the evidence they could muster from the texts supporting the festival. Although many Sunni scholars had railed through the centuries against making the Prophet's birthday a special occasion, the Committee of Proof found Hadith that suggested that some leeway existed. Several Hadith commanded Muslims to "venerate" the Prophet, without stipulating the manner in which that should be done. Verse 114 from the Surah Al-Ma'idah in the Koran suggested that the earliest followers of the Prophet considered feasting a proper way to commemorate an event of religious significance. "Eisa, the son of Maryam, said, 'O Allah, O our Lord! Send down to us a table spread from heaven, so that it may become a day of celebration for us.'" And Mohammed himself had acknowledged the glory of the day that he came into the world: "The Holy Prophet (Peace and Blessings of Allah be Upon Him) said: 'When my mother gave birth to me she saw a light proceeding from her which showed her the castles of Syria.'"

Al Qaeda's morality minister again listened without a change of expression as the Committee of Proof recited the relevant verses. "Fine," he said when they were done. "But you still can't do it. There will be men and women meeting in the streets, and that is inappropriate. You can't do it. That's it. There won't be a Mawloud festival."

Then the morals enforcer delivered a chilling message. "You need to bring us those manuscripts," he said, "and we are going to burn them."

In the gathering darkness, with Timbuktu's jihadi leaders demanding the manuscripts and the members of the Crisis Committee promising to deliver them, but stalling for time, a lone vessel left from Toya on a test run. The thirty-foot boat motored down the center of the river, passing flat mud banks, thatched huts, and low dunes silhouetted against the twilight sky. "The moments of sunset upon the river are those of the greatest intensity of life," Dubois wrote in *Timbuctoo the Mysterious*. "The canoes multiply near the villages bringing the fruit of the field to buildings to which the people will flock for tomorrow's market . . . and the great trees on the banks are so whitened at this hour by the sleeping ospreys that they seem to have been covered by a fall of snow." Swells thrashed against the vessel as it cut through the water toward Djenné. Then, with alarm, the couriers and captains heard an engine and the whir of rotor blades. A French attack helicopter swooped down low over the water and hovered above the craft. The pilots shone spotlights on the boat, blinding those onboard. "Open the footlockers," they demanded over a loudspeaker. The French warned the crew that they would sink the boat on suspicion of smuggling weapons if the couriers refused. The terrified teenaged couriers fumbled with the locks beneath the glare, flung the chests open, and then stepped aside. The pilots could see that the chests were filled with only paper. The helicopters flew off.

Shortly afterward, twenty pinasses, each carrying fifteen metal chests filled with manuscripts, motored in a convoy down the Niger from a port near Timbuktu. Haidara and Brady had decided that the boats should travel in flotillas, both to speed up the evacuation and provide, they hoped, a certain safety in numbers. Passing beyond the monochromatic emptiness of Tuareg territory, they reached a transition zone where the arid Saharan wastes give way to more fertile climes—palm trees, thickets of low bushes. Ahead lay Lake Debo, the inland sea formed by the seasonal flooding of central Mali's inland Niger Delta, "a huge basin of water . . . a veritable sea. . . . Its shores are invisible, for no distant mountains betray their boundaries," Dubois wrote.

But as they approached the lake, the Niger seemed to disappear before their eyes, swallowed up by a sea of grass. "It is in truth a singular element, being neither land nor water, but a strange mixture of both," Dubois observed. "From a depth of six to eight feet the tall grasses emerge, thick and green, and wearing all the appearance of a great field. . . . We are no longer upon the water, but seem . . . to be sliding over grassy steppes streaked with watery paths." The aquatic meadow formed an ideal sanctuary during this period of chaos for bandits. As the convoy threaded its way along channels through the grass, a dozen turbaned men brandishing Kalashnikovs emerged from the dense vegetation. They ordered the flotilla to stop. Forcing open the locks, the men thumbed through the Arabic texts and brightly colored geometric patterns covering the brittle pages.

"We will keep these," they announced.

The couriers pleaded with them and offered their cheap Casio watches, silver bracelets, rings, and necklaces. When that failed, they got on the phone with Haidara, in Bamako. He urged the bandits to release the couriers and the cargo, promising to deliver a sizeable ransom as soon as possible.

"Trust me on this, we will get you your money," Haidara said.

Haidara couldn't afford not to pay them, he would later explain: thousands of other manuscripts were already heading downriver.

The couriers waited nervously beside their metal trunks while the bandits debated what to do. At last, the gunmen, understanding Haidara's predicament, released the boats and the manuscripts. One of Haidara's agents, as promised, delivered the cash four days later.

At Brady's home in Bamako, Haidara spent fifteen hours a day talking simultaneously on eight cell phones to his team of couriers, whom he had instructed to brief him every fifteen minutes when they were on the road. Huge sheets of brown butcher paper taped to one wall tracked the names of the teenagers, their latest cell phone contacts, the number of footlockers each was carrying, their locations, and conditions en route. Brady sent text messages to her donors informing them of progress: 75 FOOTLOCKERS GOING THROUGH, OUR KIDS HAVE MADE IT ACROSS LAKE DEBO, ARE NOW IN MOPTI. During one frenetic day toward the end of the boatlift, 150 taxicabs, each carrying three footlockers and a courier, made the journey from Djenné to Bamako.

In Timbuktu, French Mirage jets bombed Al Qaeda's barracks and then targeted Abou Zeid's residence—delivering a rocket that blew out the back half of Qaddafi's former villa and wrecked the salon where the King of African Kings, then the Al Qaeda emir, had held meetings and receptions. Abou Zeid, anticipating the French attack, had vacated the premises well ahead of time.

A few months after the attack I followed a faint sand track past thorn trees and a few walled-off compounds to a rise in the desert. Behind an iron gate stood a Moorish-style villa of beige concrete, with oblong windows and turquoise ornamental trim, surrounded by a garden of pine and palm trees. "We still call this place 'Chirac's Dune,'" my Tuareg guide, Azima Ag Ali Mohammed, told me. In 2006, he explained, Qaddafi had chosen to build this desert retreat on the exact site where the French president had met hundreds of dignitaries in a Tuareg tent during a 2003 tour of Francophone West Africa. "Qaddafi was jealous of Western leaders," Azima went on, and wanted to prove that he was their equal.

We squeezed through a gap in the gate and walked through the unlocked front door. "This is where Abou Zeid held his meetings," he said, leading me into a low-ceilinged room divided by square columns. Shards of glass, marble tile fragments, and chunks of concrete littered the floor. Broken roof slabs blocked the view of the garden. As I walked around the outside of the house—skirting the charred remains of a Nissan sedan, bullet casings, and rubber hoses from Qaddafi's irrigation system—I heard a rustling. I looked up, startled, to see a white-robed herdsman leading six donkeys up and over the huge pile of rubble. "*Salaam Aleikum,*" he said, with a deferential nod of his head, then continued on his way.

After the French scored a direct hit on Abou Zeid's residence, the Al Qaeda emir summoned the Crisis Committee for a final meeting. The hospitals were overflowing with the dead and injured, Ibrahim Khalil Touré remembered, and the jihadi leader was in a somber mood. Letting his calm demeanor slip for the first time, Abou Zeid slammed his hand down on the table in the dark conference room. "There can be no mockery of us," he warned. "If we see anyone celebrating in front of his house, he will be immediately killed. If we see anybody laughing or ridiculing us, he will be killed." Abou Zeid warned Touré and the other committee members that the penalty for looting Arab shops in revenge would also be death. "The population should stay calm, and should not aid the enemy, and not mock us as long as we are here," he reemphasized. Abou Zeid dismissed the group at nine o'clock that night. The end, Touré was sure, was imminent.

The next morning, Iyad Ag Ghali packed his Land Cruiser and slipped out of town. His dreams of a caliphate unified under Shariah law had collapsed, and the protean figure that had morphed from rebel leader to presidential security adviser to jihadi had taken on a new identity: fugitive. Abou Zeid lingered in town for another four days. On Friday, January 25, after prayers, he and his lieutenants slaughtered a lamb and prepared a *méchoui*—the entire animal skinned and roasted on a spit—and ate it in the dunes. Abou Zeid placed his five European hostages in a pair of SUVs and drove out of the city in a nine-vehicle convoy. His militiamen destroyed the city's mobile phone tower and stripped the radio station of its consoles and computers. Then they turned their attention to the objects that they had mostly ignored until now: the manuscripts.

18

On Friday morning, January 25, 2013, fifteen jihadis entered the restoration and conservation rooms on the ground floor of the Ahmed Baba Institute in Sankoré, the government library that Al Qaeda in the Islamic Maghreb had taken over the previous April. For nearly a year, thousands of manuscripts left behind by the Ahmed Baba staff had been sitting in the open, stacked on shelves and lying on restoration tables, while the jihadis prayed, trained, ate, and slept around them.

Now, on the verge of being expelled from Timbuktu, the Al Qaeda fighters would exact their retribution. The men swept 4,202 manuscripts off lab tables and shelves, and carried them into the tiled courtyard. In an act of nihilistic vindictiveness that they had been threatening for months, the jihadis made a pyre of the ancient texts, including fourteenth- and fifteenth-century works of physics, chemistry, and mathematics, their fragile pages covered with algebraic formulas, charts of the heavens, and molecular diagrams. They doused the manuscripts in gasoline, watching in satisfaction as the liquid saturated them, and tossed in a lit match. The brittle pages and their dry leather covers ignited in a flash. The flames rose higher, licking at a concrete column around which the volumes had been arranged. In minutes, the work of some of Timbuktu's greatest savants and scientists, preserved for centuries, hidden from the nineteenth-century jihadis and the French conquerors, survivors of floods and the pernicious effects of dust, bacteria, water, and insects, were consumed by the inferno.

Seven months later, I walked through the Sankoré neighborhood and entered the institute, a three-story labyrinth of long hallways, Moorish-style arches, and beige stucco walls made to resemble traditional mud brick. Just inside the entrance, a white-bearded septuagenarian, wearing a white turban and matching white gown, sat on the floor, one leg extended, the other propping up a cardboard box used for manuscript storage. The box was filled with charred scraps of paper. He sifted through the blackened bits, arranging them as if assembling a jigsaw puzzle. He stared intently at the remains, mumbling to himself, lost in his futile task.

"A caretaker saw smoke rising," curator Bouya Haidara, a gnomish figure who bears no relation to Abdel Kader Haidara, told me, as he stood beside the blackened concrete pillar, the only remaining evidence, beside the charred scraps in the manuscript box, of the crime that had taken place here. The caretaker had retrieved a few scorched pages from the fire, but the rest had been destroyed. Then, leaving nothing but blackened page fragments and ashes, the jihadis followed Abou Zeid and Ghali into the desert.

And yet out of this wanton act of destruction the curators of the Ahmed Baba Institute had managed to extract a small victory. Bouya escorted me down a wide flight of stairs to the basement, leading the way by flashlight, since power had still not been restored to the city months after the occupation. He turned the key in the lock, and cast his beam over black, moisture-resistant cardboard boxes neatly arranged on dozens of metal shelves, as tidy and ordered as the stacks of a university library in the United States. During their ten months of living at the Ahmed Baba Institute, the fighters had never bothered to venture downstairs to this dark and climate-controlled storage room hidden behind a locked door. Inside were stacks containing 10,603 restored manuscripts, folios, and leather-encased volumes, among the finest works in the collection. "All of them—untouched," Bouya Haidara said.

In Bamako, Abdel Kader Haidara saw the burning of the manuscripts as a confirmation of the jihadis' intentions—and a vindication of his remarkable undertaking. Starting with no money besides the meager sum in his savings account, Haidara had recruited a loyal circle of volunteers, badgered and shamed the international community into funding the scheme by presenting it as an epic showdown between civilization and the forces of barbarism, raised $1 million—a tremendous sum for Timbuktu—and hired hundreds of amateur smugglers in Timbuktu and beyond.

In a low-tech operation that seemed quaintly anomalous in the second decade of the twenty-first century, he and his team had transported to safety, by river and by road, past hostile jihadi guards and suspicious Malian soldiers, past bandits, attack helicopters, and other potentially lethal obstacles, almost all of Timbuktu's 377,000 manuscripts. Not one had been lost en route. "Abdel Kader and I experienced something I have trouble describing. Power, strength, perseverance can't adequately articulate what it was," Emily Brady said in her online interview via Reddit. "We kept thinking that we had to lose some manuscripts—theft, bandits, belligerents . . . combat, books in canoes on the Niger River—we had to lose some, right? Well, we didn't. Not a single manuscript was compromised during the evacuation—nada, zero. They all made it."

Timbuktu had been the incubator for the richness of Islam, and Islam in its perverted form had attempted to destroy it. But the original power of the culture itself, and the people, like Haidara, who had become entranced by that power, had saved the great manuscripts in the end. Haidara would often be asked in the coming months if the effort had been worth the trouble. What would have happened, interlocutors demanded, if he had sat back and done nothing? "The only response can be 'I cannot be one-hundred-percent certain,'" he would respond. "But I think that if we had left them alone, if we had not acted, many more would have ended up like the manuscripts at the Ahmed Baba Institute."

Haidara often chose such moments to portray Timbuktu as a paragon of moderation and intellectual ferment that had fallen victim to a once-in-a-millennium conflagration. The reality, of course, is more complex and less flattering to the city's reputation. Timbuktu had witnessed the killings of scholars by the Emperor Sunni Ali in the 1300s, the rise of the anti-Semitic preacher Muhammed Al Maghili in the 1490s, the edicts of King Askia Mohammed banning and imprisoning Jews during that same decade, and the implementation of Shariah law in Timbuktu by the jihadis in the early and mid-1800s. The city seemed to be in a constant state of flux, periods of openness and liberalism followed by waves of intolerance and repression. "These Wahhabis who came to Timbuktu in 2012 represented something entirely new," Haidara always insisted, though it was clear that similar strains of anti-intellectualism, religious purification, and barbarism had coursed through the city repeatedly over the preceding five centuries.

As Abou Zeid was fleeing Timbuktu and his comrades were destroying whatever manuscripts they could lay their hands on, I boarded a flight from Algiers to Bamako to piece together for *The*

New York Review of Books the story of the jihadis' 2012 conquest and to report on the French military effort to bring them down. The country was in turmoil, elated by the sudden French intervention, yet fearful that AQIM and Ansar Dine could inflict a last burst of savage violence. On my first morning in the capital, I paid a call on Imam Chérit Ousmane Mandani Haidara, no relation to Abdel Kader, a charismatic Sufi preacher who was much admired in Mali for being the first Muslim leader to denounce jihadi rule in the north. The Mawloud festival had begun in Bamako, and pilgrims crammed the courtyard of Imam Haidara's green-domed Sufi mosque on a sealed-off street in the capital, protected by metal detectors and a battalion of red-bereted private guards. The imam received me in a dusty room above his mosque, furnished with gold-painted wingback chairs and sofas and blood-red carpets. Jihadi sympathizers had infiltrated the capital, he told me. He was fearful of assassination, too terrified to leave his compound. What's more, his moderate Islamic organization, Ansar Dine, a Sufi group with one million followers and branches across West and Central Africa, had been tainted by Iyad Ag Ghali's appropriation of the name. His followers were being harrassed by the police and army in several African countries, accused of being terrorists. "Iyad Ag Ghali is a Wahhabi, his Ansar Dine is not the same as my Ansar Dine, I am a pacifist," insisted the imam, a tall and imposing figure in his fifties, swathed in a golden boubou and a green wool scarf. "They created Ansar Dine only to make trouble for me." The Mawloud Festival at Haidara's mosque went off without any trouble, but the imam's fears of jihadist infiltration in the capital would be realized some time later, when Al Qaeda terrorists threw grenades and sprayed automatic-weapons fire at La Terrasse, a popular bar-restaurant frequented by expatriates in Bamako, killing two Westerners and three Malians.

I set out the next day for the north in a hired Toyota Land Cruiser. The tarmac quickly turned to dirt, and my driver fell in behind a half-mile-long French military convoy heading to Tim-buktu. In 1994 I had traveled with the French army during Op-eration Turquoise in Rwanda, and the scenes were vividly familiar. French flags hung from mud-brick huts, jeeps and trucks kicked up clouds of dust, and children waved from the roadside. The French intervention in Rwanda had been cloaked in ambiguity: though French president François Mitterrand had presented it to the world as a humanitarian campaign to save Tutsis from genocide, its real intent seemed to be to carve out a safe haven for the Hutu *géno-cidaires*, and prevent Paul Kagame's Anglophone Rwandan Patri-otic Front from seizing control of the country. The mission in Mali, however, was far more straightforward and was moving ahead with what seemed like near-universal approval.

From time to time on the journey north I found myself think-ing about my old acquaintance Abdel Kader, whom I had not spo-ken to since before the jihadi occupation began, and speculating on the fate of his manuscripts. I had imagined that Haidara and his col-leagues might have buried them in the desert, as people had done during French colonial times. I had no idea that at that moment a fleet of boats was heading upriver from Timbuktu, bearing seven hundred footlockers toward safe havens in Bamako.

After ten hours and 380 miles, I pulled into Mopti, a Niger River port once favored by backpackers and other adventurous travelers, and a jumping-off point to visit the Dogon people, an animist tribe that dwelled in the nearby *falaise*, or cliffs. Now hotels, travel agen-cies, and once popular cafés such as the Restaurant Bar Bozo—noted for its views of sunset over the river—all stood deserted, having shut down following the kidnappings and killings of Westerners. Here the Niger River came into view for the first time since we had left Ba-mako; the handful of pinasses that I saw motoring slowly upstream might well have been loaded with Haidara's precious cargo, though I had no awareness of the boatlift that was then in progress.

Shortly after dawn the next morning, under a slate-gray sky, my driver took me toward Konna. Our plan was to follow the French army all the way to Timbuktu and, if our timing was fortuitous, observe the moment of liberation from jihadi rule. But Malian soldiers at a roadblock just past the airport at Sévaré had other ideas. Blocked from advancing by the surly troops, we parked on the roadside, beside a pancake-flat sea of thorny acacias and desert grass, and over the next hour another twenty vehicles filled with film crews and newspaper and newsmagazine reporters took their place along the shoulder. The morning dragged on, the sun rising higher in the now cobalt-blue sky, temperature soaring into the low one hundreds, journalists kicking the dirt in frustration, the soldiers gruffly refusing repeated entreaties to let the convoy through.

A French paratroop officer roared up in a jeep and tried to intervene on our behalf, eventually directing us back down the road to the airport. Outside the front gate, a Malian colonel in crisp fatigues and Ray-Bans curtly informed the pack of journalists that he made the rules, not the French, and the "theater of operations" would remain sealed off to the press. French TV had reported that day that Malian government soldiers had murdered eleven suspected Islamists and thrown their bodies down a well in Sévaré, and some speculated that the soldiers' obstinance toward the press may have stemmed from that unsavory revelation.

At the Hotel Kanaga on the river in Mopti—the only functioning hotel for Westerners in the city—I sat at the poolside bar that night beside a handful of other reporters and aid workers, swatting away mosquitoes in the tropical heat, and listened to French radio reports of a hostage drama across the border that served as a reminder of the spillover effect of the Malian war and the potential for further turbulence in North Africa. Forty Islamic militants had seized dozens of Western employees at the In Amenas gasworks in the Algerian Sahara. Algerian security forces had attacked the terrorists, and thirty-eight hostages—including three Americans—and twenty-nine Islamists had been killed in the crossfire. The militant who had orchestrated the attack from a secret enclave in the desert was identified as none other than Mokhtar Belmokhtar, the one-eyed cigarette smuggler turned emir of Gao, on the run from French forces, and seeking revenge for the routing of his fighters in northern Mali.

In the months leading up to the French invasion, Belmokhtar's independent streak had led to ugly quarrels with his masters in the Algerian mountains, a dispute that had apparently culminated in this monumental act of terror. In October 2012 the fourteen members of AQIM's Shura Council had rebuked him in a pointed letter, later discovered by an Associated Press reporter in an abandoned Al Qaeda barracks in Timbuktu. The Council chastised him for failing to stage "spectacular attacks" in the Sahara, in contrast to his chief rival, Abou Zeid; making only a feeble effort to acquire weapons; and "poorly" managing the kidnapping of the Canadian diplomats in 2008, "trading the weightiest case (Canadian diplomats!) for the most meager price (700,000 euros)!" Most egregiously, Belmokhtar had, it seemed, aired the organization's "dirty laundry" and revealed closely guarded information to rival militant groups. "Did he not intentionally depict [himself] as the great leader in the field while depicting the organization's leadership as a failure?" the council asked. "If not for God's grace, he would have splashed out secrets to the whole world and the heavens above."

With the officious and mundane language of a performance review at a law firm or a bank, the Shura Council further rebuked him for refusing to take his superiors' phone calls, ignoring summonses to meetings, and neglecting to file expense reports. Such behavior could have "destructive effects for the entity of the organisation and would tear it apart," wrote the secretary of the Shura Council, which was dominated by former senior members of the GIA, the Islamist radicals who had murdered tens of thousands of civilians during Algeria's civil war, and the GSPC, the Salafi spinoff that kidnapped Westerners for ransom and bombed embassies and other facilities in north Africa in the early 2000s. "Why do the successive emirs of the region only have difficulties with you?" they challenged Belmokhtar. As their final insult, the council announced that they had "suspended" him from his command.

In December 2012, Belmokhtar had issued his response: he split from Al Qaeda and formed a new organization, Al Mouwakoune Bi-Dima, Arabic for "Those Who Sign with Blood," taking the name from an Islamist rebel cell in the 1990s Algerian civil war. The January 2013 carnage at the Saharan gasworks, prefaced by demands for the release of one hundred prisoners from Algeria's jails, might well have been Belmokhtar's grotesque effort to upstage his bosses, and to show that he could be every bit as ruthless and murderous toward Western hostages as the fanatic Abou Zeid.

Gao fell on January 26, and on the evening of the 27th, while I was still sitting by the roadblock at Sévaré, waiting to cross into former jihadi territory, a French armored column, supported by Tiger attack helicopters and a battalion of parachutists, entered Timbuktu without firing a shot. Mohammed Touré, Haidara's right-hand man, was one of thousands of residents who rode in cars, trucks, and motorcycles through the dusty streets, honking their horns in celebration.

"*Merci François Hollande, Merci,*" one ecstatic young man, draped in a French tricolor, chanted over and over as jeep-loads of French soldiers roared past. At the radio station, the manager patched together equipment and returned to the air, playing the first music that had been heard in Timbuktu in nine months. And hundreds of jihadis headed north, to the remote mountain sanctuary that some of them knew well. There they would make their final stand against the French army.

19

General Bernard Barrera, the newly appointed commander of French ground forces in Mali, landed in Bamako on January 21, ten days after the start of Operation Serval, and on the very day that was to mark the start of the now canceled Mawloud festival in Timbuktu. He set up a temporary headquarters in an airport hangar, flew by helicopter one week later to the just-liberated towns of Gao and Timbuktu, and established a forward command post at the U.S.-built military base in Tessalit, the gateway to the Adrar des Ifoghas massif. Iyad Ag Ghali's men had occupied the compound for nearly a year and stripped it bare. In the looted headquarters, Barrera—a third-generation infantry officer from Marseille and a veteran of Bosnia, Kosovo, Darfur, and Afghanistan—laid plans for a search-and-destroy mission against the jihadis. In Bamako, Mali's army chief of staff had predicted that the radicals would take refuge in the most impregnable corner of the Adrar des Ifoghas. "Go to the

Ametettaï Valley," he had told Barrera. "That's where you will find the enemy."

Barrera knew that they had to move quickly. He had brought a copy of Joseph Césaire Joffre's memoir of his expedition to Timbuktu in 1893–1894, and the descriptions by the future World War I commander in chief of French forces on the Western Front, of "desolate, near-desert country under a burning sun," the "scarcity of water," "intense heat," and the "mountain defiles of difficult access" weighed on him. The extreme conditions in the Adrar des Ifoghas and the hundreds-miles-long supply lines would wear down Barrera's men quickly. "We have to seize this valley in one week to ten days, or the battle is lost," he told his staff. The stakes were significant: a French withdrawal without a decisive defeat of the jihadis would give Al Qaeda in the Islamic Maghreb an enormous propaganda victory, potentially drawing thousands more recruits to the cause, and throwing Mali into deeper chaos. For Abdel Kader Haidara, who was following the looming battle in the north as best he could from his Bamako sanctuary, the crushing of the extremists was essential. Only then, he knew, could he finish his monumental task, and return the 377,000 manuscripts to their desert home.

The Amettetaï is one of four interlocking valleys in the heart of the massif, and the only one with a year-round supply of water. For decades it served as a sanctuary for Tuareg insurgents, drug traffickers, and Islamist extremists. The valley runs east to west for twenty-five miles, and is eight hundred yards wide at its western entrance. Low gray and black granite hills, eroded to rubble and pocked with caves, rise on both sides. Fields of boulders and rocks, with countless crawl spaces, cover the valley floor. Two sandy ancient riverbeds, or *oueds*, one running north to south and the other running east to west, become torrential rivers during the two or three annual rainstorms. The bare rocky hills drive the summer rain straight down into the oueds, where wells can easily reach the water table—the permeable layer beneath the earth's surface in which water saturates the soil and fills all gaps between rocks. At the north end of the valley, in the middle of the oued, stands a hamlet, Ametettaï—four abandoned stone huts built by nomadic herders. Nearby, in the shade of thorny acacias and fruit trees, four large cavities in the sand, dug by Tuareg nomads to thirty feet, contain ample reserves of water.

In late January, Mokhtar Belmokhtar, Iyad Ag Ghali, and Ab-delhamid Abou Zeid dispersed with their jihadi followers into the desert. Belmokhtar retreated to the no-man's-land along Mali's bor-der with Algeria, to carry on his campaign of carnage and hostage taking. Ghali fled north from Kidal and may have sought tempo-rary refuge in a mountainous region of Darfur, in Western Sudan. (Other reports placed him in the western Sahara region of Morocco, and the northern desert of Mauritania.) Abou Zeid and at least six hundred fighters from Al Qaeda in the Islamic Maghreb, including the men who had burned four thousand manuscripts at the Ahmed Baba Institute, retreated to the Ametettaï, where they prepared for a long siege. The fighters buried mines at the valley's entrance points, camouflaged their pickup trucks beneath acacia trees, set up sniper positions in the hills, and filled caves with food, water, guns, and ammunition. The aim of Abou Zeid and his jihadi cadre was clear: hold out in their rock-walled sanctuaries, outlast the foreigners, force them to retreat from the valley, and live to fight another day.

At the army base in Tessalit, forty-eight miles northwest of the Ametettaï, Barrera devised a three-pronged attack. One battalion from a Chadian expeditionary force—battle-hardened men used to fighting in equally harsh terrain—would enter the valley from the east. A six-hundred-man mechanized battalion, consisting of infan-try and armored vehicles, supported by four 120-millimeter mor-tars and two long-range CAESAR howitzers, would assault from the west. Four companies of troops from the 2nd Foreign Parachute

Regiment, France's rapid reaction force, would enter from the north. These four companies of Foreign Legionnaires would divide the valley in two, capture Ametettaï village, and cut off the jihadis' access to water.

On February 22, the Chadian battalion made an initial foray into the Ametettaï through a narrow opening at the valley's eastern extremity, in armored trucks and on foot. The jihadis were prepared for them. The fervor that they had displayed in Timbuktu—the fanatical certainty that had driven them to declare war on the city's music, manuscripts, and culture of tolerance—assumed a terrifying new intensity on the battlefield. Suicide bombers, wearing explosive belts filled with steel pellets, threw themselves on patrols at the entrance to the valley. Twenty-six Chadian soldiers were killed and seventy injured in close combat. Helicopters evacuated the dead and wounded, and the weary survivors returned by truck to Tessalit, the U.S.-built base being used as the French command center. They spent three days convalescing. Then they declared that they were ready to reengage. Before dawn on February 25, they joined 1,200 French soldiers for a coordinated assault. "You're going to fight determined men, men who are dug into strong defensive positions," Barrera told the troops before they departed. "We are going to suffer losses, but we have to continue fighting." He gave his men a maximum of six days to take the valley, an even lower figure than his initial assessment. "Beyond that," he told them, "we will have surpassed our physical limits."

Captain Raphaël Oudot de Dainville had arrived at Tessalit by troop transport plane from Niger on February 22—the same day that the Chadians died at the eastern entrance to the Ametettaï Valley. A third-generation military man and a 2005 graduate of the Military Academy of Saint-Cyr, considered the West Point of

France, Oudot de Dainville was an infantry officer in the French Foreign Legion, comprised of French officers and international recruits. These men, often fleeing from checkered pasts in their home countries and seeking a second chance in life, were legendary for their esprit de corps. The troops under Oudot de Dainville's command came from England, the Balkans, Poland, Russia, and half a dozen former states of the Soviet Union, and had seen action in the Côte d'Ivoire, the Central African Republic, and Afghanistan. He had led his parachutists into the Tagab Valley in Kapisa Province northeast of Kabul in the winter of 2010, where the Taliban had put up a fierce resistance, and where Oudot de Dainville had first confronted the fight-to-the-death ethos of Islamist fanatics. He considered his men to be tougher, more disciplined, and more used to hardship than their French-born counterparts. "They push everything to the extreme," he said.

Before dawn, Oudot de Dainville and his soldiers climbed into military trucks at Tessalit and headed south through the desert. They bounced on sandbags for ten hours over a moonscape of stones, pebbles, and boulders. At three-thirty in the afternoon, the men dismounted from their trucks in the oued, near the Ametettaï's northern entrance. Sappers checked for mines buried in the sand. The men walked in a tight formation through the ancient riverbed, wary of ambushes. The temperature was 122 degrees. Each man wore a helmet, flak jacket, and sixty-pound backpack filled with six plastic bottles of water, meals-ready-to-eat (MRE), and ammunition. They carried French-made M4 rifles; antitank missiles, mortar tubes, and disassembled 12.7-millimeter machine guns. The hamlet of Ametettaï was four miles from their point of entry into the valley. In between lurked hundreds of fanatical fighters, including Abou Zeid, the jihadi commander and the scourge of Timbuktu, dug into caves with enough water, food, and ammunition to hold out for weeks.

Moments after Oudot de Dainville and his men entered the

Ametettaï, the jihadis opened fire on the troops with small arms and rocket-propelled grenades. The parachutists crawled to cover behind boulders. Bullets ricocheted off the rocks and struck flak jackets and helmets. Kevlar vests saved four French soldiers; a bullet lodged between one man's helmet and his skull. The Legionnaires inched forward, taking advantage of the enemy's limited visibility, creeping up on the sides of their caves and tossing in grenades. The explosions resonated across the valley. They moved across the stony terrain, taking sniper fire from the hills, sweeping the area for fighters and weapons, tossing in more grenades and moving on.

That night they camped on rocks inside the valley, cushioning themselves as best they could with pieces of cardboard ripped off boxes of mineral water after the bottles had been consumed. Oudot de Dainville bunked down in the middle of his company. Teams of sentries kept watch. The French officer was well familiar with the fate of the French colonial commander Colonel Etienne Bonnier and his column of French and Senegalese troops, who had camped in the Sahara on the night of January 14, 1894, while on a reconnaissance mission after an exhausting thirty-five-mile march from Timbuktu. Tuareg swordsmen and cavalrymen waited in silence until the French sentries dozed off, then, at four a.m., with cries of "Kill them," charged Bonnier and his men, leaving thirteen French officers dead, as well as a military doctor, a veterinarian, and sixty-six Senegalese infantrymen. Only one French officer had survived. "It was a disaster without precedent in the history of our colonial wars in Africa," one French officer later wrote. This time French intelligence intercepted radio transmissions from Abou Zeid exhorting his men to wage jihad against "the dogs," as he called the French—an echo of the call to holy war that the Tuareg warrior chief Ngouna had made against Bonnier on the eve of the massacre. Abou Zeid was rousing his men to jihad from a cave or a crawl space a couple of hundred yards from the French position.

Inching across the stony terrain at sunrise, the Legionnaires made use of technology that their colonial counterparts didn't have: long-range guns and airpower. Oudot de Dainville's forward air controller on the ground singled out concentrations of enemy fighters and radioed for support. CAESAR howitzers pummeled the jihadis with 155-millimeter shells that could be fired with accuracy from twenty-five miles away. Mirage jets dropped four-hundred-pound bombs capable of destroying nests of fighters hidden deep underground. Tiger helicopters swooped in low across the battlefield and struck the jihadis with rockets. Abou Zeid could do little else but hunker down and wait out the onslaught.

Barrera and his logistics team worked around the clock to keep the French well supplied and their morale high. Helicopters ferried in ten tons of bottled water daily for the two battalions—an average of two and a half gallons per soldier—enough to ward off thirst and even give them a shower from a bottle once a day. Small perks—a warm Castel beer, cigarettes trucked in from Algeria, a raw onion that they mixed in with their MREs to compensate for the absence of fresh fruits and vegetables—lifted their spirits. Barrera helicoptered back and forth from his command post in Tessalit and spent hours on the battlefield, sometimes sleeping beside his men.

On the 27th of February, after five days of combat, nearing Barrera's projected limit of French endurance, French artillery and air-burst cluster bombs killed forty Islamist fighters at the eastern entrance to the valley. The air strikes came during a fierce firefight between a cell led by Abou Zeid and the Chadian battalion that had suffered heavy losses five days earlier.

"The French have hit us very badly," reported one commander in an intercepted radio transmission. "I think the game is up for us."

That day, the voice of Abou Zeid fell silent.

The massive casualties changed the tenor of the battle. "In the next few days," Barrera told me, "The morale of the jihadis fell. We could see that they were no longer fighting."

Two days after the cluster bombardment, Foreign Legion parachutists captured Ametettaï village, the jihadis' only source of water, without a shot being fired. One company of Legionnaires occupied the stone huts and established a perimeter around the wells. Oudot de Dainville's company seized the heights above the village. Holed up in their grottos and crawl spaces, the jihadis were now dependent entirely on the water that they had stashed inside. Victory, Oudot de Dainville knew, was just a matter of time.

The battle of the Ametettaï was a lopsided struggle between a modern army equipped with state-of-the-art weaponry and advanced communications systems, and a ragged band of fanatics who possessed only two advantages, strong defensive positions and a willingness to die for a cause. When their water ran low, they recklessly emerged from their caves in search of fresh supplies. Until now the only enemy combatants the French had encountered face-to-face had been preadolescent runners, employed to carry guns and ammunition between caves. But now desperate groups of fifteen or twenty jihadis charged from their grottos, shouting *"Allahu Akbar."* The fighters sometimes advanced to within sixty feet of Oudot de Dainville and his men, then gunfire cut them down.

On March 4, the French Foreign Legionnaires and the Chadian battalion met in the center of the valley and shook hands, their pacification of the Amettetaï complete. The last jihadis had slipped out of the valley in the middle of the night, leaving behind the corpses of six hundred comrades, many blown to bits. The French had suffered only three deaths. Other French forces had simultaneously rooted the extremists out of Gao and out of the Telemsi Valley along the Niger River, a stronghold of Wahhabism where the jihadis had sought refuge.

It had taken only fifty-three days for the French military to largely vanquish a rebel force that had shaken the world and come close to seizing control of a country. The extremists, Barrera said months later, had fought "with courage and tenacity," but, lacking popular support in the areas that they had controlled, relatively thin in numbers, and forced to make a final stand in a remote and uninhabited corner of the country, the Al Qaeda guerrillas could not withstand a massive assault by a modern European army. The French had not killed every jihadi in Mali, but they had crippled their ability to mount coordinated attacks with large numbers of fighters. The survivors had dispersed into the desert, no longer capable of controlling Timbuktu or any other community in the north.

Operation Serval was hailed almost universally as a model for future interventions—an example of a European nation going into a former colony and efficiently ridding it of a jihadi power, while suffering minimal losses. At the same time, the ease of the French victory underscored the weakness of the Malian armed forces, raising questions about the sustainability of the enterprise. Hollande made it clear that the army had no intention of lingering in Mali, but the fragility of the north suggested the French would find no easy exit. Small jihadi cells were still scattered throughout the desert, the potential for sporadic violence in northern Mali remained high, and for Abdel Kader Haidara and the manuscripts that he had rescued, it was quite likely that there would be no speedy return to Timbuktu.

Oudot de Dainville returned to Tessalit, drank a cold beer, washed his clothes, and took his first shower in two weeks. Then he and his men headed to the Terz Valley, just south of the Amettetaï, to search for jihadis who got away. They found it deserted.

Days later, French troops secretly flew the battered corpse of a jihadi commander recovered from the eastern entrance to the Ametettaï to Algiers and handed it over to Algerian intelligence officials for DNA analysis. Forensic investigators compared the body's genetic markers with those of two relatives of Abou Zeid, and in late March the French Foreign Ministry announced a definitive determination: the emir of Timbuktu was dead. His killing, declared Hollande, "marks an important step in the fight against terrorism in the Sahel." He had been the most ruthless and resilient of Mali's Al Qaeda commanders, and had remained a fanatic to the end. Unlike Ghali and Belmokhtar, who had opted for escape, Abou Zeid had chosen to make a last stand, knowing that his only options were victory or death.

Only one question remained about Abou Zeid: How had he died? A Mauritanian private news agency reported that the AQIM chieftain had been killed in the French artillery and cluster-bomb attack at the eastern end of the valley on February 27. A few weeks after the positive identification in the Algiers lab, however, *Paris Match* published a photo of a bloodied corpse that appeared to be his, taken on March 2 inside a crawl space beneath a granite boulder. The blood was fresh, suggesting that Abou Zeid had survived the deadly French barrage and fought until the final hours of the jihadis' resistance. The Chadian soldier who took the photo recounted that, after eight hours of close combat on March 2, the jihadis' shooting had ended abruptly with a loud explosion at seven in the evening. Abou Zeid had apparently killed himself with a grenade when he realized that there was no way out. His torso was mangled but parts of his body remained intact. Inside a pocket of the diminutive corpse, Chadian soldiers found a French passport belonging to Michel Germaneau, the seventy-eight-year-old aid worker Abou Zeid had executed three years before, following a French commando raid on an Al Qaeda desert camp. The jihadi leader had apparently kept the document as a souvenir of his murder.

Epilogue

The rain fell in sheets on the sprawling city of Bamako, turning rutted roads into obstacle courses of churned-up mud and pools of fetid brown water. It was August 2013, the height of the summer rainy season, and five months after the French defeat of the jihadis in northern Mali. Abdel Kader Haidara, who was still living in Bamako, had arranged to meet me in front of Amandine, a popular café and patisserie in a riverside neighborhood with the mellifluous name of Badalabougou, to show me what had become of the manuscripts that his teams had smuggled out of Timbuktu. His driver pulled up in a Toyota Land Cruiser and Haidara, resplendently dressed in a pale blue embroidered boubou and a maroon skullcap, beckoned to me from the curb. I leapt over pools of mud in the parking lot and climbed into the rear seat. We drove through clouds of exhaust, past battered yellow taxis, rusting buses, minivans, and packs of cheap Chinese Cub model motorbikes, known

locally as "Jakartas." Street hawkers darted in and out of traffic, selling cell phone recharge cards, inflatable plastic cheetahs, crates of
oranges, flashlights, gym shorts, cheap Ray-Ban knockoffs, fried
millet donuts, papayas, and grilled kebabs—the desperate hustle of
an impoverished city.

We turned down a wide dirt road flanked by neat rows of palm
and eucalyptus trees with homes peeking above concrete walls. I
caught a glimpse of the Niger—slow moving, olive green—at the
end of the street. A security guard opened the gate. We rolled up a
dirt driveway, passed an overgrown garden, and stopped before a
half-completed villa. "It belongs to a Savama-DCI family," Haidara
said. Haidara was keeping everything vague, fiercely protective of
the network that had participated in the rescue. "People are still at
risk," he had told me earlier.

Haidara instructed me to wait beside a storage shed and disappeared into the house. I studied the detritus scattered on the muddy
ground—a one-wheeled, rusted bicycle, a discarded Dell com-
puter—and considered that even in the more prosperous corners of
Mali, which are few, everything seemed to fall victim to neglect and
decay. After five minutes, Haidara emerged from the house with a
key. He opened the storage room, switched on a light, and beckoned me inside. Tidy, ten-foot-high stacks of wooden and metal
chests—jammed closely together, four or five stacks deep—filled
the musty, fluorescent-lit space and rose to the ceiling. Haidara told
me that they represented parts of twenty-six discrete collections,
including his own. Thousands and thousands of manuscripts had
found a refuge in this fifteen-foot-by-eight-foot room and twenty-
five others scattered across Bamako, having escaped the predations
of Al Qaeda, and made their way by road or by river past jihadi and
Malian army checkpoints, bandits, and French attack helicopters.

The smuggling operation had produced the first system-
atic effort to describe and document the collections. During the

packing in Timbuktu, Haidara, Touré, and other members of the Timbuktu team had compiled a crude handwritten database, registering the names of manuscripts, their owners, and the themes and provenance of every work, which he had later transferred to a laptop. Henry Louis Gates and the Andrew Mellon Foundation had requested that Haidara undertake precisely the same task in 1996, when he had received a grant to build the Mamma Haidara Library. But it had taken the near-destruction of Timbuktu's manuscripts to prompt him finally to get the job done. Emily Brady called the cataloguing "the first pragmatic step in being able to integrate this knowledge, to transform all this torn-up paper into something meaningful," a coherent list that could reveal for the first time, to both manuscript owners and the outside world, the depth and breadth of the accumulated scholarship of Timbuktu. Haidara had applied for a $25 million grant from Germany's Gerda Henkel Foundation so that he could build a sophisticated, computerized catalogue of all 377,000 manuscripts, as well as put into place an ambitious restoration and conservation program. "Abdel Kader knows now for the first time what the hell he has, and it thrills him," Brady had told me.

I breathed in the stale air. Haidara threw open one ornamented chest to reveal a mass of yellowing, crumbling pages and rotting leather covers stacked one on top of the other, with no protection or padding in between. "The dampness and the rain are hastening the destruction of these and many other manuscripts," Haidara told me. "They should be returned to Timbuktu as quickly as possible." The drier air in Timbuktu acted as a kind of safeguard against fungal rot, though the arid climate of his hometown was also deleterious over time, causing unprotected pages to grow brittle and fall apart. "We have begun to see . . . mold, mildew, and fungus on paper and also on leather bindings," Emily Brady had said in her Reddit interview two months earlier, part of a drive to raise $100,000 to preserve the manuscripts in Bamako by purchasing moisture traps, archival boxes, and additional footlockers.

It was anyone's guess when their return to Timbuktu would happen. The French army had swept across the north in February and March 2013, liberated Timbuktu and Gao, killed Abdelhamid Abou Zeid, and driven the jihadi army deep into the Sahara. Violence had dropped dramatically, the August election of a new president in Mali, Ibrahim Boubacar Keïta, a longtime leader of the opposition and a former speaker of the National Assembly, had put the country back on a path toward democracy, and the United Nations had approved a sixteen-thousand-man peacekeeping force, mostly comprised of soldiers from West Africa, to stabilize the north. The French were continuing to pursue notorious jihadis, among them Oumar Ould Hamaha, the influential Belmokhtar deputy known as Red Beard who had terrorized Mohammed Touré that night in Timbuktu—and who would be killed in a French air strike in northeastern Mali a few months after my visit.

But terrorist attacks were continuing sporadically in the north, and at least half a dozen Western hostages remained held in horrific conditions somewhere in the Sahara. The fates of these men varied, depending on the whims of their captors and the willingness of European governments to continue handing over large sums of cash to free them—a practice that, the U.S. State Department and other observers argued, was only strengthening the jihadis and fueling the kidnapping-for-money trade. In July 2013 AQIM shot in the head and killed Philippe Verdon, one of the two French geologists who had been seized from a hotel in Hombori in March 2011, and whom the terrorist group had accused of being a spy. In November 2013, Al Qaeda freed the four French nationals kidnapped at a uranium mine in Niger in 2010, after the French government reportedly paid a $32 million ransom, the highest amount ever given to the terrorist group. The amount was roughly equivalent to what the French had spent on all military operations during the first ten days of Operation Serval. Verdon's business partner and France's last remaining hostage, Serge Lazarevic, would be freed in December 2014 in exchange for France's release of four Islamic militants, including two Al Qaeda members who had participated in the pair's abduction. In April 2015, French Special Forces liberated the Dutchman taken hostage in the Timbuktu guesthouse three and a half years earlier. But his fellow prisoners from South Africa and Sweden are still in Al Qaeda custody.

Despite their sharply reduced mobility, the radicals were still picking off the occasional Westerner who strayed into their path. Three months after my rainy season encounter with Haidara—in November 2013—AQIM militants with connections to Iyad Ag Ghali abducted two French radio correspondents in Kidal, epicenter of rebellions, and a place of continuous unrest. The French army gave chase in jeeps and a helicopter. When the kidnappers' car broke down eight miles north of the city, they cut the journalists' throats, shot them, and jettisoned their corpses. Then they escaped into the desert.

Two months later I flew from Bamako to Kidal in a United Nations–chartered Antonov jet with civilian engineers, French officers, and contingents of United Nations soldiers and police from Senegal, Guinea, and Burkina Faso. I was the first correspondent to visit the outpost since the French reporters were murdered. The U.N. civilian staff members who had arranged my trip told me that the place was still so dangerous that I could stay for only twenty-four hours, and could not leave the U.N. compound except in an armored vehicle, with an escort of blue helmets. Stepping off the plane into the blinding sunlight and blast-furnace heat, I watched peacekeepers in turbans roar up in six camouflage-painted trucks with heavy machine guns, protecting the plane from attack. A hot wind was blowing, sending up sprays of sand. In the distance, rising above a sea of scrub, I could see a line of black hills, the Adrar des Ifoghas, where the climactic battle between the jihadists and French expeditionary forces had taken place. "Some of the terrorists have gone back in there," a French colonel told me, stubbing out a cigarette as he waited to board the plane for Bamako.

Kidal was the trouble spot where the international community's ambitions had collided with Mali's realities, a nest of both secular Tuareg militants, still aspiring to create the independent state of Azawad, and Al Qaeda in the Islamic Maghreb fighters, seeking to blend into the civilian population and keep the jihad alive. A contingent of U.N. peacekeepers had arrived the previous summer, but they were reluctant to take on either group.

"Nobody is in control here," I was told by a Guinean lieutenant, as we toured the city in a U.N. armored vehicle escorted by two pickup trucks filled with Togolese police. The security team saw me off the next morning with evident relief. In May 2014, three months after my visit, Tuareg rebels stormed government buildings, killed dozens of soldiers, and took thirty hostages in a "declaration of war." Kidal's violence radiated outward across the Sahara, keeping the region in a state of perpetual instability.

In February 2014, days after returning from my unnerving trip to Kidal, I rode north from Bamako on a rutted road, part asphalt and part dirt, for five wearying hours to observe one hopeful sign of Mali's revival: the Festival on the Niger—the four-day concert set on a barge moored in the shallows in the southern town of Ségou, which had never been under the control of the militants. The older, more famous Festival in the Desert in Timbuktu had been canceled for the second year in a row in January 2014 because of rocket attacks, ambushes, suicide bombings, and kidnappings in the north. But the impresario Manny Ansar had been invited here, to a stage alongside the Niger River, with his troupe of mostly Tuareg musical exiles, to celebrate the festival's postwar theme of "cultural diversity and national unity."

Ansar and I walked along the riverbank at dusk while waiting for the concert to begin. It was from this very stretch of the river, in December 1893, that the doomed French commander, Etienne Bonnier, had embarked with an army of French officers and Senegalese infantrymen on a gunboat bound for Timbuktu. French forces later ambushed and killed the orchestrator of the massacre, Ngouna, Ansar's great-great-grandfather, ending Tuareg resistance around Timbuktu. We stood contemplatively at the edge of neatly furrowed fields, observing a fisherman standing upright in his wooden pirogue, poling across the Niger's glassy surface in the fading light. The river had nourished Mali's precolonial empires and sustained life here for millennia. But it had also served as an avenue for war and conquest, and much of the violence that had torn apart Mali had unfolded along its now peaceful banks.

By the time we returned to the festival space, the scene had come alive. U.N. peacekeepers, Malian generals in camouflage uniforms and red berets, Western tourists, and locals filled every seat and jammed the aisles. I took a seat in the VIP section near the stage, while the impresario worked the aisles, embracing ambassadors and Malian music aficionado friends from the United States and Europe, shifting effortlessly from French to English to Tamasheq and back again. Then the lights came up, and Khaira Arby, known as the "Nightingale of the North," strolled onto the stage.

In a sequin-studded green gown and a tiara of gold coins, rows of silver bracelets jangling on her arms, the diva swept back and forth, gesticulating grandly, voice booming. In the summer of 2012 AQIM militants had trashed Arby's guitars and her recording studio and threatened to cut out her tongue if they captured her, forcing her to flee in terror to Bamako from Timbuktu. Now she extended her arms toward the audience, overcome with emotion. "I'm singing for the Tuaregs who never picked up arms against their country," proclaimed Arby, to the crowd's roar of approval. It was a gesture of reconciliation, and a plea for unity, in a nation that had been torn apart by war and occupation.

At ten p.m., Ahmed Ag Kaedi, the Tuareg guitarist from Kidal, whose guitars had been burned by Iyad Ag Ghali's henchmen, took the stage. His strident guitar playing and hypnotic wail seemed a cry of defiance. Swathed in boubous and Tuareg veils, Kaedi and his Tuareg band, Amanar, sang in Tamasheq about the beauty of the desert, about infinite skies and soaring dunes, about the joy of comradeship, and the sadness of loss and exile, their haunting call-and-response vocals and insistent guitar phrasing rising to an emotional crescendo of loneliness, melancholy, and yearning. Around one a.m., a hundred jubilant spectators climbed onto the stage, gathering around Kaedi as his driving guitar solo cut through the night. Ansar, swathed in a blue boubou, with a rakish white scarf tossed around his neck, danced and embraced the musicians, swept away by the euphoria of the moment. Assembling his exiles on this stage in Ségou, he had scored a symbolic triumph over Al Qaeda in the Islamic Maghreb—thugs and killers who had been determined to stamp out all spontaneity, art, and joy in their self-declared caliphate.

Yet the scene was bittersweet. I thought back to my visit to the Festival in the Desert in 2008, at the height of its popularity, when eight thousand people came to Essakane, one quarter of them Westerners. Tourists in safari jackets had filled the sandy streets of Timbuktu, brimming with anticipation, reveling in the sense of adventure. At the oasis, white canvas tents and traditional nomadic dwellings stitched together from the hides of goats covered the wind-rippled white dunes. It was a grand, unforgettable scene. After a day in the heat and a communal meal with a quintet of young

Australians on a months-long trek through Africa, I fell asleep in a tent before midnight. But two hours later, awakening to an infectious guitar phrase, I scaled a fifty-foot-high dune overlooking the floodlit stage. I lay back on the cool sand, stared at a sky filled with stars, and let the hypnotic vocals and guitar licks of Ibrahim Ag Habib, Tinariwen's lead singer, wash over me.

Now, six years later, I wondered whether the Festival in the Desert would ever take its place again in the dunes of Essakane. Mokhtar Belmokhtar had set up a new base in chaotic Libya, where jihadis were gaining the upper hand in many parts of the country. On June 13, 2015, two American F-15 fighter jets would drop several five-hundred-pound bombs on a gathering of jihadis in the Libyan coastal city of Ajdabiya, reportedly killing Belmokhtar and six others. But a jihadi spokesperson insisted that the bomb had missed the man whom the French military had labeled "The Uncatchable One," and who had mistakenly been reported killed several times over the years; to this date no DNA evidence has been presented to confirm his death. Iyad Ag Ghali, meanwhile, was wheeling and dealing from deep in the Sahara, offering to negotiate for the release of the remaining Western hostages in return for immunity from prosecution for war crimes. He was said to be hiding in the oasis of Tinzouatine, which occupies the no-man's-land between Algeria and Mali. The Department of State had named Ghali a "Specially Designated Global Terrorist"—but French and Algerian Special Forces had displayed little zeal in going after him. Despite his plunge into jihadism, despite the suffering he had inflicted on his countrymen, Ghali's influence among the Tuareg remained considerable, and it was widely believed that no final agreement between the armed nomads and the government could be achieved without his approval. "Iyad is not finished as a political player," Ansar, Ghali's former close friend, assured me.

Without constant surveillance and military pressure on Al

Qaeda and its partners, General Bernard Barrera told me, the threat to the region, to Europe and beyond, would not dissipate. "I don't think the jihadis have the capacity to regroup," Barrera said when I met him in his office at the Ecole Supérieure de Guerre in Paris, a vast complex founded by Louis XV in 1751 to train five hundred "gentlemen" for a career in arms, and famed as the military school where Napoleon Bonaparte had prepared for a naval career. "They can conduct little operations, with rockets, killing local people, carrying out acts of terror," Barrera went on. "We have to keep surveying them, because the terrorism could come to France. It's not just a problem for Mali. It is a problem for the West."

By 2015, however, the international community's attention was beginning to drift. In late September 2015, sixteen months after I interviewed Barrera, prosecutors brought before the International Criminal Court at The Hague a former member of Ansar Dine's "morality squad" in Timbuktu. The ex-jihadi, Ahmad Al Faqi Al Mahdi, a teacher's college graduate turned zealot in Iyad Ag Ghali's radical Islamic movement, stands accused of directing the destruction of ten Sufi shrines and a Sufi mosque in 2012. Prosecutors contend that he wielded great power as the head of the Islamic Police, and human rights groups and many Timbuktu residents welcomed the news of his arrest. At the same time, the draw-down of French troops, the continued weakness of the Malian army, and the inability of African peacekeepers to fill in the gaps allowed the terrorists to regroup. Attacks escalated throughout the year, culminating in the siege of the Radisson Blue Hotel in Bamako on November 20, 2015. Nineteen people died.

Haidara and I met again in February 2014, during the same trip in which I visited Kidal and the Festival on the Niger. He had recently returned from his second visit to Timbuktu since the French intervention, and he had come away encouraged. The first of the city's forty-five libraries had reopened, and some of their proprietors were returning home. Haidara was thinking about moving with his family back to Timbuktu as well, but the security remained precarious, with jihadis still encamped in the dunes beyond the city limits, and the Haidaras were enjoying the advantages that living in a relatively cosmopolitan city can offer. He and his first wife had located a physical therapist at a private hospital in Bamako and their five-year-old son had begun to improve both physically and mentally. "When we were in Timbuktu, there were absolutely no specialists to treat him," Haidara told me. The boy could now sit up, speak a few words, and play with a friend. "It is a bit of a *soulagement*—a relief—to see this, but it is not easy," he told me.

Displaced and impoverished by the conflict, a huge extended family was leaning on Haidara for financial support. He was buying them shoes, clothing, grain, and sheep and goats for religious festivals, and paying the school fees of a dozen nephews and nieces. "When I was young, I earned a lot of money, because I worked extremely hard, but it's all gone now. I've given it all out. I have so many dependents," he told me as we sat beside the Niger River in the garden of my guesthouse, the Villa Soudan, at dusk, sipping Cokes and watching the sky turn to amber and purple over the King Fahd suspension bridge, a gift from the government of Saudi Arabia twenty years ago. Lights flickered on in the handful of high-rises beside the river—a twenty-story bank building inspired by the Great Mud Mosque of Djenné, an unfinished hotel once owned by Qaddafi. The river meandered past weed-choked islands and paddies and plots of vegetables on both banks. Men, women, and children poked at the soil with hoes beneath the sodden sky. Bamako was one of the region's fastest growing cities, with a population that had doubled to over a million in the past decade, but even along the river, the heart of the capital, it retained the feeling of an extended

African village. "I send money to Timbuktu every month, I send money to Bamba every month. It is too much," Haidara went on. The forty-five other library owners of Timbuktu were depending on him as well. "My ambition now is to rehabilitate all these libraries in Timbuktu, so that I can bring all the manuscripts back to each family that entrusted them to me," he said. "That will give me a little bit of peace."

Before the short winter rains swept over the city, the Ford Foundation, the Prince Claus Fund, and the Swiss Cooperation Office in Mali had given Haidara thousands of dollars to relocate the manuscripts around Bamako, this time to ten new spaces high above ground: sturdily built, watertight constructions equipped with dehumidifiers to save them from rot. Now that project was finally done. The following day I took a taxi to a neighborhood a few miles from my hotel, passing half-built concrete buildings of slapdash construction, tangled phone and electrical wires, and billboards for Air Mali, the Orange mobile telephone network, and HIV-AIDS prevention, and got out in front of a four-story commercial building on the dusty main street. Haidara waved to me from the top-floor balcony. I climbed the stairs and found him in front of a large storage room—one of the new, climate-proofed facilities he'd found for the manuscripts to keep them from disintegrating further during their purgatory in Bamako. A young assistant dragged out a metal footlocker, setting it down silently beside Haidara and me.

Kneeling on a carpet he had laid down in the hallway, Haidara opened the box, gently took out the first volume from the pile, and opened it. Five hundred years old, encased in a dark brown goatskin cover, the massive manuscript was in fine condition. I pictured a robed scribe dipping his quill pen into a leather pouch filled with illuminated ink, huddled over linen paper in a murky atelier of a university in sixteenth-century Timbuktu. The manuscript that Haidara balanced in his lap was a well-known volume called

Waffayat Al Ayan Libnu Halakan—a kind of medieval *Encyclopaedia Britannica*, originally written in the mid-thirteenth century by a Kurdish scholar named Ibn Khallikan, chronicling the lives of the *ulema*, the great Islamic scholars, of the tenth through twelfth centuries. The capsule biographies were arranged alphabetically, written in blocks of squiggling Arabic script in black ink, broken periodically by illuminated single lines of red, blue, and gold. "Each time the scribe commenced a new section, he changed the color of the ink," he said. "A single copyist wrote the main text, because the writing is the same throughout, so it might have taken him six or even seven months to complete it."

But the volume that Haidara held in his hands was, in fact, a collaborative effort. Scores of scholars over the centuries had added commentaries to the original work written by Ibn Khallikan, who had studied in Damascus and lived most of his life in Cairo, filling the margins of every page with notes written in tiny Arabic characters. Haidara ran his fingers gently over these scribblings, commenting on the different textures of the ink and the variations in the handwriting. In many places the original paper had deteriorated, and new bits had been glued carefully into place, giving the manuscript a worn patchwork appearance, like a beloved article of clothing that had been mended over and over again. "Notice how many times it was restored, degraded, and restored," he said. "The great intellectuals give a work like this a lot of importance. Each notation is dated, and marked by name of the author." Exegesis followed exegesis, in the manner of Talmudic commentaries, scholars noting one another's arguments, debating fine points of law and ethics, their dialogue continuing down through the centuries. "This commentator took a phrase from the work, and he gave his opinion about a point of jurisprudence," he said, pointing to a cluster of Arabic characters squeezed into the margin. "There are several copies of this book around," including one that had been transcribed by

Timbuktu's most illustrious scholar, Ahmed Baba, for his own library. "The big difference here is the notations."

The encyclopedia functioned as a kind of pre-Internet chat room, with the conversations attenuated over hundreds of years. Such encyclopedias proliferated during Timbuktu's Golden Age, reflecting a desire to give coherence and order to Islamic scholarship from Timbuktu to Egypt and beyond, to confer recognition, even immortality upon learned men who had sought to enlarge the scope of human understanding. They were a *Who's Who* of the medieval Islamic world, and they represented an extraordinary achievement at a time when that world was a far bigger, far less interconnected place, and collating the biographies of scattered scholars required exhaustive time and effort. The vigor and durability of Timbuktu's intellectual life seemed tangible here, in both the original text and the ancient commentaries of savants through the ages. Haidara flipped through the manuscript's pages reverently before placing it gently back on top of the pile in the footlocker. He had rescued it once from the hands of jihadis in Timbuktu, and again from a waterlogged basement in Bamako. He closed the chest, locked it, and beckoned to his assistant to place it back in the storage room. The manuscript had one last journey ahead of it—back to Timbuktu— though when exactly that would take place, not even Haidara could tell.

Acknowledgments

The Bad-Ass Librarians would never have gotten off the ground without the wholehearted backing of my editors at *Smithsonian Magazine*. In the winter of 2006, I traveled to Timbuktu to write about efforts to recover and rehabilitate the manuscripts, and over the next eight years made two more trips to Mali on assignment for *Smithsonian*—a two-week journey in January 2008, to research a lengthy piece about artifact smuggling, and an August 2013 trip to chronicle Abdel Kader Haidara's rescue effort. The trips whetted my fascination for this strange and beautiful country, and laid the groundwork for the book. I'm deeply indebted to *Smithsonian*'s Carey Winfrey, Michael Caruso, Terry Monmaney, and, above all, my assigning editor and close friend Kathleen Burke, for indulging my wanderlust for a decade and for encouraging this project. Molly Roberts, Jeff Campagna, Nona Yates, Bruce Hathaway, Jesse Rhodes, Brian Wolly, and the entire editorial staff of *Smithsonian* also deserve great thanks for their support.

Robert Silvers sent me to Mali for *The New York Review of Books* in January 2013, days after the French launched Operation Serval to drive out the militants, a critical trip that brought home the country's trauma with great immediacy. Esther Kaplan of the Nation Institute provided funding for that January 2013 journey. Over the following year, the *Review* also sent me to Kidal and Timbuktu, continuing to provide me with a prestigious forum for my Mali reporting and helping me to develop my expertise about the country. I owe thanks as well to the *Review*'s Hugh Eakin, an encouraging voice throughout the project. I'm grateful, too, to Jon Sawyer and Tom Hundley of the Pulitzer Center on Crisis Reporting in Washington, DC, which financed my travel through northern Mali in January and February 2014 and published much of my reporting and photography on their web site.

Over the past decade Stuart Emmrich and Suzanne McNeille of *The New York Times* commmissioned several travel pieces that gave me a grounding in Mali's music and culture. Evan Ratcliffe and Katia Bachko at *The Atavist Magazine* allowed me to explore the relationship between Manny Ansar and Iyad Ag Ghali for my May 2015 piece, "The Desert Blues." The reporting turned up new details that enriched the book's narrative. Oliver Payne and Victoria Clark of *National Geographic* also provided a highly visible outlet and more funding for my research into the manuscript story.

I'm deeply indebted to my longtime friend Karen Crabbs, of Toguna Adventure Tours in Bamako, who has organized half a dozen trips for me through Mali since 2006, some of them at the height of the country's instability. Karen introduced me to key sources, found me fixers and translators, provided astute observations about security conditions and politics, and showed me Bamako's vibrant nightlife. It was over a dinner with her one evening in 2013 in Bamako that I first began contemplating a book on Mali, and she served as an important sounding board for the work-in-progress. Adam Thiam, Mali's most celebrated journalist, shared his reporting on the jihadist takeover of northern Mali, as well as his contact list in Timbuktu and Gao. Manny Ansar, whom I first met through Karen Crabbs in Bamako in January 2013, became a critical source of information about Malian music, Tinariwen, Tuareg culture and history, and the life of his one-time close friend, Iyad Ag Ghali. During our many rendezvous in Oslo, Berlin, Bamako, and Ségou in 2013 and 2014, Manny was unfailingly generous with his time and unlocked many memories, some quite painful, that he had stored away for years. Azima Ag Ali Mohammed, my frequent guide in Timbuktu, opened up doors to secret corners of the city. Mohammed Touré, the until know unsung hero among the bad-ass librarians, shared his stories in gripping detail. The musicologist and Tinariwen expert Andy Morgan shared his intimate knowledge of the band and of recent Tuareg history.

I owe a tremendous thanks to Abdel Kader Haidara, whom I first met in Timbuktu in 2006 and had remained in intermittent touch with over the years before returning to Mali for this book project in January 2014. Haidara devoted twenty hours of his time in Bamako and in Brussels to telling me his life story, displaying infinite patience, opening up a world to me, sharing his insights into Islam, Timbuktu Society, Sorhai culture, and, of course, the genius of the Islamic manuscripts of Timbuktu's Golden Age.

In Paris, my longtime friend and colleague Jon Randal, the legendary former foreign correspondent for *The Washington Post*, introduced me to his contacts in the French Ministry of Defense, who gave me access to key military officers involved in Operation Serval. They helped me recreate this obscure but important campaign against the jihadis in the northern desert. Thanks to Pierre Bayle, General Bernard Barrera, Captain Raphaël Oudot de Dainville, and Colonel Bruno Bert of the 2e régiment d'infanterie—régiment d'Auvergne, who hosted me at his camp in Clermont Ferrand and introduced me to his troops over a long lunch with multiple glasses of French wine and champagne. Vivienne Walt and Jeffrey Schaeffer accommodated me in style at their apartment in Sèvres-Babylone, and offered their friendship and enthusiasm for the work in progress. Thanks as well to the staff of the National Library at the Georges Pompidou Center in Paris, for facilitating my access to vital archival materials.

Stateside, former Ambassador to Mali Vicki Huddleston made herself available on repeated occasions, in person, by phone, and by email, to answer questions about the U.S. response to the growing jihadi threat in the Sahel. Former Ambassador Gillian Milovanovic, former General Chuck Wald, and former defense attaché William Mantiply also gave generously of their time. Henry Louis "Skip" Gates shared with me vivid detail about his often inspiring, sometimes exasperating encounters with Abdel Kader Haidara. Scott Johnson, Janet Reitman, Lee Smith, Kathleen Hughes, Bob and Frankie Drogin, Keith Richburg, Nicole Gaouette, Yudhijit Bhattacharjee, Clifton Weins, Michael Kimmelman, and, in London, Alex Perry, provided encouraging words and advice about the narrative, as did my father, Richard Hammer, my stepmother, Arlene Hammer, my mother, Nina Hammer, and my stepfather Mitchell Cotter. At Simon & Schuster, my editor Priscilla Painton, ably assisted by Megan Hogan, Sophia Jimenez, and Jonathan Evans, worked tirelessly on the project, whipping up my enthusiasm, helping me to find and shape the narrative, and coming up with the wonderful title. My agent Flip Brophy was, as always, a steady voice of support.

In Berlin, Paul Hockenos, Mark Simon, Sam Loewenberg, and Melissa Eddy offered their friendship and advice over many enjoyable meals and conversations. Annette Krämer devoted herself to caring for her grandson, Tom, for countless hours, easing the family burdens and making my travel and writing possible. My sons, Max, Nico, and Tom helped me retain my perspective and kept my spirits high. Above all I want to thank my partner, Cordula Krämer, for her unflagging commitment, support, and love throughout all the ups and downs of this project, for her amazing ability to hold down a challenging job and be an astonishingly good mother of a three-year-old. She is bad-ass, in the best sense of the word.

Notes

Prologue

1   *He shifted nervously in the front passenger seat*: Author interview with Mohammed Touré, Bamako, February 17, 2014.

Chapter One

8   *"Abdel Kader . . . you are the one"*: Author interview with Abdel Kader Haidara, Bamako, January 27, 2014.

8   *"You have no right to give the manuscripts away"*: Haidara interview.

9   *"I need you to come and see me"*: Haidara interview

10   *"Thanks, but I really don't want to"*: Haidara interview.

10   *"You have to come"*: Haidara interview.

10   *"You are the custodian"*: Haidara interview.

11   *"Every time they drive into the villages"*: Haidara interview.

Chapter Two

12   *"The rich king of Tombuto [who] hath many plates"*: Hassan Mohammed Al Wazzan Al Zayati (Leo Africanus), *The History and*

Description of Africa: And of the Notable Things Therein Contained (New York: Cambridge University Press, 2010), p. 824.

13 *"Salt comes from the north"*: Michael Woods and Mary B. Woods, *Seven Wonders of Ancient Africa* (London: Lerner Books, 2009).

14 *"the one with the big belly button"*: Rick Antonson, *To Timbuktu for a Haircut: A Journey Through West Africa* (Toronto: Dundurn, 2008).

15 *"The emperor flooded Cairo with his benefactions"*: Nehemia Levtzion, "Mamluk Egypt and Takrūr," in *Studies in Islamic History and Civilization*, ed. Mose Sharon, (Jerusalem: E.J. Brill, 1986), p. 190.

16 *"The great oppressor and evildoer Sunni Ali"*: John Hunwick, ed. and trans., *Timbuktu and the Songhay Empire: Al-Sa'dī's Ta'rikh al-sūdān Down to 1613 and other Contemporary Documents* (Leiden, NLD: Brill, 2003).

17 *"spend a great part of the night"*: Hassan Mohammed Al Wazzan Al Zayati, *The History and Description of Africa*, p. 825.

18 *"The land of Djenné is prosperous and densely inhabited"*: Hunwick, *Timbuktu and the Songhay Empire.*

19 *"In the year 991 in God's month of Rajab the Godly"*: Lila Azam Zanganeh, "When Timbuktu was the Paris of Islamic Intellectuals in Africa," *The New York Times*, April 24, 2004.

20 *"Drinking cow-milk and mixing the powder"*: Aslam Farouk-Alli and Mohamed Shaid Mathee, "The Tombouctou Manuscript Project: Social History Approaches," in *The Meanings of Timbuktu*, Shamil Jeppie and Souleymane Bachir Diagne, eds. (Cape Town: HSRC Press, 2008), p. 182.

24 *"God orders that slaves must be treated"*: Mahmoud Zouber, "Ahmed Baba of Timbuktu (1556–1627): Introduction to His Life and Works" in *Timbuktu: Script and Scholarship,* Lalou Meltzer, Lindsay Hooper, and Gerald Kinghardt, eds. (Cape Town: Tombouctou Manuscripts Project/Iziko, 2008), p. 25.

24 *"rise up and kill the Jews"*: Ralph A. Austen, *Trans-Saharan Africa in World History* (New York: Oxford University Press, 2010), p. 99.

25 *"The King is an inveterate enemy"*: Hassan Mohammed Al Wazzan Al Zayati, *The History and Description of Africa*, p. 825.

26 *"Why did you conquer Timbuktu?"*: Chris Gratien, "Race, Slavery, and Islamic Law in the Early Modern Atlantic," in *Journal of North African Studies* 18, no. 3 (2013): pp. 454–468.

27 *"All these people, who possess a small degree of learning"*: Heinrich Barth, *Travels and Discoveries in North and Central Africa* (London: Ward, Lock, and Co., 1890), p. 435.

28 *"They were afraid that I should practice"*: Félix Dubois, *Timbuctoo the Mysterious,* trans. Diana White (New York: Longmans, Green, and Co., 1896), p. 289.

28 *"Poetry and works of imagination"*: Ibid., p. 287.

29 *"Perhaps in the future"*: Kwame Anthony Appiah, "Africa: The Hidden History," *The New York Review of Books,* December 17, 1998.

Chapter Three

30 *"Say you're the son of Mamma Haidara"*: Haidara interview, January 30, 2014.

31 *"You? . . . Who do you think you are?"*: Haidara interview.

32 *"They form the sole population"*: Dubois, *Timbuctoo the Mysterious,* p. 20.

33 *"I have seen them set out"*: Ibid.

33 *"Stay here, don't go"*: Haidara interview.

34 *"Nobody's talking to me"*: Haidara interview.

34 *"Pay attention, you have to keep hold"*: Haidara interview.

35 *"Who led you here?"*: Haidara interview.

35 *"The ramparts of the city were of salt"*: John O. Hunwick and Alida Jay Boye, *The Hidden Treasures of Timbuktu: Historic City of Islamic Africa* (London: Thames & Hudson, 2008), p. 55.

36 *"He's dangerous. What does he want"*: Haidara interview.

36 *"It's for the town's orphans"*: Haidara interview.

36 *"My predecessors made a number"*: Haidara interview.

37 *"I gave out a lot of cows"*: Haidara interview.

38 *"tens of thousands of dollars"*: Haidara interview.

39 *"You come from where?"*: Haidara interview.

39 *"How much do you want for this?"*: Haidara interview.

41 *"You found all that?"*: Haidara interview.

41 *"When I was at the Ahmed Baba Institute"*: Haidara interview.

42 *"What's the matter with you?"*: Haidara interview.

43 *"What's the problem?"*: Haidara interview.

44 *"Who told you about that?"*: Haidara interview.

45 *"I was well paid for this work"*: Haidara interview.

Chapter Four

48   *"You know I have a problem"*: Haidara interview.

49   *"We're going to help you"*: Haidara interview.

50   *"I understood their politics"*: Haidara interview.

51   *"It blew my mind and the image stuck with me"*: Phone interview with Henry Louis Gates, October 1, 2014.

52   *"I am apt to suspect the Negroes"*: Isaac Kramnick, ed., *The Portable Enlightenment Reader*, (New York: Penguin Books, 1995).

52   *"The Negroes of Africa have by nature"*: P.H. Coetzee and A.P.J. Roux, eds., *The African Philosophy Reader*, (London: Routledge, 2003), p. 81.

52   *"It is no historical part of the World"*: Robert Dainotto, *Europe (In Theory)* (Raleigh: Duke University Press, 2007), p. 169.

Chapter Five

58   *"suffocating remoteness"*: Joshua Hammer, "Timbuktu Postcard: Still Here," *The New Republic*, November 13, 1995.

58   *"Sweeping out of the Sahara"*: Ibid.

58   *"The next Air Mali flight from Bamako"*: Ibid.

60   *"I said, 'You have to open your own libraries'"*: Author interview with Abdel Kader Haidara in Timbuktu for *Smithsonian*, March 4, 2006.

61   *"Really, we are doing good work"*: Haidara interview, March 4, 2006.

62   *"Nobody in the family had thought about collecting them"*: Author interview with Sidi Yayia Al Wangari for *Smithsonian*, March 5, 2006.

62   *"This one is rotten"*: Al Wangari interview.

62   *"It was a lending library"*: Author interview with Ismail Diadjié Haidara for *Smithsonian*, March 5, 2006.

63   *"This will protect them"*: Author interview with Mohamed Gallah Dicko for *Smithsonian*, March 5, 2006.

64   *"We're expanding our search"*: Dicko interview.

65   *"Dust is the enemy"*: Author interview with Fida Ag Mohammed for *Smithsonian*, March 6, 2006.

Chapter Six

70   *"the Zelig of air power"*: John Barry, "Lt. Gen. Charles F. Wald," *Newsweek*, December 30, 2001.

71   *"vast, ungoverned spaces"*: Author interview with Charles F. Wald, at Le Meridien Hotel, Arlington, Virginia, February 24, 2014.

73   *"It's too bad that there's no ocean here"*: Djamel Alilat, "Avec Les

Chômeurs de la vallée de Metlili (Ghardaïa)," *El Watan*, March 23, 2013.

74 *"Osama bin Laden's Ambassador"*: Duncan Gardham, "Abu Qatada Profile: 'Osama Bin Laden's ambassador man in Europe,'" *The Telegraph*, June 17, 2008.

74 *"The GIA attacked families, young people"*: Salima Mellah, *The Massacres in Algeria, 1992–2004: Extracts from a report presented by the Justice Commission for Algeria at the 32nd Session of the Permanent People's Tribunal on Human Rights Violations in Algeria (1992–2004)*, May 2004, p. 12.

75 *"The sound of gunfire"*: Ibid., p. 20.

75 *"The weaker brethren"*: Robert Fisk, "Mokhtar Belmokhtar: The new face of al Qa'ida (and why he's nothing like Osama bin Laden)," *The Independent*, January 24, 2013.

78 *"It was Abed who painted that"*: Alfred de Montesquiou, "Abou Zeid veut être le Ben Laden du Sahara," *Paris Match*, September 30, 2010.

78 *"He was manhandled [by the police] many times"*: Ibid.

78 *"Before [his father died] he had always been very open"*: Ibid.

79 *"He is ugly and even shorter than [French president Nicolas] Sarkozy"*: Ibid.

83 *"In the name of God we rise up and begin"*: Author interview with Manny Ansar, Ségou, Mali, February 6, 2014.

83 *"Tuaregs didn't go to school"*: Interview with General El Haj El Gamou, former Tuareg rebel commander, Bamako, January 25, 2014.

83 the *"eternal Saharan mystique" of "a veiled nomad"*: Pierre Boilley, *Les Touaregs Kel Adagh: Dépendances et révoltes: du Soudan français au Mali contemporain* (Paris: Éditions Karthala, 1999), p. 9.

84 *"He was Clint Eastwood, John Wayne"*: Ansar interview, February 6, 2014.

85 *"The Pakistanis are up there converting all the former Tuareg rebels"*: Phone interview with Manny Ansar, April 9, 2015.

86 *"Life is like a waiting room in an airport"*: Ansar phone interview, April 9, 2015.

86 *"twice as many prayers"*: Ansar phone interview, April 9, 2015

87 *"He began to lose his friends"*: Author interview with Abdallah Ag Alhousseyni, Leeds, England, May 6, 2014.

87 *"You know the Festival in the Desert is not something constructive"*: Ansar interview, February 6, 2014.

87 *"Iyad approached the German ambassador"*: Author interview with General El Hadj Ag Gamou, Bamako, January 25, 2014.

88 *"The Germans gave him the vehicle"*: El Gamou interview.

88 *"everybody knew about it as soon as it happened"*: Author interview with Vicki Huddleston, former U.S. ambassador to Mali, Raleigh, North Carolina, February 27, 2014.

Chapter Seven

90 *"We wove them together"*: Wald interview.

91 *"concerned"*: Huddleston interview.

91 *"What are they doing?"*: Huddleston interview.

92 *"Tell me exactly who's out there"*: Huddleston interview.

93 *"There was a resentment"*: Wald interview.

94 *"She didn't know us well at the time"*: Wald interview.

94 *"I guess you came to thank me"*: Huddleston interview.

95 *"Imam, you've got your own website?"*: Wald interview.

96 *"creating an armed terrorist group"*: Jeremy Keenan, "The Collapse of the Second Front," *Algeria-Watch*, September 26, 2006.

96 *"We knew he had close contacts"*: Huddleston interview.

97 *"Belmokhtar is probably in the crowd"*: Huddleston interview.

97 *"He looked the part of a desert warrior"*: Huddleston interview.

98 *"You'd better not be involved"*: Huddleston interview.

Chapter Eight

100 *"O infidels and apostates, your joy will be brief"*: Habib Trabelsi, "Zarqawi death 'relief' for rival rebels: experts," *Lebanonwire*, June 9, 2006.

100 *"a bone in the throat of American"*: Hall Gardner, *Averting Global War: Regional Challenges, Overextension, and Options for American Strategy* (New York: Palgrave Macmillan, 2007), p. 133.

102 *"There is a commercial aspect to what he does"*: "Desert Storm Brewing," *Jane's Terrorism and Security Monitor*, November 2, 2010.

103 *"for his Christianizing activities"*: Ahmed Mohamed, "Christopher Leggett Death: al Qaida Says It Killed American In Mauritania For Prosletyzing," *The World Post*, July 26, 2009.

103 *"He was relatively slight"*: Robert Fowler, *A Season in Hell* (New York: HarperCollins, 2011).

104 *"They would sit chanting in the full Sahara sun"*: Ibid.

104 *"I recoiled with horror at the sight"*: Ibid.

105 *"it strengthens our determination never to concede"*: Alan Cowell and Souad Mekhennet, "Al Qaeda Says It Has Killed Briton," *The New York Times,* June 3, 2009.

105 *"was attracting the dregs of the society"*: Author interview with Tiéman Coulibaly, former Malian foreign minister, Bamako, February 15, 2014.

107 *"Esprit de corps did not exist"*: Author interview with Colonel Didier Dacko, Bamako, February 18, 2014.

107 *"termination of Al Qaeda in the Islamic Maghreb"*: Huddleston interview.

108 *"one, rather unimpressive soldier"*: Craig Whitlock, "U.S. counterterrorism effort in North Africa is defined by decade of missteps," *The Washington Post,* February 4, 2013.

108 *"We won't train the guys to look for Al Qaeda"*: Phone interview with Gillian Milovanovic, former U.S. Ambassador to Mali, March 6, 2014.

108 *"It was a huge canard"*: Milovanovic interview.

109 *"their own people"*: Huddleston interview.

109 *"Don't turn the radio on"*: Author interview with William W. (Marshall) Mantiply, former defense attaché, U.S. Embassy Mali, April 16, 2014.

110 *"The French realized AQIM was a growing threat"*: Huddleston interview.

110 *"As a quick response to the despicable French act"*: "Al-Qaeda in North Africa 'kills French hostage,' " BBC News, July 26, 2010.

111 *"The [government's] attitude was, 'it was best' "*: Mantiply interview.

111 *"The level of inaction at the presidency"*: Political Officer Aaron Sampson, "As Northern Crisis Deepens, Mali Drifts," U.S. Embassy, Bamako, April 14, 2008, confidential diplomatic file released by Wikileaks.

112 *"I want to be near the Great Mosque"*: Ansar interview.

113 *"I don't think he was flipped there"*: Yochi Dreazan, "The New Terrorist Training Ground," *The Atlantic,* October 2013.

113 *"Are you sure you're not heading down"*: Ansar interview.

114 *"You are going where?"*: Ansar interview.

116 *"Arabs with short beards, Tuaregs with turbans"*: Charlotte Wiedemann, "From Holes in the Sand to a Digital Library," trans. Katy Derbyshire, Qantara.de, April 21, 2010.

Chapter Nine

116 *"The Westerners come over here"*: Wiedemann, "From Holes in the Sand."

116 *"I tried to remain as modest as I could"*: Author interview with Abdel Kader Haidara, Brussels, December 16, 2014.

118 *"The only time I ever saw him frazzled"*: Author interview with anonymous Haidara friend in Bamako, January 20, 2014.

118 *"Haidara is a man obsessed with the written word"*: Peter Gwin, "The Telltale Scribes of Timbuktu," *National Geographic,* January 2011.

120 *"impure as beads of sweat"*: Ambassador Terence P. McCulley, "The 'Frere Guide' Qadhafi Causes a Stir in Mali," U.S. Embassy, Bamako, April 17, 2006, confidential diplomatic file released by Wikileaks.

121 *"We knew that we had no chance"*: Author interview with "Yusuf," former Tuareg rebel, Timbuktu, February 15, 2014.

121 *"It's an age favorable to war"*: Jonathan Curiel, " 'Desert Blues' Never Sounded So Good as it Does with Terakaft," KQED Arts, October 8, 2012.

122 *"645 kilograms of Semtex plastic explosives"*: "Nigeria Militants a growing threat across Africa: UN," Reuters, January 26, 2012.

122 *"He was a good friend of Amadou Toumani Touré"*: "Yusuf" interview.

124 *"talked for hours"*: "Yusuf" interview.

124 *"It happened at night"*: "Yusuf" interview.

124 *"I knew Al Qaeda"*: "Yusuf" interview.

Chapter Ten

126 *"The vehicle made a single tour"*: Author interview with a young eyewitness (not for attribution), Timbuktu, February 14, 2014.

126 *"I heard the dog barking"*: Author interview with a hotel receptionist (not for attribution), Timbuktu, February 14, 2014.

127 *"at a leisurely pace"*: Young eyewitness interview, February 14, 2014.

128 *"It was a journey of revelation"*: John Gentile, "Robert Plant Documents His Time in Mali," *Rolling Stone,* November 11, 2013.

128 *"Swords turn to guitars, democracy blooms"*: Tom Freston, "Showtime in the Sahara," *Vanity Fair,* July 2007.

128 *"The festival has been vital in bringing foreigners"*: James Truman, "Mali: Where the Music Lives," *Condé Nast Traveler,* October 12, 2008.

129 *"You invite nonbelievers to your festival"*: Andy Morgan, *Music, Culture & Conflict in Mali* (Copenhagen: Freemuse, 2013), p. 44.

129 *"Manny [Ansar] congratulates us"*: Freston, "Showtime in the Sahara."

129 *"Mali's most popular female singer"*: Ibid.

130 *"The entire* etat-major *of the Malian military"*: Ansar interview.

131 *"The concert had been going on for an hour"*: "Mali: à Tombouctou, un festival avec la star Bono fait oublier Al-Qaïda," *Jeune Afrique*, January 15, 2012.

131 *"Music is stronger than war"*: Ibid.

131 *"It was us or them"*: Author interview with Adam Thiam, Malian journalist, Bamako, January 19, 2014.

132 *"putting an end to the incompetent regime"*: Afua Hirsch, "Mali rebels claim to have ousted regime in coup," *The Guardian*, March 22, 2012.

134 *"Turn off your headlights"*: Author interview with Abdel Kader Ascofaré, director of Radio Communal Bouctou, Timbuktu, February 16, 2014.

134 *"I cannot"*: Ascofare interview.

Chapter Eleven

136 *"Abdel Kader, you mustn't go now"*: Haidara interview.

137 *"Where are you coming from?"*: Haidara interview.

138 *"They're going to break into our libraries"*: Haidara interview.

139 *"Twelve bearded terrorists from all over the world"*: Author interview with Boubacar Touré, owner of the Hotel Bouctou, for *The New York Review of Books,* August 5, 2013.

140 *"Who are your clients?"*: Boubacar Touré interview.

140 *"Mr. Abou Zeid, tourism has been ruined"*: Boubacar Touré interview.

141 *"No, no, that's not acceptable"*: Boubacar Touré interview.

141 *"You take out all the bottles"*: Boubacar Touré interview.

142 *"Peuple de Tombouctou"*: Second author interview with Boubacar Touré, Timbuktu, February 14, 2014.

143 *"Don't talk like that"*: Second Boubacar Touré interview.

143 *"We're going to have to replace the imams"*: Second Boubacar Touré interview.

143 *"We used to go into forty-seven villages"*: Ascofaré interview.

144 *"I went to this celebration"*: Author interview with Ibrahim Khalil Touré, Timbuktu, for *The New York Review of Books*, August 5, 2013.

144 *"Shariah is going to come little by little"*: Ibrahim Khalil Touré interview.

145 *"Abou Zeid had a preternatural calm"*: Ibrahim Khalil Touré interview.

145 *"Everything happened little by little"*: Ibrahim Khalil Touré interview.

146 *"I saw three members of the Islamic police"*: Human Rights Watch, "Collapse, Conflict, and Atrocity in Mali: Human Rights Watch Reporting on the 2012–13 Armed Conflict and Its Aftermath," p. 88.

146 *"he frantically tried to hit the answer button"*: Ibid.

147 *"They removed the memory card"*: Ibid., p. 89.

147 *"they are a bad influence for children"*: Ibid., p. 90.

147 *"The north feels dead"*: Ibid., p. 89.

147 *"They've taken all the joie de vivre"*: Ibid., p. 72.

148 *"We were ordered to wear our beards"*: Second author interview with Ibrahim Khalil Touré, Timbuktu, February 15, 2014.

148 *"They sentenced people to be flogged"*: Author interview with Hôtel La Maison manager, August 5, 2013.

149 *"When someone is arrested, the person is brought to the commissariat"*: Human Rights Watch, "Collapse, Conflict, and Atrocity in Mali," p. 86.

149 *"He hit me forty times"*: Ibid., p. 88.

149 *"I like smoking"*: Ibid., p. 87.

150 *"urinated on himself"*: Ibid., p. 87.

150 *"I see them running, sometimes with their guns"*: Ibid., p. 92.

151 *"How does he have the strength to fire it?"*: Chris Simpson, "Time to Rekindle Timbuktu's Flame," IRIN, February 12, 2014.

151 *"We had no choice"*: Ibrahim Khalil Touré interview.

151 *"We are a city that has had Islam"*: Ibrahim Khalil Touré interview.

152 *"They would pray with their rifles"*: Ibrahim Khalil Touré interview.

153 *"Please take care of the Prince"*: Author interview with Moussa Isuf Maiga, Gao resident, in Gao, February 11, 2014.

Chapter Twelve

155 *"They went on television and assured us"*: Author interview with Sane Chirfi Alpha, Timbuktu, February 14, 2014.

155 *"We could read between the lines"*: Chirfi interview.

155 *"These manuscripts show a community"*: Phone interview with Deborah Stolk, Prince Claus Fund, August 30, 2013.

156 *"wonderful books about playing the lute"*: Author interview with Emily Brady, Timbuktu, January 23, 2014.

157 *"Abdel Kader called me"*: Brady interview.

157 *"What do we have to do?"*: Haidara interview.

157 *"I ran the library"*: Author interview with Mohammed Touré, Bamako, February 17, 2014.

158 *"It looks like ordinary baggage"*: Mohammed Touré interview.

159 *"Listen. . . . I want to bring some trunks"*: Haidara interview.

162 *"We moved them by night"*: Author interview with anonymous mule-cart driver, Timbuktu, August 6, 2013.

162 *"They were owners"*: Mohammed Touré interview.

162 *"If I talk about"*: Haidara interview.

Chapter Thirteen

165 *"They said that saints are not acceptable"*: Chirfi interview.

166 *"Beware of those who preceded you"*: Mohamad Tajuddin Mohamad Rasdi, *Rethinking the Mosque in the Modern Muslim Society* (Kuala Lumpur: Institut Terjemahan & Buku Malaysia Berhad, 2014), p. 191.

166 *"We pray to them for everything we look for in life"*: Human Rights Watch, "Collapse, Conflict, and Atrocity in Mali," p. 94.

167 *"Over the period of several days"*: Ibid., p. 113.

167 *"We knew we would be next"*: "Yusuf" interview.

168 *"We lost our dream of Azawad"*: "Yusuf" interview.

168 *"We do not want Satan's music"*: Morgan, *Music, Culture & Conflict in Mali*, p. 21.

168 *"saw my sound system and my instruments"*: Lloyd Gedye, "Tuareg Blues: A Struggle for Life, Land and Freedom," *The Con*, September 4, 2013.

169 *"When I heard the sentence I got weak"*: Author interview with Muhamen Bebao for *The New York Review of Books*, January 26, 2013.

169 *"People think it's done with a single stroke"*: Author interview with eyewitness to amputation, in Bamako, for *The New York Review of Books*, January 26, 2013.

169 *"At around three p.m. they took me to the public square"*: Human Rights Watch, "Collapse, Conflict, and Atrocity in Mali," p. 83.

170 *"It was horrible"*: NBC News Staff and Wire Reports, "Mali al-Qaida-linked group stones couple to death over alleged adultery," *NBC News*, July 31, 2012.

171 *"Aliou took two butcher knives"*: Human Rights Watch, "Collapse, Conflict, and Atrocity in Mali," p. 84.

172   *"You will not do this in Gao"*: Moussa Isuf Maiga interview.

172   *"He lived in the house"*: Mohammed Touré interview.

174   *"These manuscripts are at risk"*: Haidara interview.

175   *"Why are you whipping women"*: Ibrahim Khalil Touré interview.

176   *"What are the reasons that you women"*: Author interview with Tina Traoré, Timbuktu, February 15, 2014.

Chapter Fourteen

178   *"It's still not time"*: Brady interview.

178   *"You have to get them out"*: Haidara interview.

179   *"This is clear"*: Jemal Oumar and Essam Mohamed, "From Mashreq to Maghreb: al-Qaeda shifts focus," *Magharebia,* August 26, 2012.

179   *"I knew we didn't have much time"*: Haidara interview.

180   *"We began to panic"*: Brady interview.

180   *"We're desperate"*: Brady interview.

182   *"What are you carrying?"*: Mohammed Touré interview.

185   *"I had so many worries"*: Haidara interview.

185   *"I saw him with the manuscripts"*: Brady interview.

186   *"That is the only reason"*: Ibrahim Khalil Touré interview.

186   *"You cannot come in"*: Mohammed Touré interview.

Chapter Fifteen

187   *"the chaos and violence in Mali [threatens] to undermine the stability"*: Hillary Clinton, "Transcript: Clinton's remarks at UN Secretary General Meeting on the Sahel," U.S. Africom Public Affairs, September 26, 2012.

187   *"As each day goes by"*: Eric Schmitt, "American Commander Details Al Qaeda's Strength in Mali," *The New York Times,* December 3, 2012.

188   *"We warn all the countries"*: "Les Islamistes prêts au combat contre le CEDEAO et l'OTAN," exclusive interview on Malian television, October 22, 2012.

188   *"It was no longer a place for sin"*: Author interview with Manny Ansar for *The New York Review of Books,* January 26, 2013.

189   *"They are off to war"*: Ibrahim Khalil Touré interview.

190   *"The military returned to their camp to eat around dawn"*: Author interview with Boubacar Dialo, in Konna, Mali, February 9, 2014.

190   *"They ate, they were exultant"*: Dialo interview.

190   *"They flanked them"*: Dialo interview.

191 *"Your town was long terrorized"*: Author interview with Osman Ba, in Sévaré, Mali, for *The New York Review of Books*, January 29, 2013.

Chapter Sixteen

193 *"Bring me more tea"*: Brady interview.

194 *"The French were disgusted"*: Huddleston interview.

195 *"The French people are ready"*: Steven Erlanger, "The French Way of War," *The New York Times*, January 19, 2013.

195 *"At first we thought"*: Ba interview.

196 *"This flag lived only for nineteen hours"*: Dialo interview.

197 *"intelligence, equipment, financing, and training"*: Vicki Huddleston, "Why We Must Help Save Mali," *The New York Times*, January 14, 2013.

Chapter Seventeen

199 *"The Niger, with its vast and misty horizons"*: Dubois, *Timbuctoo the Mysterious*, p. 18.

200 *"When the jihadis arrived"*: Author interview with Mohannan Sidi Maiga, Toya, Mali, for *Smithsonian*, August 5, 2014.

200 *"Toya is off the track"*: Maiga interview.

202 *"We killed and injured hundreds of them"*: Ascofaré interview.

202 *"Normally our marabouts read"*: Ibrahim Khalil Touré interview.

203 *"That holiday does not exist"*: Ibrahim Khalil Touré interview.

204 *"Fine. . . . But you still can't do it"*: Ibrahim Khalil Touré interview.

204 *"The moments of sunset upon the river"*: Dubois, *Timbuctoo the Mysterious*, p. 35.

204 *"Open the footlockers"*: Haidara interview.

205 *"a huge basin of water"*: Dubois, *Timbuctoo the Mysterious*, p. 30.

205 *"It is in truth a singular element"*: Ibid., p. 33.

205 *"We will keep these"*: Brady interview.

205 *"Trust me on this"*: Haidara interview.

206 *"75 FOOTLOCKERS GOING THROUGH"*: Brady interview.

206 *"We still call this place 'Chirac's Dune'"*: Author interview with Azima Ag Ali Mohammed for *The New York Review of Books*, August 6, 2014.

207 *"This is where Abou Zeid held his meetings"*: Azima Ag Ali Mohammed interview.

207 *"There can be no mockery of us"*: Ibrahim Khalil Touré interview.

Chapter Eighteen

210 *"A caretaker saw smoke rising"*: Author interview with Bouya Haidara, Timbuktu, for *Smithsonian,* August 6, 2014.

211 *"All of them—untouched"*: Bouya Haidara interview.

212 *"The only response can be"*: Author interview with Abdel Kader Haidara, Brussels, December 16, 2014.

212 *"These Wahhabis who came to Timbuktu"*: Haidara interview.

216 *"spectacular attacks"*: Shura Council of Al Qaeda in the Islamic Maghreb to Shura Council of the Masked Brigade, "Al-Qaida Papers," Associated Press, October 3, 2012.

Chapter Nineteen

218 *"Go to the Ametettaï Valley"*: Author interview with General Bernard Barrera, Paris, March 18, 2014.

219 *"desolate, near-desert country under a burning sun"*: M. J. Joffre, *Opérations de la colonne Joffre avant et après l'occupation de Tombouctou* (Paris: Berger-Levrault & Cie., 1895).

221 *"We are going to suffer losses"*: Laurent Larcher, "La Bataille de L'Ametettai du général Barrera au Mali," *la Croix,* May 28, 2013.

222 *"They push everything to the extreme"*: Author interview with Captain Raphaël Oudot de Dainville, May 10, 2014.

223 *"It was a disaster without precedent"*: Louis Frèrejean, *Objectif Tombouctou: Combats contre les Toucouleurs et les Touareg* (Paris: L'Harmattan, 1996), p. 258.

224 *"The French have hit us very badly"*: Barrera interview.

224 *"In the next few days"*: Barrera interview.

226 *"with courage and tenacity"*: Barrera interview.

Epilogue

229 *"It belongs to a Savama-DCI family"*: Haidara interview.

230 *"the first pragmatic step"*: Brady interview.

230 *"The dampness and the rain"*: Haidara interview.

233 *"Some of the terrorists have gone back there"*: Author interview with anonymous French colonel, Kidal, February 3, 2014.

233 *"Nobody is in control here"*: Author interview with Mohamed Diare, U.N. minister of economy and finance of Guinea, Kidal, Mali, February 3, 2014.

236 *"Iyad is not finished"*: Ansar interview.

237 *"I don't think the jihadis"*: Barrera interview.
237 *"When we were in Timbuktu"*: Haidara interview.
238 *"When I was young"*: Haidara interview.
238 *"I send money to Timbuktu"*: Haidara interview.
239 *"Each time the scribe commenced"*: Haidara interview.
240 *"Notice how many times"*: Haidara interview.

Index

Abd Al Wahhab, Muhammad, 67, 165–66
Abou Zeid, Abdelhamid, 77–81
  and advances on Bamako, 196, 201
  AQIM and, 77, 101–5, 110, 123, 141,
    150–51, 176, 206–7, 216, 227
  and battle of the Ametettaï, 220,
    222–24, 227
  Belmokhtar and, 104, 153, 216
  capture of, 196
  death of, 227, 232
  draconian punishments and, 170–71
  El Para and, 79–81, 96
  Ghali and, 88, 141, 152, 191
  Haidara's nephew's arrests and, 174,
    185–86
  kidnappings and, 80–81, 96, 102–5, 110,
    140, 176–77, 208, 217, 227
  Mawloud festival and, 202
  and occupation of Timbuktu, 139–45,
    150–53, 163, 170, 174–77, 185–86,
    188–89, 202, 206–7, 222, 227
  physical appearance of, 140–41, 150–51,
    176

  rescuing manuscripts and, 174–75,
    185–86
  retreat of, 201, 208, 210, 212–13, 220
  smuggling of, 78–79
  war council of, 188–89
  women's protests and, 176–77
  Zakak meeting and, 123
abu Bakr Al Wangari, Mohammed, 61–62
Abu Es Haq Al Zaheli, 95
Abu Mohammed Al Maqdisi, 74
Abu Musab Al Zarqawi, 74, 99–100
Abu Qatada, 74, 104–5
Adrar des Ifoghas massif, 81, 87, 97, 110,
    123, 218–19, 234
*Advising Men on Sexual Engagement with
    Their Women*, 20
Afghanistan, 71–74, 91, 97, 99, 101, 103–
    5, 112, 153, 218, 222
Africans, Africa:
  Gates's documentary series on, 52–54
  long accepted truth about, 51–52
Aga Khan, 119
Aguelhok massacre, 131–32

Ahmed Baba Al Massufi Al Timbukti,
    22–26, 35, 242
  capture of, 10, 25–26, 41
  Haidara's prospecting work and, 41, 46
  loss of manuscripts of, 25–26
  Ahmed Baba Answers a Moroccan's Ques-
    tions About Slavery, 23
Ahmed Baba As Sudani, 62
Ahmed Baba Institute of Higher Learning
    and Islamic Research, 7–11
  conservation work of, 37, 63–64, 154
  destruction of manuscripts at, 209–10,
    220
  finances of, 10, 63, 154
  Gates's documentary and, 52–53
  Haidara's father's manuscript collection
    and, 7–8, 10, 49
  manuscript prospecting and, 10–11,
    30–48, 117, 174–75
  and occupation of Timbuktu, 174–75,
    209, 211
  physical appearance of, 9, 66, 210
  rescuing manuscripts and, 174–75
  Wald and, 95
  Zouber and, 9–11, 30–31, 42
Albarn, Damon, 128
Algeria, 5, 13, 24, 73–80, 107, 120, 123,
    125, 152–53, 171, 212–13, 220, 224,
    237
  Abou Zeid and, 77–80, 102
  AQIM and, 100–103, 109–10
  Belmokhtar and, 74–76, 102
  civil war in, 71, 74–77, 101, 217
  Haidara's prospecting work and, 37, 46
  kidnappings and, 80, 96, 99, 215–16
  and occupation of Timbuktu, 138–39,
    141
  Wald and, 90, 95
  and war in Mali, 226–27
Alhousseyni, Abdallah Ag, 87
Ali, Azima, 68
Ali, Imam, 166
Al Jazeera, 103, 110, 186
Al Qaeda, Al Qaeda in the Islamic
    Maghreb (AQIM), 71–75, 99–105,
    112, 133, 172
  and Abou Zeid, 77, 101–5, 110, 123,
    141, 150–51, 176, 206–7, 216, 227
  and Aguelhok massacre, 132

  and Belmokhtar, 73–75, 77, 90, 101–5,
    110, 122–23, 149, 153, 216–17
  and draconian punishments, 171
  and drug trafficking, 105, 110–11, 140
  and Festival in the Desert, 129
  and Festival on the Niger, 236
  finances of, 101–2, 104–5
  and Ghali, 123–24
  growth of, 109, 111
  and Huddleston, 107, 109–10
  and international intervention and
    war, 187–88, 194, 196, 206–7, 213,
    226–27, 237–38
  and kidnappings, 102–5, 110–11, 127,
    129–30, 140, 194, 216, 232–33
  Konna military operations of, 190, 196
  leadership and command structure of,
    100–101
  Mali and, 2, 73, 77, 101–3, 105, 107–8,
    110–11, 123
  manuscripts destroyed by, 209, 220
  and Mawloud festival, 203
  and occupation of Timbuktu, 2, 140–41,
    145, 147–48, 159, 170, 174, 176, 185–
    86, 188, 209–10, 216, 235–36
  relations between Tuaregs and, 123–25
  and rescuing manuscripts, 1–2, 162,
    174, 230
  retreat of, 220
  and terrorism, 2, 100–101, 105, 109–10,
    213
  and threats to manuscripts, 155–56, 198
  and unrest in Kidal, 234
  and Zakak meeting, 123–24
Ametettaï Valley, battle of the, 219–27
Amnesty International, 75
Andrew W. Mellon Foundation, 51, 54–56,
    231
Annabi, Abdu Oubeida Al, 101
Ansar, Mohammed "Manny":
  Bono and, 129–31
  and Festival in the Desert, 85, 87,
    128–30, 188
  and Festival on the Niger, 234–36
  Ghali and, 84–87, 112–14, 128, 237
Ansar Dine, 123, 170, 213
  and occupation of Timbuktu, 145, 150,
    165, 186, 238
  and war on musicians, 168

Arab Spring, 133
Araouan, 6, 23, 35–36
Arby, Khaira, 235–36
Aristide, Jean-Paul, 92
Armed Islamic Group of Algeria (GIA), 74–77, 79, 101, 216–17
Askia Ishak II, King of the Songhai Empire, 25
Askia Mohammed I, King of the Songhai Empire, 13, 16, 24–25, 62, 153, 212
Assad, Bashar Al, 72
Associated Press, 216
astronomy, 17, 19, 28, 53, 62, 66
    Ahmed Baba on, 23
    manuscript exhibits and, 61
Atlantic Monthly, The, 112–13
Australia, 127, 237
Avicenna, 18
Azzam, Abdullah Yusuf, 73, 112

Bakkay Al Kounti, Ahmed Al, 46, 66
Bamako, 4, 27, 31, 38, 42, 102, 106, 108, 120, 127–28, 156–57, 162–63, 191–94, 200–201
    Ansar and, 128, 130
    and Festival in the Desert, 131
    Gates's documentary and, 52
    Ghali and, 84, 86, 113
    growth of, 240
    Haidara's home in, 163, 173, 185, 219, 229, 239
    Haidara's personal life and, 48, 118
    Hammer's trips to, 57–59, 68, 169, 212–14, 229–30, 233–34, 239–40
    Huddleston and, 92
    and international intervention and war, 194, 196, 198, 218–19
    kidnappings and, 88
    Malian insurgency and, 136–37
    Mamma Haidara Library and, 49
    manuscripts relocated to, 240–42
    Mawloud festival in, 213
    and occupation of Timbuktu, 137, 147, 175, 179, 185, 235
    rebel advances on, 191, 193–94, 196, 198, 201
    rescuing manuscripts and, 2, 180–81, 183–84, 201, 205–6, 214, 229–32, 242
    Wald and, 91, 93

Bamba, 5–6, 8, 34, 48, 60, 240
Barrera, Bernard, 218–21, 224–26, 238
Barth, Heinrich, 27, 66
Bebao, Muhamen, 168–69
Bella Farandja, 42, 59, 138, 154, 159
Belmokhtar, Mokhtar, 73–78, 88–90, 112
    Abou Zeid and, 104, 153, 216
    Algerian civil war and, 74–75, 77
    AQIM and, 73–75, 77, 90, 101–5, 110, 122–23, 149, 153, 216–17
    desert training of, 93–94
    draconian punishments and, 171–72
    drug trafficking of, 105
    El Para and, 96
    Ghali and, 88
    Hamaha and, 172, 188, 232
    Huddleston and, 92, 95–97
    kidnappings and, 88, 96, 102–5, 216–17
    in Libya, 122, 237
    and occupation of Gao, 149, 152–53, 172, 216
    and occupation of Timbuktu, 139, 144, 188–89
    physical appearance of, 74, 103–4, 153, 216
    rebuke of, 216–17
    retreat of, 216, 220, 227
    smuggling of, 76–77, 92, 216
    Wald and, 73, 90, 93, 95
    war council of, 188–89
    Zakak meeting and, 123
Ben Ali, Zine El Abidine, 119
Ber, Hammer's visit to, 64–65
Berlusconi, Silvio, 103
Bibliothèque Fondo Kati, 63
bin Laden, Osama, 68, 72–75, 77, 80, 100, 112, 119, 133, 153
bin Naif, Prince Mohammed, 112
Boilley, Pierre, 83
Boko Haram, 124, 153, 188
Bonnier, Etienne, 223, 235
Bono, 129–31, 148
Bouteflika, Abdelaziz, 75
Brady, Emily:
    background of, 155–56
    cataloguing manuscripts and, 231
    Haidara and, 156–57, 178, 180, 185, 192–93, 205–6, 231

Brady, Emily: (*cont.*)
  and occupation of Timbuktu, 156–57,
    178, 180
  rescuing manuscripts and, 161, 178,
    180–81, 192–93, 199, 205–6, 211,
    231–32
Brown, Gordon, 105
Burkina Faso, 31
  digitizing manuscripts and, 135
  Haidara's prospecting work and, 38,
    42–43, 45–46
  and occupation of Timbuktu, 147
  and peacekeeping in Mali, 233
Bush, George W., 71, 120

Cairo, 6, 9–10, 13, 15–17, 24, 63, 241
calligraphy, 2, 17, 21–22, 160
  manuscript evaluation and, 37–38
Canada, 102–4, 216
Caroline, Princess of Monaco, 128
Chad, 6, 82, 96, 106, 220–21, 224–25, 227
Charles V, King of France, 15
Chirac, Jacques, 120, 206–7
Chirfi Alpha, Sane, 155, 164–65
Christians, 13, 46, 63, 103
Clinton, Hillary, 187
Colombia, 105–6
Commercial Bank of Mali, 146, 176, 181
Condé Nast Traveler, 128–29
Côte d'Ivoire, 26, 31, 147, 194–96, 222
Cresques, Abraham, 15

Dacko, Didier, 107
Delory, Vincent, 194
Dicko, Mohamed Gallah, 64
Djenné, 63–64, 196
  Great Mud Mosque of, 18, 26, 52, 64,
    182, 184, 190, 239
  rescuing manuscripts and, 201, 204,
    206
Djingareyber, 42, 144, 185, 202
Djingareyber Mosque, 15, 53, 69, 95, 165,
    202
Droukdel, Abdelmalek, 99–101, 109, 171
Dubai, 60, 115, 180
Dubois, Félix, 27–28, 67
  on Niger River, 33, 200, 204–5
Dyer, Edwin, 104–5, 111

Egypt, 6, 13, 24, 28, 30, 44, 49, 76, 84–85,
    95, 119, 242
El Para (Amari Saifi), 79–81
  Ghali and, 81, 87–88
  Huddleston and, 95
  kidnappings and, 80–81, 87–88, 95–96,
    100
  pursuit and capture of, 96, 107
Equatorial Guinea, 105
Essakane, 57–58, 85, 128, 188, 236–37

Faidherbe, Louis, 27
Fatimah's Hand, 43
Festival in the Desert, 57–58, 113, 128–31,
    188, 234, 236–37
  and Ghali, 85, 87, 128
  security for, 129–31
Festival on the Niger, 113–14, 234–36,
    239
Fez, 12–13, 61, 63
Fisk, Robert, 75
Ford Foundation, 55, 60, 62, 66, 157, 240
Fowler, Robert, 103–4
France, 67, 83, 120, 125
  Aguelhok massacre and, 132
  Algeria and, 75, 77, 79–80
  AQIM and, 100, 103, 109–10
  Belmokhtar and, 89–90
  in colonial period, 4–7, 11, 27–28, 30,
    33, 38, 58, 77, 97, 194, 214, 224, 226,
    235
  Ghali and, 86
  intervention and war in Mali of, 90,
    194–200, 202, 204, 206–7, 213–27,
    229, 232–34, 237–39
  kidnappings and, 100, 103, 110, 127,
    130, 152, 194, 215, 227, 232–33
  manuscript thefts and, 28
  and occupation of Konna, 195
  and occupation of Timbuktu, 148, 187
  and rebel advances on Bamako, 193–94,
    196, 198
  rescuing manuscripts and, 204
  as threat to manuscripts, 198, 204
Freston, Tom, 128–29
Gao, 6, 10, 15–16, 24, 62–64, 106, 144, 201
  draconian punishments in, 169–72
  drug trafficking in, 149

Haidara's prospecting work and, 34–35, 41, 43, 45–47
and international intervention and war, 198–99, 225, 232
Islamic Police in, 149–50, 169
kidnappings and, 105
Konna military operations and, 190–91
liberation of, 217–18
libraries in, 62–63
Malian insurgency and, 133
rebel occupation of, 148–50, 152–53, 167, 169–72, 216
Shariah Court in, 170
violence and looting in, 167
Gates, Henry Louis "Skip," 51–56
African documentary series of, 52–54
background of, 51
Mamma Haidara Library and, 54–56, 231
Gerda Henkel Foundation, 60, 231
Germaneau, Michel, 103, 110, 227
Germany, 27, 59–60, 66, 70–71
cataloguing manuscripts and, 231
Ghali and, 87–88
kidnappings and, 80–81, 87–88, 127, 140
Wald and, 93–94
Ghali, Iyad Ag, 81–88, 96–98, 111–14, 122–25, 131–33, 187, 213, 218, 236
Abou Zeid and, 88, 141, 152, 191
Aguelhok massacre and, 131–32
Ansar and, 84–87, 112–14, 128, 237
AQIM and, 123–24
army of, see Ansar Dine
childhood of, 81–82, 87
draconian punishments and, 170–71
and Festival in the Desert, 85, 87, 128
finances of, 123
Huddleston and, 96–98
Islam and, 85–88, 96–97, 112–14, 122–24, 143, 238
kidnappings and, 88, 111, 131–32, 233, 237
and occupation of Konna, 191–92, 195
and occupation of Timbuktu, 138–39, 141–44, 152, 163, 165, 188–89, 238
physical appearance of, 86, 97, 114, 122, 141

retreat of, 201–2, 207–8, 210, 220, 227
songs of, 82–84, 113–14
war council of, 188–89
war on musicians of, 168
Zakak meeting and, 123–24
Ghana, 14–15, 26, 30–31, 76
Gharyani, Abdelrahman Al, 179
Gossi, 43
Gourma Rharous, 32–34, 38–40, 46
Granada, 12, 22, 63
Great Britain, 6, 29, 31, 60, 97–98, 100, 222
kidnappings and, 104–5, 111, 126–30, 140, 152
Guardian, The, 238
Guinea, 5, 15, 31, 76, 233–34
Gwin, Peter, 118–19

Habib, Ibrahim Ag, 84–85, 113–14, 237
Habré, Hassan, 82
Hadith, 16–17, 23, 61–62, 166, 173
Ghali and, 86
Mawloud festival and, 203
and occupation of Timbuktu, 148
Haidara, Abdel Kader, 1–11, 30–51, 57–66, 95, 115–20, 154–63, 172, 178–82, 197–201, 210–14, 217, 233, 239–42
arrest of, 1
Bamako home of, 163, 173, 185, 219, 229, 239
Brady and, 156–57, 178, 180, 185, 192–93, 205–6, 231
cataloguing manuscripts and, 231
childhood and adolescence of, 3–5, 8–9, 50, 58, 117, 157, 239
children of, 59, 138, 161, 163, 185, 239
and destruction of manuscripts, 211
education and studiousness of, 4, 8–9
father of, 3–10, 30, 32–33, 44, 48–49, 157, 160
finances of, 32–33, 36–40, 42, 44–45, 47, 50, 54, 60–61, 117–18, 157, 205–6, 211, 239–40
Gates's documentary and, 53–54
honors and awards of, 60, 116
illnesses and injuries of, 43, 46–47
international and domestic profile of, 116–19

Haidara, Abdel Kader (*cont.*)
  and international intervention and war,
    197, 219, 239
  Libyan manuscript acquisition attempts
    and, 49–51
  Libyan revolution and, 120
  Malian insurgency and, 135–38
  Mamma Haidara Library and, 49,
    53–55, 115–16
  manuscript collection of, 159–60, 185,
    230
  manuscript evaluation and, 37–38
  manuscript prospecting of, 11, 30–48,
    117–18, 174–75
  mother of, 8–9
  negotiating skills of, 37, 39–40, 44–46,
    118, 205
  nephew's arrests and, 173, 185–86, 188
  and occupation of Timbuktu, 137–38,
    142, 144, 154–55, 157, 163, 174–75,
    185, 212
  personal life of, 42, 46, 48, 59, 117–18,
    136, 138, 239
  physical appearance of, 32, 44–45, 59,
    116
  property owned by, 42
  and relocation of manuscripts to Ba-
    mako, 240–42
  rescuing manuscripts and, 1–2, 157–63,
    174–75, 178, 180–82, 184–85, 189,
    192–93, 198–201, 205–6, 211–12,
    214, 226, 229–31, 242
  restoring manuscripts and, 115–16
  and returning manuscripts to Tim-
    buktu, 219, 226, 231, 240, 242
  and threats to manuscripts, 154–55,
    157, 162–63, 174–75
  Timbuktu home of, 59, 66, 138, 142,
    151, 154, 159
  wives of, 59, 138, 161, 163, 185, 239
  Zouber's meetings with, 9–10, 30–31,
    41–42
Haidara, Bouya, 210–11
Haidara, Chérit Ousmane Mandani, 213
Haidara, Ismail Diadjié, 62–63
Haidara, Mohammed "Mamma," 3–10
  childhood of, 5–6
  death of, 8
  education of, 6–7

  manuscript collection of, 3–4, 6–10,
    48–49, 160
  and son's childhood and adolescence,
    3–5, 8, 157
  son's prospecting work and, 30, 32–33, 44
  teaching career of, 3–4, 6
Haiti, 92, 94
Hamaha, Oumar Ould "Red Beard,"
    172–74, 188, 232
Hanafi, Mohammed Al, 32–34
Harvard University, 51, 53, 55
Hegel, Georg Wilhelm Friedrich, 52
Hekmatyar, Gulbuddin, 74
Hippocrates, 18, 27
*History and Description of Africa and of
    the Notable Things Therein Contained,
    The* (Leo Africanus), 12
Hollande, François, 187, 194–95, 217,
    226–27
Hotel Bouctou, 58–59, 67–68, 128
  and occupation of Timbuktu, 139–42,
    152
Hotel Kanaga, 215
Hôtel La Maison, 131, 148, 152, 169, 238
Houdas, Octave, 28
Huddleston, Vicki, 90–98, 107–10
  AQIM and, 107, 109–10
  background of, 92, 94
  Belmokhtar and, 92, 95–97
  Ghali and, 96–98
  and international intervention and war,
    90–93, 194, 196–97
  kidnappings and, 88
  Milovanovic and, 107–8
  physical appearance of, 94
  Wald and, 91–95, 107
Human Rights Watch, 146–47, 150,
    166–67, 169
Hume, David, 51–52
Hunwick, John O., 30–31

Ibn Ali, Hussein, 166
Ibn Batuta, 7, 28
Ibn Khalilkan, 241–42
Ibn Saud, Abdul Aziz Ibn Muhammed,
    166–67
Ikatel, 59
Independent, The, 75
International Criminal Court, 238

Iraq, 10, 18, 49, 99, 103, 133, 165
Islamists, Islam, 2, 15–21, 64, 66–69,
    71–76, 99, 122–25, 165–76, 212–13,
    215–17, 222, 241–42
  Abou Zeid and, 78–79, 102, 140–41,
    143
  Ahmed Baba Institute and, 7–9, 66
  Ahmed Baba on, 23
  Algerian civil war and, 71, 74–75, 217
  and attacks on shrines and cemeteries,
    179, 187
  Belmokhtar and, 73–74, 76
  draconian punishments and, 170–71
  Ghali and, 85–88, 96–97, 112–14,
    122–24, 143, 238
  Haidara's nephew's arrest and, 173–74
  Haidara's prospecting work and, 34–35,
    38, 41, 46
  Huddleston and, 93
  and international intervention and war,
    188, 196, 219, 224, 233, 238
  Jews and, 24
  jurisprudence and, 4, 6–7, 17–19, 23,
    34–35, 46, 117
  kidnappings and, 80, 215–16, 233
  Leo Africanus and, 12
  in Mali, 68, 81, 89, 133, 149
  manuscript exhibits and, 61
  Mawloud festival and, 202–3
  and occupation of Gao, 149–50, 167,
    169, 171
  and occupation of Konna, 191
  and occupation of Timbuktu, 142–43,
    145–51, 155, 159–61, 165, 167–69,
    173–76, 181, 185, 238
  open vs. inflexible, 24–25
  and overthrow of Touré, 133
  Qaddafi and, 120
  and rebel advances on Bamako, 193,
    196
  rescuing manuscripts and, 159–61, 181,
    185, 200–201
  sexuality and, 20
  Sunni Ali and, 15–16
  in Timbuktu, 17–19, 21, 24–26, 68–69,
    156, 165, 212
  Wald and, 91–93
  Western stereotypes of, 46
  Zouber's education and, 9–10

Islamic Police:
  in Gao, 149–50, 169
  in Timbuktu, 1–2, 145–47, 149–50,
    159–61, 168–69, 173–76, 181, 185,
    200, 238
Islamic State of Iraq and Syria, 72, 133
Israel, 73, 82, 109
Italy, 13, 103, 105
Jane's Terrorism and Security Monitor, 102
Jazeera, Al, 103, 110, 186
Jeune Afrique, 131
Jews, 15, 63
  anti-Semitism and, 24–25, 212
  in Timbuktu, 23–25, 46, 212
jihadis, jihad, 26–28, 46, 67, 71–76, 160, 239
  Abou Zeid and, 78–79, 96, 102, 104,
    151–52, 171, 174, 176–77, 188–89,
    196, 201, 207, 220, 222, 227
  and advances on Bamako, 196, 198
  Algeria and, 75, 78–79
  AQIM and, 2, 101–2, 105, 110–11,
    122–24
  and attacks on shrines and cemeteries,
    165–67, 179
  Belmokhtar and, 74–76, 90, 92, 96, 104,
    112, 153, 171–72, 188–89, 220
  draconian punishments and, 171
  Droukdel and, 99–100
  El Para and, 80–81, 95–96, 107
  Ghali and, 87–88, 111, 122–24, 133,
    168, 171, 188–89, 191–92, 201–2,
    208, 220, 237
  Huddleston and, 92–93, 97, 107–8
  and international intervention and war,
    90, 194–96, 198, 213, 215, 217–27,
    232, 234, 238
  kidnappings and, 102, 105, 189, 232
  in Libya, 237
  Malian insurgency and, 89, 133, 135
  military operations in Konna of, 190–91
  and occupation of Gao, 148, 150, 153,
    171–72
  and occupation of Konna, 191–92,
    195–96
  and occupation of Timbuktu, 20, 139–
    40, 143–48, 151–52, 155, 157–58,
    162–63, 165–67, 174–77, 178–80,
    182, 185–86, 188–89, 200–202, 204,
    207, 209, 214, 221

jihadis, jihad (*cont.*)
  rescuing manuscripts and, 158, 174–75,
    178, 182, 192, 200–201, 211, 230
  retreat of, 201–2, 210, 220
  and threats to manuscripts, 27–28, 155,
    157, 162, 210–11
  and unrest in Kidal, 234
  Wald and, 90, 95
  and war on musicians, 168
Joffre, Joseph Césaire, 27, 219
Juma Al-Majid Center for Culture and
  Heritage, 60, 115, 180

Kaedi, Ahmed Ag, 168, 236
Kagame, Paul, 214
Kant, Immanuel, 52
Kebede, Liya, 128
Keïta, Ibrahim Boubacar, 232
Khadijah, 43
Khalil Ibn Ahmad, Al, 18
Khartoum, 6
Kidal, 101, 105, 110, 168, 172, 236, 239
  Ghali and, 81–82, 85, 97, 111, 123, 133,
    170, 220
  violence and unrest in, 233–34
King Abdulaziz University, 112
Kitchener, Horatio Herbert, 6
Konaré, Alpha, 64
Konna, 215
  rebel occupation of, 191–92, 195–96
  rebel operations in, 189–91, 196
  rescuing manuscripts and, 182, 192
Korans, Koran, 3–4, 16–17, 22, 26–27,
    61–63, 78, 173
  Ahmed Baba on, 23
  in Ber, 65
  Haidara's education and, 9
  Haidara's father's manuscript collection
    and, 4, 6
  Haidara's prospecting work and, 39–40,
    44
  manuscript exhibits and, 61, 66
  Mawloud festival and, 117, 203
  and occupation of Timbuktu, 143,
    146–47, 150, 174
  physical appearance of, 160
  sexuality and, 20–21
  and war on musicians, 168
Kuwait, 7, 10, 40, 49, 174

Ladders of Ascent, The (Ahmed Baba), 23
Laing, Alexander Gordon, 4, 35
Lake Debo, 18, 205–6
Lazarevic, Serge, 233
Leggett, Christopher, 103
Leo Africanus (Hassan Mohammed Al
  Wazzan Al Zayati), 7, 12–14, 17, 25
Léocour, Antoine de, 194
Library of Congress, 61, 116
Libya, 13, 37, 49, 76, 101
  Abou Zeid and, 78–79
  and attacks on shrines and cemeteries,
    179
  bombing of, 133, 237
  French intervention in, 197
  Ghali and, 81–82
  manuscript acquisition attempts of,
    49–51
  revolution in, 60, 119–22, 133
  terrorism and, 70–71
Libya Hotel, 169–70
Lindh, John Walker, 97
Loiseau, Hervé Djamel, 97
London Underground attacks, 98

Maghili, Muhammed Al, 24, 212
Mahdi, Ahmad Al Faqi Al, 238
Maiga, Mohannan Sidi, 199
Mali, 22, 56, 63–69, 71–73, 87–94, 116–18,
    155–56, 158, 162–63, 240
  Abou Zeid and, 77, 80, 104
  AQIM and, 2, 73, 77, 101–3, 105, 107–
    8, 110–11, 123
  Belmokhtar and, 73, 76, 90, 104
  in colonial period, 4–7, 11, 27–28, 30,
    33, 38, 58, 97, 194
  coup in, 132–33, 135, 155, 181
  draconian punishments and, 171
  drug trafficking and, 105–6, 110, 194
  El Para and, 87, 96, 107
  and Festival in the Desert, 57, 128–31
  and Festival on the Niger, 113, 234,
    236
  Gates and, 51–52
  Ghali and, 81–84, 88, 96–97, 111–12,
    122–23, 237
  Haidara's prospecting work and, 31–32,
    35, 38, 41–43, 117
  Huddleston and, 94, 96–97, 107–9

international intervention and war in,
90–93, 187–88, 194–200, 202, 204,
206–7, 213–27, 229, 232–34, 236–39
Islam in, 68, 81, 89, 133, 149
kidnappings and, 80–81, 87–88, 102–3,
105, 111, 127–28, 130, 232
languages spoken in, 4, 28, 38–39, 109,
134, 156, 158
Libyan manuscript acquisition attempts
and, 49–50
Libyan revolution and, 120–21
military of, 106–11, 125, 127–28, 130–
33, 135–36, 138, 146, 152, 181–84,
189–90, 192–96, 201, 211, 215, 218,
230, 235
northern, 15, 81, 83, 87, 91, 94, 96, 101,
104, 111, 122, 124, 128, 167–68, 174,
179, 182, 187–88, 193–94, 198, 213,
216, 219, 221, 226, 229, 232, 234–35
and occupation of Timbuktu, 151,
187–88
peacekeeping in, 232–35
and rebel advances on Bamako, 193–94,
198, 201
rebel insurgency in, 5–6, 50, 58–59, 65,
68, 72, 81, 83–84, 89, 96, 108–9, 112,
122–25, 132–39
and rebel operations in Konna, 189–91
rescuing manuscripts and, 174, 181–84,
201, 205, 211, 230
tourism in, 58–59, 101–2, 130
and unrest in Kidal, 234
Wald and, 90–91, 93–94
Zouber and, 9–10
Mamma Haidara Commemorative Library, 60–61, 154, 173
building and rebuilding of, 54–56, 231
creation of, 49–50, 53–55
exhibitions from, 61, 116
finances of, 49, 53–55, 60, 66, 115
opening of, 56
physical appearance of, 66
press on, 115–16
rescuing manuscripts of, 159–61, 181, 186
Mantiply, Marshall, 106–7, 111, 132
manuscripts:
of Ahmed Baba, 23–26, 41
Ahmed Baba Institute and, 7–8, 10–11,
49, 63–64, 66, 174–75, 209–10, 220

ajami, 17
in Ber, 65
cataloguing of, 41, 49, 54, 60, 230–31
in colonial period, 27–28
copying of, 2, 4, 17–18, 21–22, 28,
37–38
damage and destruction of, 26–27, 36,
38, 44, 54, 62, 65, 119, 157, 160–61,
178, 199, 204, 209–13, 220, 231
digitizing of, 54, 60, 64, 115–16, 135,
154, 186
evaluations of, 31–34, 37–40, 44, 116
exhibitions of, 61, 66, 115–16, 154
fragments of, 41, 63
funding for, 60, 155, 157, 161, 163,
180–81, 192, 231–32, 240
Gates's documentary and, 53–54
of Haidara, 159–60, 185, 230
and Haidara's childhood and adolescence, 3–4, 8
of Haidara's father, 3–4, 6–10, 48–49,
160
Haidara's nephew's arrest and, 173
hiding of, 2–3, 7–8, 11, 28–29, 35–36,
40, 54, 65
illuminated, 1–2, 6, 63
Jews and, 24
Libyan attempts at acquisition of, 49–51
losses of, 25–26, 54
Mamma Haidara Library and, 49–50,
54–55, 61, 159–61, 181, 186
Mawloud festival and, 202
medieval Arabic and, 95
and occupation of Konna, 192
and occupation of Timbuktu, 138,
154–55, 157, 174–75, 178, 180, 204,
209–10, 214, 221
physical appearance of, 4, 21–22, 33–34,
36, 38–39, 44, 62, 65, 159–60, 231,
240–41
preservation of, 31, 37, 48, 54–55,
57–60, 62–64, 115–16, 154–55, 157,
186, 209, 231–32
prospecting for, 10–11, 30–48, 117–18,
174–75
provenances of, 31, 41, 45, 231
purchases of, 33–34, 37–40
reading of, 46, 117, 119, 241–42
and rebel advances on Bamako, 193

manuscripts: (*cont.*)
  relocated to Bamako, 240–42
  rescuing of, 1–2, 157–63, 172–75, 178,
    180–86, 188–89, 192–93, 198–201,
    204–6, 211–12, 214, 226, 229–32, 242
  restoration and repair of, 38, 44–45, 60,
    63, 115–16, 209, 211, 231, 241
  and retreat of rebels, 208, 210, 212–13
  returning them to Timbuktu, 219, 226,
    231–32, 240, 242
  subject matter of, 2, 4, 17–21, 23, 28, 38,
    41, 44, 46, 53, 61, 66, 155–56, 160,
    209–10, 231, 241–42
  thefts of, 28, 157, 205–6
  threats to, 27–28, 154–57, 162–63, 174–
    75, 193, 198–99, 204, 208, 210–11
  Timbuktu market for, 13–14, 28
  trading for, 37–38, 44–45
  translations of, 28, 31, 116
  and visiting academics in Timbuktu, 17
  writing and collecting of, 3–4, 7–8, 17–
    18, 37–38, 53–54, 57–63, 66, 154–55,
    160, 174, 202, 241–42
Marrakesh, 10, 26, 41, 63
Massina, 38, 46, 66, 118
Mauritania, 14, 58, 83, 88, 106–7, 124,
    149, 168, 220, 227
  AQIM and, 103, 109–10, 122
  kidnappings and, 103
  and occupation of Timbuktu, 147
Mawloud festival, 117, 202–4, 213, 218
Mbeki, Thabo, 64
Mecca, 15–16, 24, 61, 67, 73, 112, 166
Milovanovic, Gillian, 107–8, 111
Mitterrand, François, 214
Mohammed, Azima Ag Ali, 206–7
Mohammed, Fida Ag, 64–65
Mohammed, Prophet, 16–18, 24, 43,
    67–68, 85, 117, 120, 165–66, 189
  Mawloud festival and, 202–3
  and occupation of Timbuktu, 148
Mokeddem, Mohamed, 78
Monde, Le, 90
Mopti, 106, 127, 194, 200–201, 214–15
  and Festival in the Desert, 131
  and occupation of Timbuktu, 151, 179
  rescuing manuscripts and, 158, 206
Morocco, 12–13, 16–17, 22–26, 28, 31, 37,
    46, 59, 76, 142, 220

Ahmed Baba's capture and, 10, 25–26
Jews and, 24
Mamma Haidara Library and, 56
Timbuktu besieged, invaded, and occu-
    pied by, 7, 10, 25–26, 54, 160, 165
Moussaoui, Zacarias, 97
Mubarak, Hosni, 119
Mukham, The, 18
Musa I, Emperor of Mali, 15, 95

National Geographic, 118–19
National Movement for the Liberation of
    Azawad (MNLA), 121
Netherlands, 60, 155
  kidnappings and, 80, 126–30, 140, 152,
    233
  rescuing manuscripts and, 180–81
New Republic, The, 58, 156
Newsweek, 139
New York Review of Books, The, 213
New York Times, The, 195, 197
Niafounké, 46, 57–58, 168
Niger, 106, 121, 194, 221, 238
  AQIM and, 101–4, 122
  kidnappings and, 102–4, 232–33
Nigeria, 5–6, 30–31, 54, 71, 96, 124, 153,
    157, 160
Niger River, 4–6, 10, 14–16, 18, 27, 57–58,
    63–64, 67, 83–84, 94, 134, 156, 163,
    167–69, 192, 195, 225, 239–40
  and Festival on the Niger, 113–14,
    234–36, 239
  Gates's documentary and, 52
  Haidara's prospecting work and, 32–34,
    36–37, 40–41, 46–47
  Malian insurgency and, 136–37
  and occupation of Gao, 148–49, 153,
    167
  and occupation of Timbuktu, 137,
    142–43, 189
  physical appearance of, 199–200, 204
  rescuing manuscripts and, 158, 182–83,
    199–201, 204–5, 211, 214, 230
  Tuaregs' migrations and, 14
9/11, 68, 71, 89, 97, 100
North Atlantic Treaty Organization
    (NATO), 119, 121, 133, 197
Northwestern University, 31
Obama, Barack, 110, 194

Observations on the Feeling of the Beautiful and Sublime (Kant), 52
"Of National Characters" (Hume), 51–52
Omdurman, 6
On the Lawfulness of Tobacco Usage (Ahmed Baba), 23
Oudot de Dainville, Raphaël, 221–26

Pakistan, 68, 85–86, 98, 101, 139
    Belmokhtar and, 73–74
    Ghali and, 86
Palestinian Liberation Organization (PLO), 82
Paris Match, 78, 227
Philosophy of History (Hegel), 52
Plant, Robert, 128
Prince Claus Fund for Culture and Development, 60, 155, 180, 240

Qaddafi, Muammar Al, 49–51, 60, 70–71, 83, 119–22, 152, 239
    downfall of, 122, 124–25, 133, 197
    former villa of, 120, 152, 206–7
    Ghali and, 82
    grand canal of, 50, 169–70
    Libyan revolution and, 119–22
Qaeda, Al, *see* Al Qaeda, Al Qaeda in the Islamic Maghreb
Qatub, Mohammed, 112
Qatub, Sayud, 112
Qazwini, Al, 36

Radio Azawad, 170, 201, 208
Radio Communal Bouctou, 133–34, 143, 170, 201
Ripley's-Believe It or Not!, 51–52
Rumsfeld, Donald, 71
Rwanda, 194–95, 214

Saifi, Amari, *see* El Para
Salafi Group for Preaching and Combat (GSPC), 76–77, 79–80, 88, 90, 92, 99–101, 217
Salafis, Salafism, 68, 73, 99, 168, 179, 217
    Ghali and, 86–87, 96, 113
Sanagou, Amadou, 132
Sangaré, Oumou, 129
Sankoré, 3, 5, 8, 25, 42, 131, 154, 175–76, 209–10

Sankoré, University of, 13, 23, 53
Sankoré Mosque, 5, 25, 53, 59, 61–65, 118, 148, 202
Sarkozy, Nicolas, 79, 110, 197
Saudi Arabia, 7, 40, 49, 60, 64–68, 72, 139, 166, 174, 239
    Ghali and, 112–13, 122
Savama-DCI (Association for Manuscript Preservation and Valorization for the Defense of Islamic Culture), 60, 64, 157, 162, 172, 200, 230
Ségou, 64, 113–14, 130, 234, 236, 245
    in colonial period, 33
    rescuing manuscripts and, 183–84
Senegal, 5, 31, 42, 61, 100, 132, 150, 235
    and peacekeeping in Mali, 233
    and war in Mali, 223
Serval, Operation, 196, 218, 226, 233
Sévaré, 136, 182–83, 192–95, 215, 217
sex, sexuality, 19–21, 156
Shariah law, 1, 67, 113, 123–24, 193, 207–8, 212
    draconian punishments and, 170, 172
    Haidara's nephew's arrest and, 173–75
    and occupation of Gao, 149, 170
    and occupation of Konna, 191
    and occupation of Timbuktu, 143–46, 148, 167–69, 173–74, 176, 185, 187
    and war on musicians, 168
Shekau, Abubakar, 153
Shi'ites, Shi'ism, 67, 99, 119, 166, 202
Sidi Yahya Mosque, 123–24, 142
Signifying Monkey, The (Gates), 51
Songhai Empire, 13, 16, 18, 52, 133, 153
    Haidara's prospecting work and, 32, 34
    histories of, 27, 31
    Jews in, 24–25, 63, 212
Sorhai tribe, 4, 8, 32, 42, 66, 68, 118, 133–34, 170, 199, 245
South Africa, 63–64, 116, 154, 233
Soviet Union, 73–74, 109, 112, 222
Spain, 12, 15, 62–63, 101, 103, 105
"Still Here" (Hammer), 58
Stolk, Deborah, 155
Sudan, 6, 13, 27, 72
Sufis, Sufism, 5, 16–17, 23, 46, 67, 117, 160, 213
    attacks on shrines of, 166–67, 179, 187, 238

Sufis, Sufism (*cont.*)
    Ghali and, 81
    Mawloud festival and, 202–3
    reformers and, 26–27
Sunni Ali, King of the Songhai Empire,
    15–16, 212
Sunnis, 67, 112, 179, 203
Sweden, 126–30, 140, 152, 233
Syria, 49, 72, 133, 203

Tablighi Jama'at, 85–86, 97–98
Taghaza, 25, 35–36, 83
Taliban, 71–72, 91, 97, 222
Tariq al Fattash, 13
Tariq Al Sudan, 18, 26–28
"Telltale Scribes of Timbuktu, The"
    (Gwin), 118–19
terrorists, terrorism, 78, 112, 124, 153,
    171, 193, 227
    Abou Zeid and, 79–80, 102, 141
    Algeria and, 77, 79
    AQIM and, 2, 100–101, 105, 109–10, 213
    in Bamako, 213
    Belmokhtar and, 73–74, 90
    drug trafficking and, 106
    El Para and, 79, 96, 107
    Ghali and, 98, 237
    Huddleston and, 92, 98, 107
    and international intervention and war,
        188, 213, 234, 238
    kidnappings and, 80, 105, 216, 232
    Libya and, 70–71
    on 9/11, 68, 71, 89, 97, 100
    and occupation of Timbuktu, 139, 141
    Wald and, 93
Tessalit, 132, 218, 220–22, 224, 226
Timbuctoo the Mysterious (Dubois), 28,
    200, 204–5
Timbuktu, 1–10, 12–23, 57–69, 83, 106,
    115–21
    Ahmed Baba's manuscripts and, 23
    and attacks on shrines and cemeteries,
        165–67, 179, 187, 238
    Belmokhtar and, 96–97, 101
    cataloguing manuscripts and, 231
    in colonial period, 27–28, 33, 235
    as commercial, literary, and cultural
        crossroads, 12–17, 58, 61, 115–16,
        212, 242

Crisis Committee of, 144–45, 150–51,
    164, 175–76, 185–86, 203–4, 207
destruction of manuscripts in, 26–27,
    209–11
draconian punishments in, 168–71
education in, 3, 9, 12–13, 16–17, 51,
    148, 151, 163, 172, 241
and Festival in the Desert, 57–58, 85,
    129–30, 234, 236–37
Gates and, 51–54
Ghali and, 84
Golden Age of, 1, 3, 7, 10, 12–13, 16–17,
    23, 25, 53–54, 58, 61, 174, 242
growth of, 14–15
and Haidara's childhood and adoles-
    cence, 3–5, 9
Haidara's home in, 59, 66, 138, 142, 151,
    154, 159
Haidara's prospecting work and, 30–32,
    34, 37–42, 44–45, 47–48
Hammer's trips to, 58–59, 64–69, 123–
    24, 139, 148, 164–65, 167, 206–7,
    210, 214–15
hiding manuscripts and, 2–3, 7
Huddleston and, 94–97
insurgency in, 58–59, 72, 133–39
and international intervention and war,
    198–200, 202, 206–7, 214–15, 217,
    223, 226, 232, 239
Islamic Police in, 1–2, 145–47, 149–50,
    159–61, 168–69, 173–76, 181, 185,
    200, 238
Islam in, 17–19, 21, 24–26, 68–69, 156,
    165, 212
isolation of, 4, 58, 61
Jews in, 23–25, 46, 212
jurisprudence in, 17–19
kidnappings and, 126–29, 152, 189, 233
Konna military operations and, 190
Leo Africanus and, 12–13
liberation of, 217–18
Libyan manuscript acquisition attempts
    and, 49–50
Libyan revolution and, 120–21
Mamma Haidara Library and, 54–55
manuscript evaluation and, 37–38
manuscript market in, 13–14, 28
manuscript writing and collecting
    in, 3–4, 7–8, 17–18, 37–38, 53–54,

57–63, 66, 154–55, 160, 174, 202, 241–42

Mawloud festival in, 202–4, 218

Moroccan siege, invasion, and occupation of, 7, 10, 25–26, 54, 160, 165

naming of, 14

physical appearance of, 5, 95

physical appearance of manuscripts of, 21–22

as progressive society, 17–20, 46

Proof Committee of, 203–4

protests in, 176–77

rebel occupation of, 2, 20, 137–82, 185–89, 200–204, 206–7, 209–12, 214, 216, 221–22, 227, 235–36, 238

and rebel occupation of Konna, 191

rescuing manuscripts and, 1–2, 157–63, 172–75, 178, 180–86, 192, 199–201, 204–5, 211–12, 214, 226, 229, 231

retreat of rebels from, 201, 207–10, 212–13

returning manuscripts to, 219, 226, 231–32, 240, 242

scholarship in, 12–13, 16–20, 25–28, 46, 53–54, 61, 165, 231

Shariah Court of, 148, 169, 174

subject matter of manuscripts of, 17–21

Sufi reformers in, 26–27

Sunni Ali and, 15–16

and threats to manuscripts, 155, 162

tourism in, 61, 67–68, 95, 126–28, 130, 139–40, 155, 164, 179, 201, 236

treatment of women in, 146–47, 175–76

university library of, 51–52

violence and looting in, 138–39, 144, 146, 150, 169, 179–80

Wald and, 94–95

weather in, 54–55, 137–38, 231

Touré, Ali Farka, 57–58, 67–68, 82, 128–29, 139, 168

Touré, Amadou Toumani, 88–89, 128

AQIM and, 110–11

and Festival in the Desert, 130–31

Ghali and, 96–97, 111, 122

overthrow of, 132–33

Qaddafi and, 120

Wald and, 91–94

Touré, Boubacar, 58–59

and occupation of Timbuktu, 139–42, 152

Touré, Ibrahim Khalil:

and occupation of Timbuktu, 144–45, 148, 150–52, 176, 185–86, 189, 207

rescuing manuscripts and, 185–86

Touré, Mohammed, 217

arrested and detained, 173–75, 182–86, 188, 232

cataloguing manuscripts and, 231

and occupation of Timbuktu, 172–73, 189

rescuing manuscripts and, 157–59, 162–63, 172–75, 181–86, 188–89

Touré, Vieux Farka, 129

Trans-Saharan Counterterrorism Initiative, 106

Traoré, Dioncounda, 194

Travels and Discoveries in North and Central Africa (Barth), 27

Trevor-Roper, Hugh, 29

Tripoli, 4, 13, 49–50, 63, 70–71, 81–82, 119–21, 179

Truman, James, 128–29

Tuaregs, 17, 64, 76, 80, 87, 102, 116, 119, 122–25, 127–29, 158, 206–7, 223

annual migrations of, 14

in colonial period, 5–6

draconian punishments and, 170

drug trafficking and, 105

and Festival in the Desert, 57–58, 85, 87, 128–31

and Festival on the Niger, 235–36

Ghali and, 81–88, 96–97, 111–12, 122–25, 138–39, 141, 237

Haidara's prospecting work and, 38–40

Huddleston and, 96–97, 108

insurgency of, 50, 58–59, 65, 68, 72, 81, 83, 89, 96, 108–9, 112, 122–25, 133–35, 137–38, 219, 234–35

Libyan revolution and, 120–21, 133

and occupation of Gao, 167

and occupation of Timbuktu, 137–42, 144, 148, 167, 170, 179

and overthrow of Touré, 133

physical appearance of, 26, 67, 131

relations between AQIM and, 123–25

rescuing manuscripts and, 205

retreat of, 167–68, 180

and unrest in Kidal, 234

and war on musicians, 168

Zakak meeting and, 121, 123–24

Tunisia, 13, 17, 28, 37, 76, 101–2, 119
Turquoise, Operation, 214

United Nations, 100, 103, 105, 122
  and peacekeeping in Mali, 232–35
  Security Council of, 119, 187
United Nations Educational, Scientific and
  Cultural Organization (UNESCO), 7,
  31, 61, 95
  and threats to manuscripts, 162–63

Vanity Fair, 128–29
Verdon, Philippe, 232–33
Villa Soudan, 158, 239

Waffayat Al Ayan Libnu Halakan (Ibn
  Khalilkan), 241–42
Wahhabis, Wahhabism, 66–69, 112–13,
  117, 151, 166, 179, 212–13, 225
Wald, Charles F. "Chuck," 70–73, 90–
  95

air strikes and, 90–93
background of, 70–71
Belmokhtar and, 73, 90, 93, 95
El Para and, 107
Huddleston and, 91–95, 107
Wangari, Sidi Yayia Al, 61–62
Wangari Library, Al, 62
Washington, D.C., 61, 108, 111, 116, 194

Yemen, 72, 133

Zakak, 121, 123–24
Zawahiri, Ayman Al, 100, 133
Zayati, Hassan Mohammed Al Wazzan Al,
  see Leo Africanus
Zouber, Mahmoud, 48–49, 64
  education of, 9–10
  Haidara's meetings with, 9–10, 30–31,
    41–42
  Haidara's prospecting work and, 11,
    30–31, 41–42

About the Author

JOSHUA HAMMER was born in New York and graduated from Princeton University with a cum laude degree in English literature. He joined the staff of *Newsweek* as a business and media writer in 1988, and between 1993 and 2006 served as a bureau chief and correspondent-at-large on five continents. Hammer is now a contributing editor to *Smithsonian* and *Outside*, and a regular contributor to *The New York Review of Books*, and has written for publications including *The New Yorker*, *The New York Times Magazine*, *Vanity Fair*, *Condé Nast Traveler*, *The Atlantic*, and *The Atavist Magazine*. He is the author of three nonfiction books and has won numerous journalism awards. Since 2007 he has been based in Berlin, Germany, and continues to travel widely around the world.

حمد المنعم باسمه دوامنا المختتم بالخلاص لك حمى حمى الهي
وقد وراءة مغنى الظلام لا تختما ومحمد واماص تغد سا
لك رحمة وعلما واسبغ على اوليائه نعما عمما وبعث بهم
غرا وعجما واوقاهم مختما ومنهى وارحم عظلا وحلما